INTERNATIONAL STUDENTS AND SCHOLARS IN THE UNITED STATES

INTERNATIONAL STUDENTS AND SCHOLARS IN THE UNITED STATES

COMING FROM ABROAD

Edited by

Heike C. Alberts and Helen D. Hazen

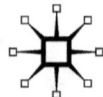

INTERNATIONAL STUDENTS AND SCHOLARS IN THE UNITED STATES
Copyright © Heike C. Alberts and Helen D. Hazen, 2013.
Softcover reprint of the hardcover 1st edition 2013 978-1-137-02446-6
All rights reserved.

First published in 2013 by
PALGRAVE MACMILLAN®
in the United States—a division of St. Martin's Press LLC,
175 Fifth Avenue, New York, NY 10010.

Where this book is distributed in the UK, Europe and the rest of the world, this is by Palgrave Macmillan, a division of Macmillan Publishers Limited, registered in England, company number 785998, of Houndmills, Basingstoke, Hampshire RG21 6XS.

Palgrave Macmillan is the global academic imprint of the above companies and has companies and representatives throughout the world.

Palgrave® and Macmillan® are registered trademarks in the United States, the United Kingdom, Europe and other countries.

ISBN 978-1-349-43852-5   ISBN 978-1-137-02447-3 (eBook)
DOI 10.1057/9781137024473

Library of Congress Cataloging-in-Publication Data

    International students and scholars in the United States : coming from abroad / edited by Heike C. Alberts and Helen D. Hazen.
       p. cm.

    1. Students, Foreign—United States 2. Education, Higher—United States I. Alberts, Heike C. II. Hazen, Helen, 1975– III. King, Russell, 1945– British students in the United States: motivations, experiences, and career aspirations.

LB2376.4.I58 2013

378.1982—dc23   2012031272

A catalogue record of the book is available from the British Library.

Design by Newgen Imaging Systems (P) Ltd., Chennai, India.

First edition: February 2013

10 9 8 7 6 5 4 3 2 1

Transferred to Digital Printing in 2013

Contents

List of Figures and Tables — vii

Foreword — ix
Wei Li

1. Introduction — 1
   Helen Hazen and Heike Alberts

   ### Part 1   Migration Patterns and Experiences

2. British Students in the United States: Motivations, Experiences, and Career Aspirations — 25
   Russell King, Allan Findlay, Jill Ahrens, and Alistair Geddes

3. The Emerging Brain Circulation between China and the United States — 47
   Wan Yu

4. "Too Many Things Pull Me Back and Forth" Return Intentions and Transnationalism among International Students — 65
   Helen Hazen and Heike Alberts

5. German Faculty in the United States: Return Migration Intentions, Reform, and Research Networks — 89
   Heike Alberts

   ### Part 2   Diversity

6. International Faculty: A Source of Diversity — 111
   Rebecca Theobald

7. International Students and Diversity: Challenges and Opportunities for Campus Internationalization — 131
   Kavita Pandit

Part 3 Challenges and Support

8. Succeeding Abroad: International Students in
   the United States   145
   Alisa Eland and Kay Thomas

9. African Students in the US Higher-Education System:
   A Window of Opportunities and Challenges   163
   Jane Irungu

10. Supporting and Mentoring International Faculty:
    Issues and Strategies   181
    Ken Foote

11. Teaching and Learning with Accented English   199
    Heike Alberts, Helen Hazen, and Rebecca Theobald

12. Conclusion   219
    Heike Alberts and Helen Hazen

List of Contributors   227

Index   231

Figures and Tables

Figures

1.1	International student enrollments in the United States, 2001/02–2010/11	6
1.2	Country of origin of international students in the United States, 2010/11	8
1.3	International scholars in the United States, 2001/02–2010/11	9
3.1	Chinese students in the United States by academic level, 2001–2011	53
5.1	German scholars in the United States, 2001–2011	91
6.1	Total number of international scholars in the United States, 1996/97–2010/11	113

Tables

2.1	Motivations for studying abroad	29
2.2	Main sources of funding for studies in the United States	33
2.3	Perceived benefits of studying outside the United Kingdom	34
4.1	Initial motivations for coming to the United States to study	72
4.2	Advantages and disadvantages of the United States	75
4.3	Advantages and disadvantages of the home country	76
6.1	Full-time instructional faculty in degree-granting institutions by selected faculty status, gender, and race/ethnicity	114
8.1	Comparison of teacher- and learner-centered pedagogical approaches	152
11.1	Correlation between student attitudes and exposure to foreign languages and NNIs (significance of χ^2)	210

Foreword

Forty years after Diane Crane's book *Invisible Colleges: Diffusion of Knowledge in Scientific Communities* highlighted the ways in which scientists communicate and collaborate, it is clear that today's scientific communities have become even more invisible, with drastically improved modern communication technologies facilitating collaborations without the need for face-to-face interactions. With the accelerated pace of globalization, these communities have also become more transnational in nature, taking the form of "knowledge diasporas" (Welch and Zhen 2008). At the same time, formal higher-education institutions can be argued to be more "visible," both literally and figuratively. This is due to the increasingly transnational flows of students and faculty members of different racial/ethnic backgrounds in academia. Academic exchanges of international students and scholars are not a new phenomenon, but in the past two decades such exchanges have become faster in pace and broader in scope: higher-education sectors in Western countries increasingly seek international students as academic and financial assets to boost enrollment and to raise revenue. The rapid economic growth of some low-per-capita-income countries over this same period means that study abroad is now a reality for more than just a privileged few. Thus, many students from newly affluent or middle-class families are now also receiving higher education beyond their national boundaries, with some eventually going on to take academic positions overseas.

Many receiving countries in the Global North, as well as countries experiencing rapid economic development in the Global South, have begun to issue policies to proactively recruit such talent to keep and improve their country's global standing. Some international treaties also include stipulations to promote skilled migration (such as the TN visa in NAFTA that encourages skilled Canadian and Mexican professionals to work in the United States). Moreover, the recent global economic downturn has not only hastened some existing trends but also shaken, if not altered, the global geopolitical and economic power balance. As such, notions such as a one-way "brain drain" for sending countries and "brain gain" for receiving countries have shifted to an emphasis on the transnational nature of "brain exchange" or "brain circulation." In these ways, the internationalizing of academia should not be, and often no longer is, a zero-sum game between sending and receiving countries, or between domestic and foreign-born academics. However, how to make such trends fair and just, with positive impacts for all parties involved, remains to be addressed with policy interventions.

Several questions are critical to tackling this outstanding challenge: How do the experiences of students and faculty from different countries and various backgrounds differ? Why and how do international academics make the decision to stay in their host country or return to their country of origin? Who will stay and who will return and when? How do transnational connections and activities facilitate "invisible colleges"? What are the impacts of internationalization efforts in higher education on domestic academics of different racial backgrounds? These are issues of particular significance to the United States that, to date, remains the world's largest and strongest magnet for foreign-born academics, and is therefore at the forefront of such debates. Within these changing global and US contexts, *International Students and Scholars in the United States: Coming from Abroad* is a timely and welcome addition to the existing literature on "academic migrations." It is, therefore, a privilege and pleasure to write a foreword for this book.

Coming from Abroad combines academic analysis of the experiences of foreign-born academics and the diversification of academia with implementable suggestions for international academics to thrive, and for university administrators to guide and assist them, in academia. The chapters are written by a diverse group of scholars and practitioners, ranging from leading scholars and academic administrators to seasoned service professionals, from faculty members to PhD students. About half of the authors are themselves former international students, most of whom are now international faculty (countries of origin represented include China, Germany, India, Kenya, and the United Kingdom), contributing to the diversity of personal and professional perspectives offered. Collectively, the chapters address academic migration at different career stages, including both international students and foreign-born faculty; and along two axes: from the Global South to the Global North (African and Chinese students) and North to North (British students and German faculty).

Focusing on the United States as the most significant receiving country for international students provides a number of contributions to the literature. First, a number of previously understudied groups are included in the analyses. In particular, Irungu's chapter on African students and Hazen and Alberts' work on the return migration intentions of international students from a range of countries uncover trends among previously under-researched groups and call for more balanced research on different groups. Second, this volume incorporates a wide range of research methods and approaches, ranging from quantitative to largely qualitative, and including mixed methods of survey, focus groups, and interviews. The approach taken by Alberts, Hazen, and Theobald of presenting voices from both sides of the classroom in analyzing teaching by nonnative English-speaking instructors is especially refreshing and useful. They compare and contrast students' interactions with international instructors in the classroom with the voices of foreign-born instructors to facilitate possible dialogue and search for the best and most feasible ways for both sides to benefit from their interactions. Third, on a theoretical level, several chapters critique the broad brushstrokes that have thus far typically been used in pursuing an internationalization agenda within academia. In particular, as Pandit and Theobald point out in their respective chapters, domestic diversity agendas and internationalization goals may intersect but do not replicate one another. As such, it is important to consider carefully how an internationalization agenda might affect preexisting diversity concerns and future goals.

Despite the accomplishments and advances made by this edited volume, there is, of course, always more research needed to further our knowledge on the subject of foreign-born academics. Here I would highlight two major areas for future study:

1. *More comparative, transnational, and longitudinal work*: Given the accelerated internationalization of the higher-education sector, and the increasing numbers of foreign-born academics working in academia, more work with comparative, transnational, and/or longitudinal approaches is warranted. Hazen and Alberts' chapter on the return migration intentions of international students demonstrates the value of comparative work on the differential experiences of students from various countries at the same academic institution. Along these lines, more comparative work—for instance directly comparing different groups in the same receiving institutions/regions/countries or the same group in different receiving institutions/regions/countries—would add considerable insight to our understanding of academic migrations, which could be used to develop more culturally sensitive and considerate

policies toward foreign-born academics. Another dimension that has so far been largely unaddressed is the significant East to West migration that is occurring among academics, with those from current or former socialist countries moving to Western countries, the United States included. Some works on South-to-North migration (such as from China to the United States) imply but do not explicitly address the particular analytical angle of this East-West dimension. The break up of the Soviet Union in the early 1990s resulted in a large exodus of Soviet and other Eastern scientists to Western countries, with persistent impacts on today's "Invisible Colleges." Another dimension that should receive more scholarly attention is transnational work—the existing literature often focuses on either sending *or* receiving areas/countries but rarely connects the two. Simultaneous research conducted in both sending and receiving regions could provide some unique angles of analysis and policy implications, especially when addressing the complex issues of "brain drain/gain/circulation/exchange." Moreover, much current research takes a cross-sectional snapshot approach. Truly longitudinal work, while more difficult to tackle in terms of both time required and logistics involved, will tease out much more detail about changing attitudes, behaviors, and experiences of foreign-born academics as well as the opportunities and constraints enabling or discouraging such changes.

2. *Confronting issues of race and racialization:* While not implying or suggesting to privilege one group, one type of research, or one ideological or political stance over others, there is a need to directly confront issues of race and racialization in our research. Foreign-born academics are often exposed to, and to a certain extent already buy into, media portrayals of different population groups while still in their countries of origin. Once they arrive, these academics experience the racial reality of the United States or other receiving countries. The preconceived racial images or beliefs held by foreign-born academics often manifest themselves in this new context, and can reinforce existing racial hierarchies via skewed thinking processes and actions. Some academics join the racialized majority with certain privileges, while those from racialized minorities become deprived of such privileges, irrespective of their class, gender, or human capital (Li and Yu 2012). When it comes to a discipline or academia as a whole then, the impacts and results are far reaching. A recent president of the Association of American Geographers, Audrey Kobayashi, recently wrote that "it is easier to celebrate diversity than to address racism" and

"before we can celebrate diversity we need to address the ongoing, real, and socially damaging effects of racism" (Kobayashi 2012, 3). Several chapters in this book either explicitly address, or implicitly allude to, these issues of race and experiences by people from racial minority backgrounds. This represents an important step, and invites further research to directly tackle issues of race, racialization, and the impacts of racism on both domestic and foreign-born academics. Such research helps tease out how, and how much, one's race makes a difference, and how to level the playing field so that all academics—racial majority and minority, domestic and international—have an equal chance to survive and succeed.

In short, I congratulate the achievements of Alberts and Hazen and all their contributors in providing such a fine volume of solid academic analysis and useful practical solutions. I look forward to future works by them and others to broaden and deepen our understanding of the complex relationships around globalization, racialization, and internationalization of higher education.

Wei Li, Arizona State University

Works Cited

Crane, D. 1972. *Invisible Colleges: Diffusion of Knowledge in Scientific Communities*. Chicago, IL: University of Chicago Press.
Kobayashi, A. 2012. "Can Geography Overcome Racism?" *AAG Newsletter* 47(5): 3.
Li, W., and W. Yu. 2012. "Racialized Assimilation? Globalization, Transnational Connections, and US Immigration." In *Race, Ethnicity, and Place in a Changing America*, 2nd edition, edited by J. Frazier, E. Tettey-Fio, and N. Henry, 33–44. Syracuse, NY: Syracuse University Press.
Welch, A., and Z. Zhen. 2008. "Higher Education and Global Talent Flows: Brain Drain, Overseas Chinese Intellectuals, and Diasporic Knowledge Networks." *Higher Education Policy* 21: 519–37.

1

Introduction

Helen Hazen and Heike Alberts

Knowledge flows increasingly freely in today's global society. Human beings, in whom this knowledge is embedded, are now also highly mobile (Meyer, Kaplan, and Charum 2002), resulting in an integrated global market for the highly skilled. Academics are a significant stream within this global flow of talent. While early educational exchanges were often associated with policies to promote cultural, social, and political ties between specific countries, more recently expansions in international student migrations have been attributed also to declining transport costs and improving technologies (OECD 2010). In addition, increased demand for higher education has in some cases outpaced the capacity of individual countries to provide quality higher education, motivating students to seek opportunities internationally (Bhandari and Blumenthal 2009). Such factors led to a tripling of the number of students studying outside their country of citizenship between 1980 and 2008 (OECD 2010, 313). By 2008, approximately 3.3 million students were pursuing tertiary education abroad, the majority (79%) in the affluent countries of the Organisation for Economic Co-operation and Development (OECD) (OECD 2010).

Academic careers are often characterized by significant geographical flexibility; indeed, international mobility is frequently considered an integral part of academic work (McNamee and Faulkner 2001; van de Bunt-Kokhuis 2000). As such, "the idea of an extreme volatility of highly skilled people, who are submitted attractive offers and hence are susceptible to move from one place to another overnight, is gaining momentum" (Meyer, Kaplan, and Charum 2002, 310). Academics are nonetheless subject to barriers to migration (see Richardson 2009), and a deeper understanding of their migration patterns is called for.

While international students dominate flows of international academics, significant numbers of individuals also move to take up positions in other countries with their degree in hand. These positions include academic faculty posts, as well as postdoctoral and other research jobs; individuals in these positions are often referred to collectively as "international scholars." International students and scholars share some of the same motivations, such as the desire to improve their economic circumstances, take advantage of more promising opportunities elsewhere, and experience another culture. Similarly, they encounter many of the same challenges, including cultural dislocation and language issues. There is also a lot of continuity among these two groups as a significant number of international students eventually become international scholars. Efforts to investigate common ground are, therefore, warranted. However, these groups are also distinctive in some ways, particularly in how they are recruited, whether or not they will be remunerated for their work overseas, and their typical age and stage of life. It is therefore important to avoid inaccurate generalizations when analyzing migration patterns of academics. Even among students a distinction has to be made between undergraduate and graduate students in terms of their opportunities to obtain external funding, the degree to which they are actively recruited, and their likely degree of commitment to an academic lifestyle, among other things. This volume attempts to carefully draw out commonalities in the experiences and context of academic migrants, while recognizing variations in the patterns that typify different groups.

The United States is a particularly important case study within discussions surrounding academic migrations owing to its dominant, and rapidly evolving, global position in hosting international students. For several decades, the United States has been one of the most significant recipients of international students, and is today host to the largest number of international students worldwide. However, in the face of increasing competition from other countries (Bevis and Lucas 2007; Mooney and Neelakantan 2004; NAFSA 2003), improving opportunities in major sending countries such as India and China (Mooney and Neelakantan 2004), tightening immigration restrictions and hostility toward foreigners in the United States (Dollag 2004; Hindrawan 2003), and economic constriction, the United States risks losing its position as the primary global recipient of international student and faculty talent (McHale 2011; Lin, Pearce, and Wang 2009; Florida 2005; NAFSA 2003). As Florida (2005, 147) points out, international students are the "canaries of the global competition for talent," with fluctuations in international student enrollments indicating wider trends in highly skilled migrations. A declining share of international students in the United States could therefore be followed by a decline in the share of highly skilled migrants more generally. The United States may have to make a coordinated and proactive effort to maintain its attractiveness to international students (NAFSA 2007, 2003).

Framing Academic Migration

While the migration of international academics has traditionally been framed within the "brain drain" discourse, with Western countries seen as overwhelmingly benefiting from their ability to attract global talent and draining skills from the low-income world, the reality today is far more complex. New players are emerging on the scene as providers of world-class education, some low-income countries now actively send students abroad to transfer knowledge back to the home country, and many student and faculty migrations have been revealed to be circular rather than unidirectional. Indeed, "mobility" may be replacing "migration" among the highly skilled, reflecting the idea that the movements of highly skilled migrants today are often short term (Vertovec 2002). As a result, many scholars now argue that the terms "brain circulation" and "brain exchange" more accurately describe the increasingly multidirectional nature of international migrant flows and the growing awareness that these movements are beneficial for both sending and receiving nations (Bhandhari and Blumenthal 2011; Brooks and Waters 2011; Goldin, Cameron, and Belarajan 2011; Johnson and Regets 1998; Gaillard and Gaillard 1997). Nonetheless, migrant flows from less to more developed regions continue to dominate (Meyer, Kaplan, and Charum 2002). Since the 1990s, there has also been increasing attention to the transnational position of migrants, recognizing that many migrants maintain close ties to both home and host country, even when the two are geographically distant. Migrants are understood to "develop and maintain multiple relations—familial, economic, social, organizational, religious, and political—that span borders" (Glick Schiller, Basch, and Szanton Blanc 1992, 1). Thus, they remain embedded within their country of birth while creating ties to, and potentially even settling permanently in, a new host country.

While global forces have led to increasing numbers of students seeking the best education available from a worldwide pool of universities, institutions and governments for their part have developed internationalization policies to try to capitalize on these cross-border flows. Three main rationales are given for implementing internationalization agendas: economic, political, and academic. From an economic point of view, internationalization prepares individuals for international careers, also benefiting the country as a whole by importing talent and knowledge. Within the political realm, internationalization is seen as contributing to national security, while in academia internationalization is in line with liberal education goals (Childress 2009). Although the notion of internationalization in higher education is supposed to involve the integration of international/intercultural approaches throughout all aspects of university life, in reality many universities have largely focused on recruiting international student and faculty talent in order to further their research agendas and attract investment and fee-paying students (Kelly 2009; Kim 2009; Waters 2008).

International Academics in the United States

In the United States' early years international educational exchanges were not always considered positive as the large number of students going to Europe served as a reminder that European institutions were superior to American universities. By 1900 the quality and reputation of American universities was improving, however, and the United States began to attract foreign students looking for a good education and research opportunities (Bevis and Lucas 2007). By the 1920s, the paradigm shift was complete, as international exchanges began to be actively promoted. A milestone was the opening of the Institute of International Education (IIE) as a clearinghouse for international exchanges in the United States in 1919. The IIE published lists of foreign scholarship opportunities, organized exchanges of professors, assisted in the creation of a student visa, and established more uniform evaluation of academic credentials from other education systems (Bevis and Lucas 2007). Today the IIE continues to be active in promoting and documenting international academic exchanges, and publishes annual *Open Doors* reports—the most important source of data on international students and scholars in the United States.

The most recent *Open Doors* report shows that 723,277 international students studied at US institutions in the 2010/11 academic year, numbers having increased on an annual basis with very few exceptions since the 1950s (Institute of International Education 2011a). Since the mid-twentieth century, the migration of students and faculty has increased rapidly worldwide, but particularly in the United States. By 2008, 19 percent of all students enrolled outside their country of citizenship were studying in the United States, making the United States host to by far the largest share of international students worldwide. The United Kingdom, with 10 percent of international students, ranks a distant second (OECD 2010, 314), but illustrates the significance of English-speaking countries in dominating the list of major host countries. The consistently high ranking of US research institutions, coupled with generous funding in certain fields, makes the United States a very attractive destination for international students (Goodman and Gutierrez 2011).

Despite these advantages, the United States' share of the international student market declined from 24 percent of international student enrollees globally in 2000 to 19 percent in 2008 (OECD 2010, 314). Furthermore, there are now about a dozen countries in the world where international students account for a larger proportion of the country's student body than in the US (Florida 2005). Increases in foreign student enrollments in the United States stopped in the 2002/03 academic year and declined over the next two years, even as other countries' international student enrollments continued to expand (Institute of International Education 2011a; Lin, Pearce, and Wang 2009). This decline has been linked to the terrorist attacks of September 11, 2001, after which the PATRIOT Act and the Border Security and Visa Reform Act of 2002 tightened immigration rules and intensified screening procedures for foreigners (Florida 2005). These reforms were designed to address concerns raised over the potential security risks posed by international students, related to fraudulent admissions of students and lack of monitoring (Borjas 2002). While stricter rules, and accompanying delays in issuing visas and increased visa rejection rates, had an influence on students (and scholars) from all countries (see Florida 2005), students from Muslim regions and countries that were seen as sponsors of terrorism were most affected. Hardening attitudes toward immigrants more broadly led to increasing discomfort for both students already in the United States and students contemplating a course of study there (Lin, Pearce, and Wang 2009; Alberts 2007; Bevis and Lucas 2007; McCormack 2007; Field, Mooney, and Neelakantan 2004). In response, numerous initiatives have been proposed or implemented to streamline the student-visa process and reduce the hardships imposed (Bevis and Lucas 2007; NAFSA 2003). In particular, the US government has made an effort to speed up visa procedures and offer opportunities for practical training after graduation in order to encourage renewed growth in international student numbers. However, critics argue that other laws and regulations, for instance related to obtaining drivers licenses and social security numbers, have simultaneously made the situation more difficult for international students (McCormack 2007); furthermore, demand for visas and permanent residency status ("green cards") outpace the supply, resulting in delays (Jasso et al. 2010).

Since 2006, international student numbers in the United States have once again begun to rise, with each progressive year hitting a new record high in terms of international student enrollments (figure 1.1). As reported in the *Chronicle of Higher Education*, "higher-education officials attribute the growth to stronger recruitment efforts by universities, the rising numbers of students who seek education abroad, and continued efforts by the U.S. government to smooth the visa-application process" (McCormack 2007, A1). In many US universities, international students today account for a significant proportion of the student body, especially in certain disciplines and at the more prestigious universities. For example, international students constitute more than 20 percent of enrollments in advanced research programs in the United States (OECD 2010), and community colleges are now beginning to attract international students (McCormack 2007). Nonetheless, some policymakers and scholars continue to voice concerns that the United States may be losing its premier position in

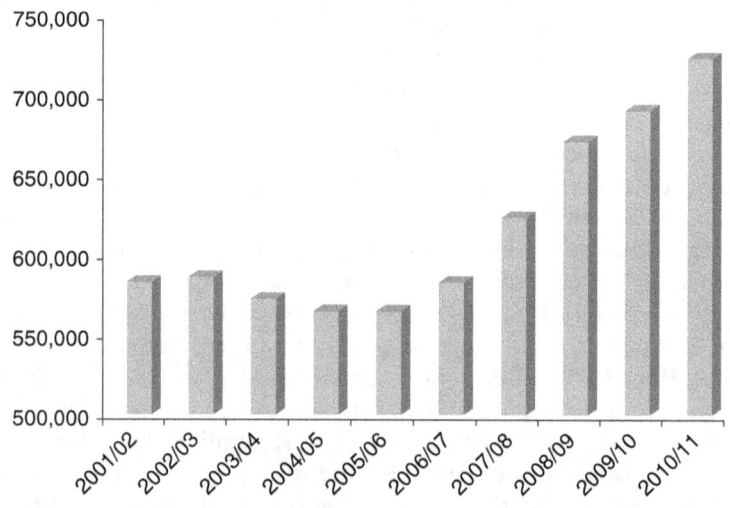

Figure 1.1 International student enrollments in the United States, 2001/02–2010/11
Source: Institute of International Education (2011a)

terms of recruiting and keeping global intellectual talent (McHale 2011; Lin, Pearce, and Wang 2009; Florida 2005) because of current weaknesses in the US and global economy and budget problems at the scale of individual universities (NSF 2010) that make it harder for students to obtain funded positions.

The contributions that international students make in the United States are increasingly being recognized, and universities compete aggressively for international enrollees. The number of international students that a university hosts is sometimes even interpreted as a marker of prestige (Lee 2010; Hazelkorn 2009). International students have long been considered significant contributors to the United States' knowledge economy (Lin, Pearce, and Wang 2009). In 1999, it was estimated that approximately one-quarter of those holding H1-B visas (the United States' visa category for highly skilled workers) had previously been enrolled in US universities, for instance, and some 40 percent of the United States' foreign-born population holds tertiary degrees (Solimano 2003, 5). Increasingly, international students are also being recognized for bringing more immediate economic benefits (Bhandari and Blumenthal 2011; Gürüz 2011). According to the US Department of Commerce, international students contribute nearly US$20 billion per year to the US economy through tuition and living expenses (Institute of International Education 2010), making higher education the fifth largest service export sector in the United States (Bhandari and Blumenthal 2011). With almost 70 percent of international students' funding originating from outside the United States (Institute of International Education 2010), and international students often paying higher tuition rates than domestic or local students (Khoser 2007), international students provide a much-needed financial injection into US tertiary education.

Regionally, South and East Asia are by far the dominant sending regions of international students to the United States, with China, India, and South Korea ranking first, second, and third in terms of student enrollments (figure 1.2). Fully 46 percent of international students are accounted for by these top three sending countries. Canada, Japan, Taiwan, and Saudi Arabia are also significant, although each country makes up less than 5 percent of total international enrollments (Institute of International Education 2011a).

Over the past ten years, approximately equal numbers of international students have arrived in the United States to pursue graduate as undergraduate studies, with a slight dominance of graduate students in most years. A far smaller proportion—over the last decade typically about 5 to 8 percent of the total number of international

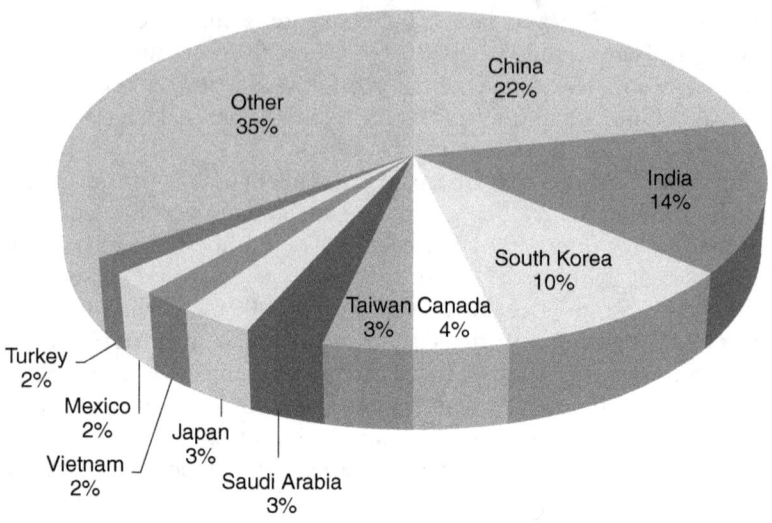

Figure 1.2 Country of origin of international students in the United States, 2010/11
Source: Institute of International Education (2011a)

students—arrive as nondegree seeking students (Institute of International Education 2011a). Business, management, and engineering comprise the top fields of study, accounting for approximately 40 percent of all enrollments in 2010/11. Beyond this, physical and life sciences, math and computer science, and the social sciences accounted for about 9 percent of students each (Institute of International Education 2011a). Waters and Brooks (2010) suggest that international students from low-income contexts tend to select fields of study on the basis of their potential to improve "employability" or "positional advantage," in order to justify the expense and effort of pursuing international study. The dominance of students from low-income countries such as India and China may, therefore, help to explain the large proportion of students pursuing subjects that enhance job prospects in a straightforward manner such as business, engineering, and computer science. Since 2006, foreign-born students—mostly Chinese, Indians, and South Koreans—have earned over 50 percent of US doctoral degrees in mathematics, computer science, physics, engineering, and economics (Bhandari and Blumenthal 2011).

International faculty members and other international scholars are also prominent on US campuses, although it is difficult to determine exactly what proportion of the faculty in the United States is

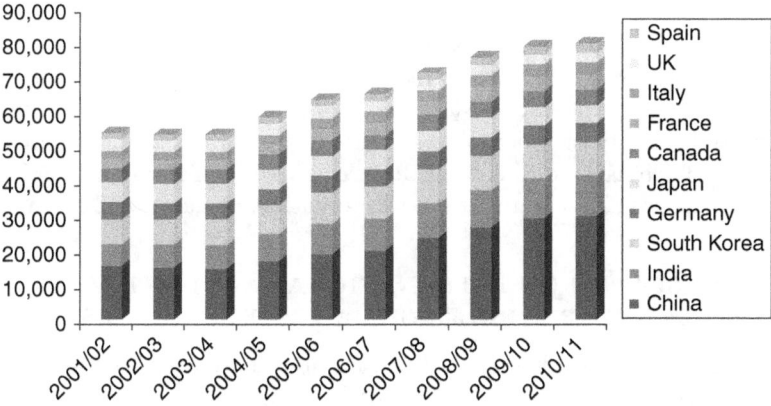

Figure 1.3 International scholars in the United States, 2001/02–2010/11
Source: Institute of International Education (2011b)

international owing to the lack of detailed data. Some estimates are available, however. Lin, Pearce, and Wang (2009) report that 22 percent of the faculty at four-year teaching colleges was foreign-born in 2003, approximately double the percentage of immigrants in the overall US population at that time. The Institute of International Education (2011b) reports that there were over 115,000 international scholars in the United States in 2010/11, and that their number has increased significantly over the past few years—the number was under 97,000 as recently as 2005/06. As with international students, a few countries dominate the flow of scholars coming to work in the United States; together, the top ten countries of origin account for roughly two-thirds of all international scholars in the United States. China is in a class of its own as a sending country, with over 30,000 scholars in the United States in 2010/11, but scholars from India (almost 12,000) and South Korea (over 9,000) are also numerically important (Institute of International Education 2011b). Beyond this, most other major sending countries are European (figure 1.3). This large proportion of East and South Asian academics represents a significant shift from the early years of international academic migrations when most international faculty were White males from Anglophone countries (Theobald 2009).

In 2010/11, two-thirds of international scholars were concentrated in just four fields—the biological and biomedical sciences (24.5%), health sciences (17.0%), engineering (12.9%), and physical sciences (11.5%). A large proportion of academic migrants are also drawn to a small number of "magnet" locations, both at the national and subnational scale. Indeed, international students and scholars are often concentrated at just a few institutions, often those that are most prestigious and receive most research funding (Gürüz 2011; Smetherham, Fenton, and Modood 2010). In 2010/11, the top recipient of international talent was Harvard University, with 4,459 international scholars, followed by Berkeley (2,929), Columbia (2,819), and Stanford (2,754) (Institute of International Education 2011b).

Research on International Student and Scholar Migrations and Experiences

As international student and scholar numbers have risen, and increasing attention is focused on processes of globalization, there has been a burgeoning interest in international academics. One body of literature, targeted at international students themselves, provides advice on succeeding in the US education system (e.g., Bailey 2011; Gebhard 2010; Lipson and Goodman 2008; Badke 2003); similar advice is available for international faculty (e.g., Alberts 2008; Wu 2003; Sarkisian 2000). A separate literature, aimed at contributing to academic debates and of greater relevance here, explores the characteristics and context of international student and faculty migrations (e.g., Bhandari and Blumenthal 2011; Gürüz 2011; Bevis and Lucas 2007). This literature examines, among other things, the characteristics and intentions of the migrants, the impact of the migrations on host and home societies, and the barriers and challenges experienced by migrants. Many studies investigate the experiences and characteristics of student migrants, often focusing on migrants from particular countries or regions (e.g., Brooks and Waters 2011; Liu-Farrer 2011; Waters 2008). Generally, less is known about the experiences and career trajectories of international faculty (Saltmarsh and Swirski 2010). Here we consider this literature on international academic migrations by theme.

Motivations for and Barriers to International Academic Migrations

In trying to understand the motivations for international academic migrations, many researchers list pros and cons of the migration process. Authors routinely cite advantages such as opportunities for career advancement, the appeal of experiencing a different culture, and the potential for personal development (e.g., Waters and Brooks 2010; Inkson and Myers 2003; Osland 1995). Financial concerns may also stimulate a move, with the search for research funding or affordable undergraduate studies directing students to particular countries and particular institutions within those countries. However, other factors such as high quality of life, open career structures, and the reputation of institutions are also important in attracting academic migrants (Ackers 2005; Mahroum 1998).

Despite the characterization of academics as having significant geographical flexibility, scholars are nonetheless embedded in a number of restrictive contexts, including the institutional, national, and social structures of their host country (Richardson 2009). In particular, national and institutional contexts impose specific requirements for individuals pursuing academic careers, including immigration restrictions and professional training requirements that may or may not transfer abroad (Kaulisch and Enders 2005; van de Bunt-Kokhuis 2000). Such factors suggest that we should not overstate the degree of flexibility that scholars have in their own careers, nor the ease with which academics are able to operate within new institutional and national contexts.

Characteristics and Patterns of International Academic Migration Flows to the United States

The demographic characteristics of faculty and students who undertake migrations to the United States are a popular theme in the literature. Studies have highlighted the increasing proportion of non-White, and particularly Asian, students in the migrant stream, many also exploring the particular challenges that this brings related to factors such as racial difference and working in a second language (e.g., Alberts 2007; Lee and Rice 2007). Among faculty, studies have noted the dominance of male, more senior, and non-White faculty in academic migrant flows. For instance, van de Bunt-Kokhuis (2000) found that higher ranking and male faculty are more likely to move, as are those with science backgrounds. Lin, Pearce, and Wang (2009) note the dominance of male and non-White faculty in international faculty flows to four-year teaching institutions. A number of studies reflect on the significance of this for institutional diversity, noting that international non-White faculty may constitute a more significant source of diversity than domestic non-White professors (e.g., Theobald 2009).

Stay rates of international academic migrants are often hard to obtain owing to a lack of data. Some statistics are available, however. Finn (2010) reports in his study of science and engineering graduates that 60 percent of students on a temporary visa when they graduated in 1997 were still in the United States ten years later. Rates of stay vary significantly among discipline and students' countries of origin, however. For instance, Johnson and Regets (1998) reported that students who stay more than four years after getting their PhD are far more likely to be employed in science and development than teaching. A few studies have investigated how migrants decide whether or not to return to their home country after graduation. For example, Zweig (1997) found that opinions on returning to China among Chinese migrants to the United States, including students and scholars, varied according to age, sex, and social background in China. Overall, however, there is a dearth of studies on international student and scholar return intentions and postgraduation movements.

Challenges of Pursuing an International Career

Many authors have highlighted the challenges of pursuing an international academic career. International students' difficulties in adapting to their new circumstances have been particularly well documented, including the challenges of transitioning to work and community life in a new context (e.g., Saltmarsh and Swirski 2010), the strain a move can have on personal and professional life (e.g., Richardson and Zikic 2007), and the impact of the transition on learning (e.g., Scheyvens, Wild, and Overton 2003). A large literature discusses the emotional, social, and psychological challenges of an international move (e.g., Sherry, Thomas, and Chui 2010; Cemalcilar and Falbo 2008; Sümer, Poyrazli, and Grahame 2008; Templer, Tay, and Chandrasekar 2006; Harris 2004).

Other studies have tried to identify those groups most at risk of experiencing problems while studying abroad, although consistent patterns across studies are elusive. For instance, Kwon (2009), in a study of gendered differences in international students' adjustment to the United States, concluded that women report experiencing greater challenges than men. Rosenthal, Russell, and Thomson (2008) found that female students not only experienced more psychological stress, but were also sometimes victims of sexual harassment or physical abuse. By contrast, Lee (2009) found that Asian women tend to adjust more easily than men. Other scholars have compared the experiences of different racial or ethnic groups. Many studies conclude that non-White students, particularly those working in a second language, experience significant challenges in adapting to new circumstances. For example, Lee and Rice (2007) found that students from the Middle East, Africa, East Asia, Latin America, and India reported far greater difficulties in adapting to US institutions than did students from Canada and Europe. Lee (2007, 28) reports racism directed at non-White international students and argues that a foreign accent is often interpreted as a sign of lesser intelligence, with incidents such as "less-than-objective academic evaluations; loss of employment or an inability to obtain a job; difficulty in forming interpersonal relationships with instructors, advisors, and peers; negative stereotypes and inaccurate portrayals of one's culture; negative comments about foreign accents; and so on" all related to ethnic discrimination. By contrast, Kwon (2009) found no significant differences in feelings of intimidation/isolation, homesickness, and loneliness among ethnic groups (although students whose English proficiency was poor did report having greater trouble adjusting), illustrating again how case specific the challenges faced by international academics may be.

Benefits and Disadvantages of Academic Flows for Sending and Receiving Countries

Another body of literature focuses not on individuals but on the benefits and disadvantages of international flows of students for host and sending countries. McHale (2011) argues that three main rationales exist for recruiting international students: revenue generation, knowledge production, and the development of a productive immigrant pool. Lee (2007) lists further benefits in the US context: improving the United States' intellectual capital, generating a positive regard toward the United States and building goodwill between countries, and broadening the perspectives of US students. She goes on to argue that "positive exchanges are essential to improving diplomatic relations, increasing international awareness, and furthering multiculturalism, all critical components of a thriving global society" (2007, 28).

International students can also provide a significant financial prop for domestic education systems (OECD 2010). Indeed, many countries, including the United States, have attempted to strategically position themselves in order to obtain a share of the lucrative international student market (Walker 2010). The importance of international students in financially supporting universities has even led to some concerns that standards may be lowered to admit or maintain high numbers of international students, as Baas (2007) reports in Australia.

Concerns about academic migrations within the United States are generally situated within a broader immigration literature that perceives immigration as a threat to domestic job stability. Beyond this, the impact of international faculty on American students has also received academic and popular press coverage (e.g., Gravois 2005; Neves and Sanyal 1991), with concerns being raised over the effectiveness of international academics as teachers. While most research on the topic has concluded that American students benefit overall, particularly from exposure to other cultures and new perspectives (e.g., Alberts 2008), a minority of commentators have argued that students may suffer from conflicting learning styles and even an inability to understand their international professors and teaching assistants (e.g., Borjas 2002).

For the sending country, too, the benefits and disadvantages of international academic migration flows must be carefully weighed. On the plus side, exchanges can generate benefits as students bring money, values, equipment, and ideas back to their home country, with international academics acting as "'carriers' of knowledge across borders" (Altbach 1989, 126). Even if academic migrants do not return permanently many remain in contact with their home country, transferring ideas and resources (Altbach 1989). For countries with less well-developed tertiary education sectors, sending students abroad for advanced training may even provide a cost-effective way to further domestic economic goals (OECD 2010).

Despite the potential advantages of international exchanges, concerns continue to be voiced over the loss of intellectual capital associated with academic migrations, since the flow of the highly skilled remains directed mainly toward affluent industrialized nations (Solimano 2003; Meyer, Kaplan, and Charum 2002; Cheng and Yang 1998), with a clear dominance in the flow of talent from East to West (Brooks and Waters 2009). Critical scholars have argued that international student flows are a reflection of persistent inequalities at the global scale (e.g., Cheng and Yang 1998), and questioned the inequity of industrialized nations gaining the greatest benefit from brain drain–type flows (e.g., Solimano 2003).

Inequalities and discrimination related to migration flows are also reflected within student populations. Lee and Rice (2007) and Lee (2007) discuss discrimination against international students of color and question the burden being placed on students from low-income countries in seeking a world-class education. At a finer scale, access to international study opportunities may serve to reproduce social advantage and disadvantage within countries (Waters and Brooks 2010; Findlay et al. 2006). Waters and Brooks (2010, 227) conclude that "there is a pressing need to examine further the uneven and often exclusive geographies of international student mobility."

Contributions of this Book

Despite this burgeoning of the international student body and increasing efforts toward the internationalization of education, US universities have shown mixed success in handling the challenges presented to them by globalization (Stearns 2009). A good understanding of the issues faced by international students and faculty is a critical first step toward devising effective strategies to help scholars meet the challenges of working abroad, in order to realize their full potential and enable them to contribute effectively to both home and host societies.

Through this volume, we add to existing scholarship in several ways. First, we examine both international students and faculty in the same volume, emphasizing continuity and commonalities between the two groups. Second, our volume contains chapters about several subpopulations that have not received much attention so far: African students and students and faculty from countries at a similar level of development as the United States. Third, several chapters address the issue of possible return migrations and the emergence of "brain circulation" and "knowledge diasporas," both recently emerged research areas. Fourth, we critically examine the contributions of international student and faculty migrations to broader internationalization efforts, questioning for instance whether international academics can provide the quick fix to diversity challenges that is often hoped. Finally, we provide targeted suggestions of ways in which these findings can be put to good use in improving the experiences of international academics and maximizing their potential contribution to the United States and their home countries.

The book is composed of three parts. Part one deals with the migration patterns and experiences of international students and faculty in the United States, including several case studies of international academics from different world regions. Focusing on the lived experiences of international migrants, this section includes analysis and discussion of migration trends and motivations. Part two focuses on diversity, considering how international academic migration patterns intersect with domestic diversity goals. Part three focuses on the challenges international academic migrants face, and how institutions can better support them to overcome these challenges. Overall, the book is designed to consider how we can use our understanding of trends and motivations of academic migrations to direct policy and goals within higher education for maximum benefit to migrants' home and host societies.

In part one Russell King, Allan Findlay, Jill Ahrens, and Alistair Geddes argue that British students are attracted to the United States by the promise of getting a world-class education at a prestigious US institution and the prospect of an international career. Wan Yu explores recent changes in the migration patterns of Chinese students, with particular attention to the increase in undergraduate migrants as well as return migrations. Continuing the theme of return migrations, Helen Hazen and Heike Alberts explore the factors international students consider in their return migration decisions, and Heike Alberts considers the reasons that keep many German faculty in the United States. Taken together, these chapters focus on the strengths of the US education system that attract international students and faculty from around the world, while also emphasizing the case-specific nature of these patterns. These cases also contribute to the growing body of evidence that international student and faculty migrations are not necessarily permanent, but part of a global circulation of talent.

In part two, Rebecca Theobald discusses the contributions international faculty make to the US higher-education system in the context of institutional attitudes toward diversity and internationalization. Continuing the topic of diversity, Kavita Pandit argues that increasing diversity through attracting international students and faculty cannot replace efforts to meet domestic diversity goals. Both authors emphasize the benefits of internationalization, but also point out some of the tensions that can arise as a result.

In part three, Alisa Eland and Kay Thomas investigate the challenges international students face in the United States and offer concrete advice for faculty, administrators, and staff in international offices supporting international students. Jane Irungu focuses specifically on the challenges African students face in the United States, and argues that international student programs need to be targeted to their particular needs. Ken Foote turns attention toward international faculty, providing a comprehensive overview of the challenges they face and strategies for supporting them. Heike Alberts, Helen Hazen, and Rebecca Theobald explore the challenges faced by non-native English-speaking instructors who teach American students, arguing that both students and teachers have to work together to ensure fruitful teaching and learning experiences. Collectively, these chapters raise awareness of issues faced by international students and scholars and offer strategies to address these.

Overall, this volume provides background information about trends and patterns in international scholar migrations, examines issues related to international scholar migrations through the lens of recently developed theoretical frameworks, and provides concrete suggestions toward ensuring that all parties benefit from the presence of international students and faculty. This book therefore speaks to academics, the international migrants themselves, and the support personnel serving them.

Works Cited

Ackers, L. 2005. "Moving People and Knowledge: Scientific Mobility in the European Union." *International Migration* 43(5): 99–131.
Alberts, H. 2008. "The Challenges and Opportunities of Foreign-Born Instructors in the Classroom." *Journal of Geography in Higher Education* 32(2): 189–203.
———. 2007. "Beyond the Headlines: Changing Patterns in International Student Enrollment in the United States." *GeoJournal* 68: 141–53.
Altbach, P. 1989. "The New Internationalism: Foreign Students and Scholars." *Studies in Higher Education* 14(2): 125–36.
Baas, M. 2007. "The Language of Migration: The Education Industry versus Migration Industry." *People and Place* 15(2): 49–60.
Badke, W. 2003. *Beyond the Answer Sheet: Academic Success for International Students*. Lincoln, NE: iUniverse.
Bailey, S. 2011. *Academic Writing: A Handbook for International Students*. New York: Routledge.
Bevis, T., and C. Lucas. 2007. *International Students in American Colleges and Universities: A History*. New York: Palgrave Macmillan.
Bhandari, R., and P. Blumenthal. 2011. "Global Student Mobility and the Twenty-First Century Silk Road: National Trends and Directions," In *International Students and Global Mobility in Higher Education: National Trends and New Directions*, edited by R. Bhandari, and P. Blumenthal, 1–23. New York: Palgrave Macmillan.
———. 2009. "Global Student Mobility: Moving towards Brain Exchange," In *Higher Education on the Move: New Developments in Global Mobility*, edited by R. Bhandari, and P. Blumenthal, 1–15. New York: Institute of International Education.
Borjas, G. 2002. "Rethinking Foreign Students: A Question of the National Interest." *National Review* 54(11). Available at: http://www.hks.harvard.edu/fs/gborjas/publications/popular/NR061702.htm. Accessed: September 5, 2011.
Brooks, R., and J. Waters. 2011. *Student Mobilities, Migration, and the Internationalization of Higher Education*. London: Palgrave Macmillan.
———. 2009. "A Second Chance at 'Success': UK Students and Global Circuits of Higher Education." *Sociology* 43(6): 1085–1102.
Cemalcilar, Z., and T. Falbo. 2008. "A Longitudinal Study of the Adaptation of International Students in the United States." *Journal of Cross-Cultural Psychology* 39(6): 799–804.

Cheng, L., and P. Yang. 1998. "Global Interaction, Global Inequality, and Migration of the Highly Trained to the United States." *International Migration Review* 32(3): 626–53.

Childress, L. 2009. "Internationalization Plans for Higher Education Institutions." *Journal of Studies in International Education* 13(3): 289–309.

Dollag, B. 2004. "Wanted: Foreign Students." *The Chronicle of Higher Education* 51(7): A37.

Field, K., P. Mooney, and S. Neelakantan. 2004. "Fixing the Visa Quagmire." *Chronicle of Higher Education* 51(7): A40–1.

Findlay, A., R. King, A. Stam, and E. Ruiz-Gelices. 2006. "Ever Reluctant Europeans: The Changing Geographies of UK Students Studying and Working Abroad." *European Urban and Regional Studies* 13: 291–318.

Finn, M. 2010. "Stay Rate of Foreign Doctorate Recipients from U.S. Universities, 2007." Oak Ridge, TN: Oak Ridge Institute for Science and Education.

Florida, R. 2005. *The Flight of the Creative Class: The New Global Competition for Talent*. New York: HarperCollins.

Gaillard, J., and A. Gaillard. 1997. "The International Mobility of Brains: Exodus or Circulation?" *Science, Technology & Society* 2(2): 195–228.

Gebhard, J. 2010. *What Do International Students Think and Feel? Adapting to U.S. College Life and Culture*. Ann Arbor, MI: University of Michigan Press.

Glick Schiller, N., L. Basch, and C. Szanton Blanc. 1992. *Towards a Transnational Perspective on Migration*. Annals of the New York Academy of Sciences 645.

Goldin, I., G. Cameron, and M. Belajaran. 2011. *Exceptional People: How Migration Shaped Our World and Will Define Our Future*. Princeton and Oxford: Princeton University Press.

Goodman, A., and R. Gutierrez. 2011. "The International Dimension of US Higher Education: Trends and New Perspectives." In *International Students and Global Mobility in Higher Education. National Trends and New Directions*, edited by R. Bhandari, and P. Blumenthal, 83–106. New York: Palgrave Macmillan.

Gravois, J. 2005. "Teach Impediment. When the Student Can't Understand the Instructor, Who Is to Blame?" *The Chronicle of Higher Education*, April 8: A10–12.

Gürüz, K. 2011. *Higher Education and International Student Mobility in the Global Knowledge Economy*. Albany, NY: State University of New York Press.

Harris, H. 2004. "Global Careers: Work-Life Issues and the Adjustment of Women International Managers." *Journal of Management Development* 23: 818–32.

Hazelkorn, E. 2009. "Higher Education Rankings and the Global 'Battle for Talent.'" In *Higher Education on the Move: New Developments in Global*

Mobility, edited by R. Bhandari, and P. Blumenthal, 79–92. New York: Institute of International Education.

Hindrawan, J. 2003. "International Student Recruitment since 9/11." *World Education News and Reviews*, March/April. Available at: http://www.wes.org/ewenr/03March/PFFeature.htm. Accessed: August 21, 2011.

Inkson, K., and B. Myers. 2003. "The Big OE: Self-Directed Travel and Career Development." *Career Development International* 8: 170–81.

Institute of International Education. 2011a. "Fast Facts." Available at: http://www.iie.org/en/research-and-publications/open-doors. Accessed: May 25, 2012.

———. 2011b. "International Scholars." Available at: http://www.iie.org/Research-and-Publications/Open-Doors/Data/International-Scholars. Accessed: May 25, 2012.

———. 2010. "Press Release: International Student Enrollments Rose Modestly in 2009/10, Led by Strong Increase in Students from China." Available at: http://www.iie.org/Who-We-Are/News-and-Events/Press-Center/Press-Releases/2010/2010-11-15-Open-Doors-International-Students-In-The-US. Accessed: July 28, 2011.

Jasso, G., V. Wadhwa, G. Gereffi, B. Rissing, and R. Freeman. 2010. "How Many Highly Skilled Foreign-Born Are Waiting in Line for U.S. Legal Permanent Residence?" *International Migration Review* 44(2): 477–98.

Johnson, J., and M. Regets. 1998. "International Mobility of Scientists and Engineers to the United States—Brain Drain or Brain Circulation?" Issue Brief, Division of Science Resources Studies, NSF 98–316, June 22.

Kaulisch, M., and J. Enders. 2005. "Careers in Overlapping Institutional Contexts: The Case of Academe." *Career Development International* 10(2): 130–44.

Kelly, A. 2009. "Globalisation and Education: A Review of Conflicting Perspectives and Their Effect on Policy and Professional Practice in the UK." *Globalisation, Societies and Education* 7(1): 51–68.

Khoser, K. 2007. *International Migration: A Very Short Introduction*. Oxford: Oxford University Press.

Kim, T. 2009. "Transnational Academic Mobility: Internationalization and Interculturality in Higher Education." *Intercultural Education* 20(5): 395–405.

Kwon, Y. 2009. "Factors Affecting International Students' Transition to Higher Education Institutions in the United States." *College Student Journal* 43(4): 1020–36.

Lee, J. 2010. "International Students' Experiences and Attitudes at a US Host Institution: Self Reports and Future Recommendations." *Journal of Research in International Education* 9(1): 66–84.

———. 2007. "Neo-Racism toward International Students." *About Campus* (Jan-Feb): 28–30.

Lee, J., and C. Rice. 2007. "Welcome to America? International Student Perceptions of Discrimination." *Higher Education* 53(3): 381–409.

Lee, S. 2009. "Gendered Differences in International Students' Adjustment." *College Student Journal* 43(4): 1217.

Lin, Z., R. Pearce, and W. Wang. 2009. "Imported Talents: Demographic Characteristics, Achievement and Job Satisfaction of Foreign-Born Full Time Faculty in Four-Year American Colleges." *Higher Education* 57: 703–21.

Lipson, C., and A. Goodman. 2008. *Succeeding as an International Student in the United States and Canada.* Chicago, IL: University of Chicago Press.

Liu-Farrer, G. 2011. *Labour Migration from China to Japan: International Students, Transnational Migrants.* New York: Routledge.

Mahroum, S. 1998. "Europe and the Challenge of the Brain Drain." IPTS Report 29. Available at: http://www.jrc.ed/pages/iptsreport/vol29/english/SAT1E296.htm. Accessed: April 18, 2012.

McCormack, E. 2007. "Number of Foreign Students Bounces Back to Near-Record High." *Chronicle of Higher Education* 54(12): A1.

McHale, J. 2011. "Structural Incentives to Attract Foreign Students to Canada's Postsecondary Educational System: A Comparative Analysis." In *International Students and Global Mobility in Higher Education. National Trends and New Directions*, edited by R. Bhandari, and P. Blumenthal, 167–91. New York: Palgrave Macmillan.

McNamee, S., and G. Faulkner. 2001. "The International Exchange Experience and the Social Construction of Meaning." *Journal of Studies in International Education* 5: 64.

Meyer, J., D. Kaplan, and J. Charum. 2002. "Scientific Nomadism and the New Geopolitics of Knowledge." *International Social Science Journal* 53(168): 309–21.

Mooney, P., and S. Neelakantan. 2004. "No Longer Dreaming of America." *The Chronicle of Higher Education* 51(7): A41.

NAFSA. 2007. "An International Education Policy for U.S. Leadership, Competitiveness, and Security." Available at: http://www.nafsa.org/public_policy.sec/united_states_international/toward_an_international/. Accessed: September 3, 2011.

———. 2003. "In America's Interest: Welcoming International Students." Report of the Strategic Task Force on International Student Access. Available at: http://www.nafsa.org/uploadedFiles/NAFSA_Home/Resource_Library_Assets/Public_Policy/in_america_s_interest.pdf. Accessed: September 3, 2011.

Neves, J., and R. Sanyal. 1991. "Classroom Communication and Teaching Effectiveness: The Foreign-Born Instructor." *Journal of Education for Business* 66(5): 304–8.

[NSF] National Science Foundation, Division of Science Resources Statistics. 2010 (July). Foreign Science and Engineering Students in the United States. Arlington, VA (NSF 10–324).

OECD. 2010. "Education at a Glance, 2010." Available at: http://www.oecd.org/dataoecd/45/39/45926093.pdf. Accessed: July 27, 2011.

Osland, J. 1995. *The Adventure of Working Abroad.* San Francisco, CA: Jossey-Bass.
Richardson, J. 2009. "Geographic Flexibility in Academia: A Cautionary Note." *British Journal of Management* 20: 160–70.
Richardson, J., and J. Zikic. 2007. "The Darker Side of an International Academic Career." *Career Development International* 2: 164–86.
Rosenthal, A., J. Russell, and G. Thomson. 2008. "The Health and Wellbeing of International Students at an Australian University." *Higher Education* 55: 51–67.
Saltmarsh, S., and T. Swirski. 2010. "'Pawns and Prawns': International Academics' Observations on Their Transition to Working in an Australian University." *Journal of Higher Education Policy and Management* 32(3): 291–301.
Sarkisian, E. 2000. *Teaching American Students: A Guide for International Faculty and Teaching Assistants in Colleges and Universities.* Cambridge, MA: Derek Bok Center for Teaching and Learning, Harvard University.
Scheyvens, R., K. Wild, and J. Overton. 2003. "International Students Pursuing Postgraduate Study in Geography: Impediments to Their Learning Experiences." *Journal of Geography in Higher Education* 27(3): 309–23.
Sherry, M., P. Thomas, and W. Chui. 2010. "International Students: A Vulnerable Student Population." *Higher Education* 60: 33–46.
Smetherham, C., S. Fenton, and T. Modood. 2010. "How Global Is the UK Academic Labour Market?" *Globalisation, Societies and Education* 8(3): 411–28.
Solimano, A. 2003. "Globalizing Talent and Human Capital: Implications for Developing Countries." Santiago: UN. Available at: http://www.andressolimano.com/articles/migration/Globalizing%20Human%20Capital,%20manuscript.pdf. Accessed: August 5, 2011.
Stearns, P. 2009. *Educating Global Citizens in Colleges and Universities: Challenges and Opportunities.* New York: Routledge.
Sümer, S., S. Poyrazli, and K. Grahame. 2008. "Predictors of Depression and Anxiety among International Students." *Journal of Counseling and Development* 86: 429–37.
Templer, K., C. Tay, and N. Chandrasekar. 2006. "Motivational Cultural Intelligence, Realistic Job Preview, Realistic Living Conditions Preview, and Cross-Cultural Adjustment." *Group and Organization Management* 31: 154–73.
Theobald, R. 2009. "New Faces in Academic Places: Gender and the Experiences of Early-Career Foreign-Born and Native-Born Geographers in the United States." *Journal of Geographical Sciences* 57: 7–22.
Van de Bunt-Kokhuis, S. 2000. "Going Places: Social and Legal Aspects of International Faculty Mobility." *Higher Education in Europe* 25(1): 47–55.
Vertovec, S. 2002. "Transnational Networks and Skilled Labour Migration." Paper presented at the Ladenburger Diskurs "Migration" Gottlieb

Daimler- und Karl Benz-Stiftung conference, Ladenburg, February 14–15.

Walker, P. 2010. "Guests and Hosts—the Global Market in International Higher Education: Reflections on the Japan-UK Axis in Study Abroad." *Journal of Research in International Education* 9: 168–84.

Waters, J. 2008. *Education, Migration, and Cultural Capital in the Chinese Diaspora*. New York: Cambria Press.

Waters, J., and R. Brooks. 2010. "Accidental Achievers? International Higher Education, Class Reproduction and Privilege in the Experiences of US Students Overseas." *British Journal of Sociology of Education* 31(2): 217–28.

Wu, X. 2003. "Challenges of Accommodating Non-Native English Speaking Instructors' Teaching and Native-English Speaking Students' Learning in College, and the Exploration of Potential Solutions." MA Thesis, University of Wisconsin-Stout.

Zweig, D. 1997. "To Return or Not to Return: Politics vs. Economics in China's Brain Drain." *Studies in International Comparative Development* 32(1): 92–125.

1
MIGRATION PATTERNS AND EXPERIENCES

2

British Students in the United States

Motivations, Experiences, and Career Aspirations

Russell King, Allan Findlay, Jill Ahrens, and Alistair Geddes

Introduction: Laura Spence and Beyond

Twelve years ago, the British educational press, and indeed the mainstream media, were consumed by the story of Laura Spence—a super-bright pupil from a Newcastle comprehensive school who, despite having five straight As at "A" level (the final secondary school exams in Britain), had been refused a place to study medicine at Oxford after an interview there. General outrage at Oxford's snobbishness ensued, with the criticism that Oxford favored applicants from the United Kingdom's fee-paying independent schools (which include the elite but perversely named "public schools"), thereby excluding excellent applicants from state schools like Laura, especially if they come from deprived parts of the country with strong local accents. Laura instead went to the United States to Harvard on a funded scholarship, completed her biochemistry degree there, and returned to do postgraduate medical training at Cambridge—the other UK university that constitutes the top duo known collectively as "Oxbridge."

How typical is Laura's story? Are there many British students who, as Oxbridge "rejects," or fearful of being turned down for a place at the United Kingdom's two ancient and most prestigious universities, apply abroad to widen their chances of success at other globally recognized institutions? Brooks and Waters (2009a) argue that there are indeed those like Laura who apply to US universities as a "second chance at success"; but our research suggests that there are many other explanations for the increase in international study. Since the United States is the most important destination for people from the United Kingdom studying abroad, the findings of this chapter are particularly important in producing a more robust understanding of the key drivers of international student mobility between one advanced economy and another. We suggest that there are some movers for whom study abroad is part of a carefully strategized plan of international career enhancement, while for others it is a product of their class habitus and family networks (see Bourdieu 1977). We also argue that there are those who are looking for "something different" yet, at the same time, desire a "knowable" destination, familiar to them for example from film and television and without any great linguistic challenge.

In the next section we describe our research project and its aims and methods. The main body of the chapter is made up of three sections that correspond to our three key research topics: students' motivations for study in the United States; their experiences there; and their future career plans. The conclusion emphasizes the motivational and strategic nature of UK student migration to the United States, targeted especially at universities perceived to be of high international standing. In terms of the link between study abroad and future career plans, fears about a putative British "brain drain" are shown to be largely unfounded, since most students abroad plan to return to the United Kingdom.

Survey and Methods

We need to draw a distinction at the outset between two types of international student mobility: credit mobility and degree mobility. Credit mobility entails a period abroad of up to one year (a summer school, a semester, or a junior year abroad), the key feature of which is that the student then returns to his or her home university and completes the program of study there, bringing back the credit for the time spent abroad (course credit, grades, etc.). Degree mobility (sometimes referred to as diploma mobility) is when a student goes abroad for the entire degree program—typically a bachelor's, master's, or doctoral qualification—and stays abroad for a minimum of one year, but usually longer. Our study examines degree mobility only. Our previous research on credit mobility—mainly on the

Erasmus student exchange scheme within Europe (Findlay et al. 2006; King and Ruiz-Gelices 2003)—will be referred to in passing, where it offers instructive comparisons with the results of research on degree mobility reported below.

The research reported here was commissioned by the United Kingdom's Department for Business Innovations and Skills (BIS). Survey and field research took place over 18 months from March 2008 to August 2009. The two reports to BIS—a main synthesis report (Findlay and King 2010) and a supplementary metadata analysis (Findlay, Geddes, and Smith 2010)—were published in January 2010. These reports are quite brief and summarize key findings mainly for a policy audience. In this chapter and a recently published paper (Findlay et al. 2012), we delve deeper into our research findings and explore them in a way that is both more detailed and more academic.

Behind the research lay two general concerns: first, that not enough is known about the scale and characteristics of UK outward degree mobility; and, second, that we need to understand how to interpret the significance of this outflow. Should the UK government be concerned that many of the "brightest and best" students are being "lost" to overseas universities, from which they might not return, thereby constituting a brain drain reminiscent of the loss of British scientists abroad in the 1960s? Or should the authorities be worried that not enough British students are going abroad, and that many are thereby missing out on the added value that an international education and cosmopolitan outlook can bring, leading in turn to a loss of competitiveness in a globalized labor market where international experience and intercultural skills count for more and more?

Our survey methods were fourfold; only the data from the third and fourth are used extensively in this chapter:

1. A metadata analysis of statistical sources on global and UK student mobility (see Findlay, Geddes, and Smith 2010).
2. A questionnaire survey of the university application intentions of 1,400 final-year school students in two regions in England, with special reference to applications to study abroad (see Ahrens et al. 2010).
3. A questionnaire survey of 560 UK students studying abroad for degrees at universities in the United States (218), Ireland (200), Australia (108), and other European countries (34).
4. Face-to-face interviews with 80 UK students studying abroad, half of them in the United States.

The survey of 560 UK students studying abroad was designed to draw the broad contours of the phenomenon of UK outward student mobility. It had five main sections: status at present (degree course, university, means of financing studies, prior international mobility); school background (type of school, exam results, languages learnt/spoken, help from school to apply abroad); decision making to study abroad (ratings of the importance of various factors, including future career plans); experience of studying abroad (perceived value, social contacts, problems, etc.); and general information about the respondent (age, sex, ethnicity, parents' education and occupations). The face-to-face interviews covered a similar range of issues, but were more in-depth, and included "softer" topics like shifting identity.

Before we discuss our main empirical results, let us briefly mention some secondary data that give an idea of the importance of the United States as a destination for UK degree students and the trends over time. Whatever definition of international students is used,[1] the United States emerges as by far the most important destination, with four times the number of UK students compared to the second most important host country, and about 40 percent of the total stock of UK students abroad. UK students in the United States numbered 6,744 in 1998, and have increased steadily to 8,783 in 2010, according to data synthesized from OECD and UNESCO (Findlay, Geddes, and Smith 2010, 6, updated). Looking at the Institute of International Education (IIE) figures for the decade 2000–2010, 50–60 percent of UK students in higher education in the United States are undergraduates, 28–33 percent are graduate students (master's and doctoral), and the rest (8–15%) are on "other" programs of study, mostly postgraduate and vocational diplomas (IIE data summarized in Findlay, Geddes, and Smith 2010).

In the rest of the chapter we present a mix of questionnaire and interview data; we also draw on a recent comprehensive review on international student mobility, which surveys and evaluates the relevant international literature (King, Findlay, and Ahrens 2010).

Motivations and Characteristics

A review of the literature suggests that the reasons why students choose to move internationally for their studies have remained fairly stable over time. One interpretation of this is that students and their advisors (tutors, parents, etc.) are "rational actors" looking for the best outcome in terms of study opportunities and the economic and career benefits deriving therefrom. "Lifestyle" and "experience" also play a role; however, these factors are less amenable to economic quantification (King, Findlay, and Ahrens 2010, 23–35).

Based on what the literature suggests and on our prior experience of researching credit-mobile students (Findlay et al. 2006; HEFCE 2004), we presented our respondents (UK-origin degree-mobile students) with a list of six potentially relevant factors motivating their decision to study abroad and asked them to rate their importance on a four-point scale (very, some, or no importance, and not applicable). Table 2.1 presents the results for the whole sample of respondents, as well as for the US subsample. The data show rather clear patterns. Two factors, attending a world-class university and having a unique adventure, are of paramount importance for most respondents, and are of great or some importance for around nine out of ten respondents. Hence the combination of "adventure" and a "world-class education" seems to encapsulate the essence of studying abroad (especially in the United States) for UK students. The third factor, career planning, also has considerable relevance; we come back to this factor later in the chapter. The remaining three factors are of lesser importance, although one can imagine that the fees issue may well rise up the table in the coming years, given that university fees are set to triple in the next academic year (2012/13).

Table 2.1 Motivations for studying abroad

	Percentage of responses to each question			
	Overall sample (n=560)		US subsample (n=218)	
	very important	some + very important	very important	some + very important
1. I was determined to attend a "world-class" university	55.0	88.7	71.9	91.6
2. I saw studying abroad as an opportunity for a unique adventure	50.4	87.9	56.7	92.6
3. I saw this as the first step to an international career	33.8	68.7	42.6	77.4
4. There were limited places for my desired course at UK universities	24.1	42.5	20.3	37.3
5. I was worried about rising student fees in the UK	18.6	33.9	10.6	25.0
6. My family encouraged me to study outside the UK	11.6	27.3	8.2	21.6

Source: Authors' survey 2008/09.

Comparing the total survey findings with the US subsample shows that UK students in the United States are more highly motivated by the first three factors, and less so by the other three than the sample as a whole (which included students in Canada, Australia, Ireland, and several other European countries). This indicates to us that British students in the United States are *particularly* attracted by the desire to attend a world-class university and the prospect that this offers for an international career, as well as the "life experience" of studying in the United States.

The pattern of responses in table 2.1 confirms students' awareness of a global hierarchy of universities. Oxford, Cambridge, Harvard, Yale, and other Ivy League institutions seem to dominate most people's mental lists of world-class universities; these rankings are confirmed (but also produced) by published rankings of universities nationally and worldwide. The "world-class university" syndrome is seen to be the most important decision-making factor (see also Findlay, Geddes, and Smith 2012), although we probably need to reflect on methodological issues of questionnaire design and autosuggestion to fully appraise this conclusion.[2]

Abundant interview evidence confirms the importance of university reputation in UK students' decisions to go to the United States. For many, especially at undergraduate level, it was a matter of applying to the United States alongside simultaneous applications to top UK universities like Oxford, Cambridge, Edinburgh, Durham, and the London colleges; or at postgraduate level combining an undergraduate degree from a top-tier (or "Russell Group") research university with a highly ranked US institution. For example, Jake, now a final-year Harvard undergraduate, was interested in music and visual arts and applied to several places in the UK (Goldsmiths, King's, Surrey) and in the United States (Georgetown, Harvard, Yale). When he was offered a place at Harvard, his reasons for accepting were clear: "It was just Harvard; I couldn't justify turning it down...it's a top brand-name...so it was a no-brainer really." Mansour had done his first degree at the London School of Economics (LSE), then an MPhil at Oxford, and became aware that the top doctoral programs in his field (economics and finance), which would equip him best for an academic career or a fast-track position in the private sector, were in the United States. Now on a funded five-year PhD program at New York University, he contrasted the intensity of the doctoral training there, "where you get involved in writing joint papers with your professor," with the three-year UK PhD, "where you are pretty much left on your own." Isabella had followed her undergraduate degree at Oxford with a master's at Yale and now a PhD at Columbia. She was aware of her good fortune in stringing together such a sequence of prestigious institutions. During a year abroad after Oxford, working in Bethlehem in the West Bank, she received "the offer and a great funding package from Yale...the admissions officer emailed me...she even called me there to talk about the program." She then continued to a fully funded PhD at Columbia in New York, "which is such an amazing city to live in." She went on to say: "The universities in the US have incredible resources and you notice that in many fields...great libraries, well so does Oxford actually, but there is also a lot of funding for other things...[like] visiting speakers."

There are obvious linkages between the motivations of students and their characteristics—whether they are undergraduate or postgraduate, their UK school history (state versus independent, etc.), parental background, and prior mobility to and contacts with the United States. Brooks and Waters (2009b, 197) summed up the key characteristics of their interviewees thus: "The vast majority of our respondents...came from high socio-economic groups, had attended private secondary schools, and had achieved high levels of academic attainment." They argue that such students are motivated to acquire the "right" credentials and other embodied life and travel experiences, which can subsequently be converted into confirmed or enhanced social status and economic capital (Waters and Brooks 2010). In this way, and following Bourdieu's (1986) "forms of capital," students who study in an international arena, especially if they attend high-prestige universities, accumulate multiple and mutually reinforcing forms of capital, including "mobility capital" (Murphy-Lejeune 2002), human capital (in the form of a world-class education), social capital ("connections" and access to networks), cultural capital (languages and intercultural skills), and, career-wise, economic capital (high-income employment).

All this rings true for our own research subjects, with one exception—Brooks and Waters' (2009b, 197) statement that "the vast majority" of their respondents had attended private sector secondary schools (even though no precise figures are given). From our questionnaire results, we found that our sample (both the total of 560 and the US subsample of 218) divided roughly evenly into those who had attended private schools and those who were from the state sector. This equal division still represents an overconcentration from the private/independent sector, which accounts for only 11 percent of the United Kingdom's senior school pupils (Findlay and King 2010, 18, 25), but our data do not support the notion of the "vast majority."[3] Instead, our findings suggest that degree mobility plays a role in maintaining status for students from privileged backgrounds, and in acquiring cultural capital for students from less-privileged origins.

School background aside, other aspects of the respondents match the above characterization of UK students in the United States. High academic standards were confirmed by the finding that four out of five respondents had three or more A or B grades at "A" level, the key secondary-level qualification for university entry. Most came from family backgrounds where their parents, too, were university educated. Prior mobility history and connections to the United States were indicated by several questionnaire variables. One in five respondents had been born outside the United Kingdom, and the same proportion (mostly the same individuals) had dual nationality. One in fourteen had studied at international schools outside the United Kingdom. More than half of the respondents had lived abroad for more than six months prior to moving to the United States, and half of these respondents had lived in the United States for more than six months before becoming university students there. Finally, one in five had family/relatives in the United States.

Some of the reasons for taking up a university offer from the United States depended on whether the student was moving there at undergraduate or postgraduate level. Our sample was distributed in three roughly equal proportions: undergraduate students (32 percent), students doing master's or other short postgraduate courses (37 percent), and doctoral students (29 percent). The breadth of the liberal arts approach of many US universities appealed to many undergraduate respondents wary of the structure of most British university degrees, which require students to specialize at a very early stage. For Jake, this had been especially important:

> I didn't know what I wanted to study. I did a fairly eclectic mix of "A" level subjects, biology, music, English, and geography, so a bit of a mix... So I didn't know what to study and I really could only apply to one subject [in the UK]... I hadn't really been to America, but I kind of liked the idea of going off to a new culture... But it was really just the subjects... I guess also the liberal arts system, the fact that I can do a lot of different courses unrelated to my subject... more than if I went to somewhere in Britain.

Megan, who was at the same Ivy League university as Jake, had a similar reaction:

> The choice of courses is absolutely amazing, just ridiculous. There are... I don't know over 4,000 courses you can take, and you take four each semester. And the things you learn about... you learn to appreciate the fact that you are doing so many different things.

Table 2.2 Main sources of funding for studies in the United States

	Percentage of respondents			
	Undergraduate (n=69)	Master's (n=81)	Doctoral (n=63)	Total (213)
Self-financing	5.9	24.4	1.6	11.6
Parental support	58.8	23.1	0.0	27.9
Grant from host institution	19.1	15.4	85.5	36.7
Bank loan/employer/other	16.2	37.1	12.9	23.7

Source: Authors' survey 2008/09.

Funding, too, was important for undergraduates, especially those whose means-tested circumstances enabled them to secure partial or even full funding at top universities whose fees would otherwise have been way in excess of what they could afford, and much more expensive than the UK university fees (£3,145 at the time of the survey, rising to £9,000 currently). For doctoral students, scholarships and teaching assistantships were even more vital in attracting them to the United States, with PhD funding so hard to obtain in the UK system. Table 2.2 shows the differential pattern of funding sources across the three respondent groups.

Several students wrote snippets of reaction to the funding issue in the open text box on the questionnaire. The following two examples are from postgraduate respondents:

> Yale pays me $50,000 a year to go here—Oxford would give me nothing.

> Although I was accepted as a PhD candidate by my first-choice university in the UK, I did not secure funding from the Arts and Humanities Research Council, and was unable to take up my place.

The interviewees naturally went into more detail. Here is a fairly typical quotation from Jake:

> I am on fairly significant financial aid...and this year they upped the financial aid for everyone...So this year it costs the same amount to send me to Harvard as it does to send my sister to Leeds, if you factor in the housing, the food...it costs pretty much the same...I think the financial system [in the United States] is very beneficial...because the way they work it out, you pay what you can afford. Theoretically, it shouldn't be a barrier to anyone.

While one might quibble about the precise figures and economic calculations in the quotations above, the key point is that funding in the United States, especially for graduate programs, is more generous and readily available than in the United Kingdom.

Experiences

Students were very satisfied overall with the experience of studying in the United States. This is clearly indicated by table 2.3, which is based on a question in the survey that asked respondents to rate the various benefits from their study abroad using a four-point scale (extremely worthwhile, worthwhile, slightly worthwhile, not at all worthwhile). The data are presented in two sets. The first set gives the responses for all US-based respondents who regarded their experience as being "worthwhile" or "extremely worthwhile." There were no significant differences by level of study (undergraduate,

Table 2.3 Perceived benefits of studying outside the United Kingdom

	Percentage of respondents				
	US sample: all respondents (n=218)		UG only: extremely worthwhile		
	extremely worthwhile (%)	extremely ww + worthwhile (%)	US (n=69) (%)	Australia (n=51) (%)	Ireland (n=150) (%)
1. Enhanced academic and professional knowledge	82.5	96.2	80.3	66.7	56.0
2. General career prospects	71.0	93.8	68.3	60.1	43.5
3. Relevance to developing an international career	65.1	91.4	62.3	51.9	28.5
4. Maturity and personal development	57.3	90.5	55.5	50.9	46.5
5. Knowledge and understanding of another country	41.7	78.2	40.4	32.4	30.5
6. New ways of thinking about the UK	40.8	71.6	39.4	38.0	38.5

Source: Authors' survey 2008/09.

master's, or doctoral level), so we have not disaggregated the data in this way. We observe from these data the extremely positive impression of the "US experience" across the first four benefits: academic and personal knowledge, general career enhancement, relevance to an international career, and personal development. For each of these factors, over 90 percent of respondents marked "extremely worthwhile" or "worthwhile." The second set of results in the table compares undergraduates in the United States with the same group in Australia and Ireland (we limit this comparison to undergraduates because postgraduates are proportionally fewer in the latter two destinations). Here students in the United States score more positively on every single one of the six "benefit" measures. Some of the differences are marginal, but those which are clearest are, in a sense, the most important—enhanced academic, professional, and career prospects.

We leave further discussion on career aspirations until the next section of the chapter, so let us now hear some students' voices about their experiences of other aspects. We heard before (from Isabella, above) about the great atmosphere of being in New York City, and others confirmed the special experience of living in one of the world's most iconic and vibrant cities. For instance Ali, doing a master's at Columbia, said:

> And that's the luck of being at Columbia, the access to things in New York...such a great city...For instance, there's a calendar of events every week that has people coming from the United Nations and people from financial institutions...And being in New York is really nice [laughs].

Others preferred the more informal atmosphere of certain institutions on the West Coast. Emily described her choice to go to Berkeley rather than MIT in Boston in the following way:

> The whole atmosphere is phenomenal, it's incredibly driven, incredibly motivated and intelligent, and also supportive because I applied to a couple of schools...MIT is the biggest one where everyone I spoke to was...like a gladiator going into a ring every day, where you have to fight and fight because the egos are so immense. Whereas at Berkeley you call everyone by their first name, everyone is allowed to talk to everyone, it's really nice.

Emily's comment about the high-pressure work environment was echoed in practically every student interview we carried out. Here are two quotations from many we could have selected. The first is from Megan, an undergraduate at Harvard and a keen swimmer:

> Now I'm pretty much adjusted, but in the beginning there was a lot [of pressure]. The time commitment was ridiculous...it felt like a 24-hour job...I would have ten or 12 hours of lectures or classes a week and then loads of training and swimming competitions...so the time commitment is just ridiculous. It's just tiring and you do a lot of running around, and you don't have any down-time basically. That is a big adjustment and on top of that you are 4,000 miles from home, which doesn't help the situation. But you do get used to it.

Sally had done a year of history at Cambridge but then took a break before transferring to Columbia for the rest of her degree because she wanted broader training for her intended career as an international affairs journalist:

> The workload is just insane...This is a lot more work than I ever, ever remember there being at Cambridge...So the downside is the quantity of the work but...I love the work but...I don't have any time to eat or sleep!

The intensive work schedule and consequent lack of social life—especially for undergraduates, it seems—stand in contrast to the impression gained from Waters and Brooks' (2010) research, which argues for understanding degree-mobile British students as "accidental achievers" for whom the desire to prolong a "carefree student lifestyle" was often a key factor. These authors (2010, 226) see the tension between deliberate "strategy" and the "accidental" accumulation of capital (in its various forms) as part of the "aesthetic disposition" and "taken-for-grantedness" of the habitus of the British (upper) middle class. Such a view sees "excitement" and "adventure" associated with studying abroad as merely expressions of the reproduction of privilege that is firmly grounded in the social networks of family and friends (Brooks and Waters 2010). But, delving into the school and family backgrounds of our student interviewees, we see at least some of them acting more independently, without much parental social capital back up, or help from school tutors. Ben, another of our Harvard interviewees, described his secondary school in Bedfordshire as "just a state school...my local school...we had no history at the school of any students applying outside the UK."

The pressure-cooker study environment of the Ivy League colleges was appreciated by many as a rite of passage with considerable personal development and career-building potential. Ben said that "it made me a lot more confident, because I have been pushed outside my comfort zone... Because I had to take all these different courses, now I am more willing to try different things." Sally continued her statement above as follows:

> I look fondly back at my days at Cambridge when I had less work to do, and I think that the work regime goes a little too far the other way here. I think that you can't perform your best in every subject, because you are just trying to do too much in one semester... But I don't regret it, it's the degree I wanted to do. Most of the time I love it, except for the exam in Chinese!

At less elite universities, however, some of the reactions were a bit different. Charlotte, at a university in California, remarked on her study program as follows:

> In England when you are going to university you are already specializing in one subject. Over here they don't do that, you are spending the entire first year doing science, English and history, etc. It's like high school. You have to do a language, and sciences, which I don't like, because I've already done that, I'm wasting my time doing it again. I'm a sociology major and I have to take so many credits to graduate and only so many of those can be sociology and the rest have to be other things, like it has to be a well-rounded education, which is a bit weird.

Turning now toward the more limited negative experiences mentioned, we note two other aspects that some interviewees raised. One was the financial squeeze on those who had little or no scholarship or institutional support. In most of these cases the slack would be taken up by parental or other family support. But the specific issue here was the difficulty of accessing part-time paid work and the incompatibility of this with the usually intense study plan. The second comment was a certain disillusionment with the quality of some teaching. Mansour remarked: "Here they couldn't care less about teaching, it's just 100 percent research." Ali, a master's student at Columbia, was a little less direct, "The teaching is not as good as I thought it would be. The impression I had before coming here was that the teaching would be leaps and miles ahead of UK education, but it is not."

A related problem was the assessment system (especially at undergraduate level) where "everything counts," including seminar contributions. On this latter point some interviewees remarked how their American classmates spoke up "just to be heard" even when they had nothing really to say. One interviewee even spotted their seminar tutor, a teaching assistant, putting a tick against each student's name when they spoke.

Career Aspirations and Future Plans

Reference back to table 2.1 (item 3) and table 2.3 (items 2 and 3) leaves us in no doubt that career aspirations are one of the main driving forces and perceived benefits of studying abroad, especially for British students in the United States. From table 2.1 we see that more than three-quarters of the questionnaire respondents rated studying for a degree in the United States as either "very important" or "important" in developing an international career. In table 2.3 we see that 90 percent of respondents saw studying for a US degree as "extremely worthwhile" or "worthwhile" in developing either general career prospects or an international career. And the "career pay-off" was seen as considerably stronger by US-based respondents than by those studying in Australia or Ireland. These comparative findings are based on reasonably robust sample sizes and so can be regarded as significant.

The general value of an international education from a prestigious overseas university for the student's CV and potential employability was nicely summed up by Donna, an undergraduate at Columbia:

> There is so much talk in the newspapers of the devaluing of degrees, so I think this is a way of making your CV stand out a little more. You didn't just get a degree, you went halfway round the world to get a degree.

The lack of credence given to "strategy" among degree-mobile British students discussed by Waters and Brooks (2010) appears different not only from our own findings but also from studies of other degree-mobile groups. For example, earlier work by Waters (2009, 2006) on East Asian students in Canada suggests that these students (and their families who are often also very much involved in the decision-making process) are in fact engaged in careful strategizing with regard to their choice of university and program, geared to attaining "positional advantage" in a crowded but increasingly "credentialized" graduate labor market. We can see strong echoes of this in our research on UK students, especially postgraduate students, in the United States. Earlier we heard how Mansour had elected to go to NYU, following LSE and Oxford, because a "good" American PhD was, in his view, the best way to cap off a prestigious series of universities for an academic career or high-level private section position in his field, financial economics. Later in his interview he set out his preferred pathway:

> I want to pursue an academic career and my first preference would be to get into the academic job market here [in the United States]. So I will apply to a bunch of Assistant Professor-type positions at some good schools and if I can get into a top-50 research university that would be an interesting start to a career.

But, like many students studying abroad, Mansour was keeping other options open too, like returning to the United Kingdom to either find an academic job there, or using his qualifications for a remunerative post in the private sector, which he thought would yield a higher income but not the less regimented lifestyle that came with academia.

In addition, across our entire sample of UK-origin students, not just those in the United States, we found that the group who had been internationally mobile before going abroad to university was also more likely to link their mobility as a student to the prospect of an international career after graduation (Findlay et al. 2012, 128). In other words, "mobility capital" reproduces itself. Mansour's case illustrates this well. Mansour is of Persian-Indian-Zoroastrian origin, with extended family links to Mumbai and California. Although he was brought up and school-educated in the London area, he had been born in Australia and had often visited relatives in India. Unsurprisingly then, Mansour felt he was "already quite international" before he moved to New York. His open geographical vision for his future career reflected his earlier life experiences of travel and residence, as well as those of his father who had himself moved from India to the United Kingdom to do his PhD.

Other interviewees, more essentially "British" (or "English," "Scottish," etc.) in their self-identities, saw a return to the United Kingdom as inevitable. They linked their future geographical mobility to their continued identification with Britain, although they appreciated the special value of their US academic and social experience. Typical of this group was Megan:

> My friends [back home in Wales] would joke and say "Oh you sound really American" and stuff. But in terms of identity I consider myself

British, strongly. I have never considered myself changing into American...if you know what I mean...At this point, I strongly believe that I wouldn't consider staying in the US because...I don't know...as I said, I haven't travelled around a lot, but as a country I know what it stands for and I know what the UK stands for. And the UK is my home and the US is definitely not my home...I am comfortable here and I am very happy here, but it is not my home. I am not saying I feel like an outsider...I just feel very affiliated with my Britishness.

But even the outwardly cosmopolitan Mansour, with his international background and his love of New York, felt occasionally "detached" from the "British" side of his identity:

I can't wait to hear the British accent...I always fly back with British Airways and it's such a pleasure to hear the accent...Another big thing I miss, probably the biggest thing I miss...is the British sense of humor...It's very different here and people can be very serious...so dreadfully serious here.

The survey also asked about where students intended to go after completion of their US degree. Fewer than one in five intended to stay outside the United Kingdom more or less permanently; the majority intended to return to the United Kingdom, either at the end of their program of study or after a period of work or further study elsewhere (either in the United States or in another location).

We leave the final word in this section to Jake. The quotation below is long because we want it to exemplify the many factors that can influence an individual's decision about what to do next and where to go at that complex juncture at the end of a first degree:

I can tell you what I can't do: I can't get a job [here in the United States], it just can't happen. It's an absolute nightmare. Especially if you are not a science person. If you were in the sciences, it's a lot easier now—they have just extended the amount of time you can stay, up to two years now. You need employment, authorized employment. If you are doing anything else other than sciences, it is 12 months and there is a lot of paperwork. And your bachelor's degree is not that valuable, because obviously you need to justify it...your employer needs to justify it. So I won't be working here, although I would like to...I have a girlfriend, she's British...she doesn't like it here and wants to go back...So that's another factor. Other than that I am applying to MIT, in two departments there, computing and technology-related...So if I get into that, I would do that. I really like Boston, I think it's a lovely city and just right for me. So that would be another two years. After that I would consider going back to Britain. I mean...it is lovely here and I wouldn't mind working in either country. Ideally I would like to work for a company that works in both countries, so I could continue to come here. Eventually I will go back...it's just that I quite like it here...and the master's would be fully funded. If I don't get in...[I may] get a job in Britain. So it's all up in the air, so fifty-fifty at the moment.

As well as epitomizing the uncertainty of future plans for many UK students studying abroad—even those like Jake in the final year of their program—the above testimonial highlights the many factors at play in such decisions. There are several sources of uncertainty: to go straight into employment or continue studying; to stay in the United States or return to the United Kingdom; the key role of financial considerations, such as the difficulty of getting work in the United States after a bachelor's degree and the lure of a fully funded master's place; and last but not least, the influence of personal factors such as family ties and intimate friendships. While Jake seems to prioritize the MIT master's over the wishes of his girlfriend, others might react differently, making (return) migration a love-related move (cf. King 2002 on "love migrations"). Different countries also have different admission and retention policies toward international students. Some want to attract and retain talented foreign students for their own labor market after these students have graduated (notably Australia and Canada), while other countries are not so keen, although certain preferential provisions may be put in place, as Jake points out, for areas like science, technology, and medicine (see Suter and Jandl 2008 for a full comparative analysis).

Also important to bear in mind here is the broader picture whereby the United Kingdom is a huge net importer of international students—globally, second only to the United States. In fact, the incomers outnumber the outgoers by at least tenfold. UK students studying abroad represent less than 2 percent of those in the UK higher-education system (Findlay and King 2010, 9). The policy issue, then, is not so much how to reduce a brain drain that hardly exists outside a few high-profile academics and scientists who have moved to the United States, but rather how to encourage more UK students to enrich their talents by embarking on an international intellectual adventure. With UK student fees set to rise by a quantum leap, the market place might prove to be the most effective driving force for this to happen. More certainly the majority of UK students interested in degree mobility will continue to look to the United

States and other major English-speaking destinations, although they may face increased competition for places from students from other countries. Moreover, the effect of such competition is not limited to students, but is also being felt by institutions themselves. Lack of supply of suitably qualified applicants is rarely an issue for universities of high standing, such as many of those in the United States included in the present study. Nonetheless, interviews that we had with the international student officers in these institutions (Findlay and King 2010) made clear that issues around recruiting the best student talent from anywhere in the world, rethinking global position and reach, and student diversity and the "student experience" are all attracting much attention.

Conclusion

Our chapter has highlighted several key areas in which we have contributed new information and fresh perspectives, including themes for further study. First, we have presented up-to-date secondary data on UK outward flows, with particular reference to the United States, which is by some measure the principal destination for degree mobility.[4] Second, our research illustrates the way in which international student mobility, driven by a search by some students for a world-class university, is embedded in complex relations linking globalization, pedagogy, and society (Findlay et al. 2012, 119). The US case, more than any other location where we have studied the phenomenon, illustrates the power of these forces in driving students to seek out a university they perceive to be of high global standing.

Third, we have added to the still-limited literature that links student mobility to ongoing mobility patterns after graduation (Findlay et al. 2012; Carlson 2011; King and Ruiz-Gelices 2003). Theoretically, therefore, we argue that the study of student migration/mobility should not be confined to a framework that separates study abroad from the wider life-course aspirations and plans of students. This is an area of future research, employing longitudinal surveys or, failing that, in-depth interviews of mature-aged respondents tracing their movements back through time.

Fourth, we have shed useful light on the vexed question of potential British brain drain by collecting data on rates of intended future mobility. Although it should be firmly borne in mind that migration intentions often do not match outcomes, worries over brain drain are unfounded. For the United States, less than a quarter of British students studying overseas intend to stay abroad long term. Many plan to return after further study or work experience abroad. Hence, when they do return, they will have further enhanced their human capital to the overall benefit of the United Kingdom's economy and society.

Notes

1. Foreign students can be recorded on the basis of citizenship, birthplace, or country of prior domicile or prior education. Most countries use the citizenship criterion, but in certain cases this can be highly misleading. For instance, in Germany citizenship for the second-generation locally born children of immigrants has until recently been denied. Further problems arise with dual citizenship. For details see Findlay, Geddes, and Smith (2010).
2. The suggestion (in the questionnaire) of being at a world-class university may trigger enhanced positive responses, as may the universities' own self-promoting publicity internalized by students after they have arrived. Against these concerns, abundant interview evidence suggests that the perception of world-class status was a real and meaningful part of the decision making at the time of the application.
3. Moreover the division between state and independent is not a simple dichotomy. For instance, "grammar schools" can be either state or independent, some state schools are selective, and individual students may have had experience of both sectors. For instance Megan, one of our interviewees at an Ivy League university, had been to a comprehensive school for most of her secondary education, but then moved to an independent boarding school for the "sixth-form" (the final two years of high school).
4. The United States is less dominant for UK outward credit mobility, for which complete statistics are not available outside the Erasmus data on intra-European exchange flows. Our own earlier research on credit mobility did derive estimates based on primary survey data collected from UK higher-education institutions, and these show that the United States is by far the main non-European destination (Findlay, et al. 2006; HEFCE 2004).

Works Cited

Ahrens, J., R. King, R. Skeldon, and M. Dunne. 2010. *"Motivations of UK Students to Study Abroad: A Survey of School-Leavers."* Working Paper No. 64. Brighton: University of Sussex, Sussex Centre for Migration Research.

Bourdieu, P. 1986. "The Forms of Capital." In *Handbook of Theory and Research for the Sociology of Education*, edited by J. Richardson, 241–58. New York: Greenwood Press.

———. 1977. *Outline of a Theory of Practice*. Cambridge: Cambridge University Press.

Brooks, R., and J. Waters. 2011. *Student Mobilities, Migration and the Internationalization of Higher Education*. Basingstoke: Palgrave Macmillan.

———. 2009a. "A Second Chance at 'Success': UK Students and Global Circuits of Higher Education." *Sociology* 43: 1085–102.

———. 2009b. "International Higher Education and the Mobility of UK Students." *Journal of Research in International Education* 8: 191–209.

Carlson, S. 2011. *"Just a Matter of Choice? Student Mobility as a Social and Biographical Process."* Working Paper No. 68. Brighton: University of Sussex, Sussex Centre for Migration Research.

Findlay, A., A. Geddes, and F. Smith. 2010. *"Motivations and Experiences of UK Students Studying Abroad: Statistical Sources—Summary Metadata Report."* London: BIS Research Paper, No. 8A.

Findlay, A., and R. King. 2010. *"Motivations and Experiences of UK Students Studying Abroad."* London: BIS Research Paper, No. 8.

Findlay, A., R. King, A. Stam, and E. Ruiz-Gelices. 2006. "Ever-Reluctant Europeans: The Changing Geographies of UK Students Studying Abroad and Working Abroad." *European Urban and Regional Studies* 13: 291–318.

Findlay, A., R. King, F. Smith, A. Geddes, and R. Skeldon. 2012. "World Class? An Investigation into Globalisation, Difference and International Student Mobility." *Transactions of the Institute of British Geographers* 37: 118–31.

HEFCE [Higher Education Funding Council for England]. 2004. *"International Student Mobility."* HEFCE Issues Paper 30.

King, R. 2002. "Towards a New Map of European Migration." *International Journal of Population Geography* 8: 89–108.

King, R., A. Findlay, and J. Ahrens. 2010. *International Student Mobility Literature Review*. London: Final Report to HEFCE.

King, R., and E. Ruiz-Gelices. 2003. "International Student Migration and the European 'Year Abroad': Effects on European Identity and Subsequent Migration Behaviour." *International Journal of Population Geography* 9: 229–52.

Murphy-Lejeune, E. 2002. *Student Mobility and Narrative in Europe: The New Strangers*. London: Routledge.

Suter, B., and M. Jandl. 2008. "Train and Retain: National and Regional Policies to Promote the Settlement of Foreign Graduates in Knowledge Economies." *Journal of International Migration and Integration* 9: 401–18.

Waters, J. 2009. "Transnational Geographies of Academic Distinction: The Role of Social Capital in the Recognition and Evaluation of 'Overseas' Credentials." *Globalisation, Societies and Education* 7: 113–29.

———. 2006. "Geographies of Cultural Capital: Education, International Migration and Family Strategies between Hong Kong and Canada." *Transactions of the Institute of British Geographers* 31: 179–92.

Waters, J., and R. Brooks. 2010. "Accidental Achievers: International Higher Education, Class Reproduction and Privilege in the Experiences of UK Students Overseas." *British Journal of Sociology of Education* 31: 217–28.

3

THE EMERGING BRAIN CIRCULATION BETWEEN CHINA AND THE UNITED STATES

Wan Yu

INTRODUCTION

It has been widely acknowledged that a country's development is highly related to its human capital resources, including highly skilled intellectuals. The spatial mobility of the highly skilled has accelerated in the context of globalization and has received increasing scholarly and public attention over the past several decades, with terms such as "brain drain," "brain gain," and the recently coined "brain circulation" (Breinbauer 2007; Johnson and Regets 1998; Baghwati and Partington 1976; Adams 1968) used to describe the movements of these highly skilled migrants. A large part of the research on this topic has focused on student migrants, especially students in higher education, who are also considered as potential permanent immigrants (Tremblay 2005).

Nowadays, China is the top sending country of student migrants to many universities in high-income countries. According to the *2011 Open Doors Report*, the number of Chinese students in the United States had reached 157,558 by 2010/11, representing 21.8 percent of the total international student body, making China the top sending country of foreign students to the United States (Institute of International Education 2011). The composition of Chinese students in the United States has changed over time, shifting from primarily graduate to undergraduate students, as reported in the **2009** *Report of the Development of Chinese Overseas Educated Talents* (RDCOET). Moreover, highly skilled migrants from the United States are increasingly returning to China; indeed, the United States is the top sending country of highly skilled Chinese returnees, with 28 percent of Chinese students in the United States eventually returning to China (Wang 2009).

The increasing circulation of international students between the United States and China has drawn not only academic but also public attention. In the United States, international students have long been appreciated for contributing to the development of the higher-education sector and generating tuition revenue, but potential negative consequences are increasingly being spotlighted, especially as international student numbers have risen and the US economy has experienced a downturn. Of particular relevance here is whether students returning to their home countries from the United States are a human capital loss for the United States, or even a waste of taxpayers' money. China, for its part, is concerned about the consequences of both an unprecedented increase in the out-migration of high school and college graduates and an ever larger flow of highly skilled Chinese returning from the Global North. The Chinese government is considering how to adjust the domestic job market to accommodate this large influx of highly skilled returnees and how to evaluate their impact on China's future. In summary, the effects of highly skilled migrations on China and the United States are not entirely clear, as growing rates of return migration increasingly complicate the picture.

Using the framework of brain circulation, this chapter argues that these increasing flows could become a win-win situation, as student migrants benefit the receiving country's economy via their tuition payments and living expenses during their stay, and contribute to their countries of origin with their professional skills after their return.

Conceptual Framework

Scholarly investigations of student migrants in higher education derive from theoretical debates on highly skilled migration, which assume that well-educated and highly skilled intellectuals are crucial for a country's global competitiveness in economic, social, and political arenas (Daugeliene 2009; Kuznetsov 2006). Public concerns regarding highly skilled migrants began in the early 1960s when European scholars expressed concerns about the mass migration of scholars from Europe to the United States. Since then, theoretical debates on highly skilled migrants have shifted among different terms that emerged in different periods, including brain drain since the 1960s, "brain overflow" since the 1970s, brain gain since the 1980s, and brain circulation since late the 1990s (Breinbauer 2007). I focus mainly on brain drain and brain circulation as they are the most relevant to this case study.

Brain Drain

The term brain drain first emerged in theoretical debates in the late 1960s to represent the loss of human capital through trained persons leaving a country (Lee and Kim 2010; Saxenian 2005). One common approach to viewing brain drain is through push and pull factors, explaining the emigration of skilled migrants through the effects of external forces. Usually, push factors in countries of origin include bad economic and political conditions, as well as limited job opportunities for skilled laborers; while pull factors to host countries include better public and social resources, an open-minded society, a larger job market, and better occupational opportunities, to name just a few (Breinbauer 2007). In regards to student migrations, many studies investigate push and pull factors in terms of the global political and economic forces underlying the migration flows and demonstrate that the migration of highly skilled professionals, especially students, is sensitive to global economic and political contexts (Chen and Barnett 2000; Altbach 1991). The combination of push and pull factors influence student migrants' choices of whether to seek higher education abroad and whether to return to their home countries after graduation. Traditionally, once highly skilled migrants went abroad, few returned to their country of origin, a phenomenon interpreted as brain drain for sending countries (Commander, Kangasniemi, and Winters 2004; Straubhaar 2000; Meyer and Brown 1999).

Some scholars, arguing from a political structuralist perspective, state that although personal and family choice plays an important role in skilled migrants' decision making, individual countries are influential through implementing policies to maintain their human capital. Governments can adjust their emigration as well as immigration policies to attract or to discourage highly skilled migrants. Thus, the migration of skilled professionals is considered not just to be the outcome of migrants' individual choices but also of the ability of countries to successfully compete for talents (Zweig, Fung, and Han 2008; Chacko 2007; Biao 2005; Mahroum 2005).

While most studies on brain drain have a pessimistic tone, a few scholars have argued that brain drain is not always an obstacle to the development of countries of origin (e.g., Commander, Kangasniemi, and Winters 2004). Daugeliene (2007) believes that the brain drain can have a positive effect on a country's knowledge-based economy in the long term because the emigration of skilled migrants contributes to the home country's economic development through increasing remittances and potential returns in the future. To capture this idea, terms such as the "optimal brain drain" (Lowell, Findlay, and Stewart 2004; Stark 2004) and "beneficial brain drain" (Beine, Docquier, and Rapoport 2001) have been coined to describe the potential benefits skilled migrants' home countries may obtain in the long run.

Brain Circulation

The term brain circulation was first introduced by Cao (1996) from research on the return migration of highly skilled Asian personnel from the United States. This concept describes "the mobility of [highly skilled personnel] who have marketable expertise and international experience and who tend to migrate for the short term or make temporary business visits in a country (or countries) where their skills are needed" (Cao 1996, 273). Many scholars argue that the emergence of brain circulation challenges the conventional dichotomy of brain drain versus brain gain as highly skilled migrants flow in both directions (Le 2008; Chen 2007; Blitz 2005; Saxenian 2002; Johnson and Regets 1998). Instead, a two-way flow of skills, capital, and technology is believed to benefit both sending and receiving countries (Saxenian 2005), and can create a win-win situation if the highly skilled migrants contribute to the receiving countries during their stay and their countries of origin after their return (Li and Yu 2012).

When skilled professionals cross borders between home countries and receiving countries, they are not merely viewed as migrants but also as knowledge carriers who enable the transmission of professional knowledge as well as the exchange of intellectual resources between the Global North and Global South (Blitz 2005). In addition to the technological aspect, brain circulation can also create a snowball effect for a nation's economic development: highly skilled migrants return and contribute to the knowledge-based economy; the thriving knowledge-based economy, in turn, provides more opportunities for skilled professionals, which further promote the circulation of highly skilled migrants (Kuznetsov 2006).

In regards to international students, scholarly attention has focused on the global economic and geopolitical context affecting student migrants, their demographic characteristics, and their return plans after graduation. In the past two decades, the United States has received an unprecedented number of international student migrants in higher-education institutions (Wadhwa et al. 2009). Similar experiences are shared by many other major immigrant receiving countries, including Canada, Australia, and New Zealand (Lu, Zhong, and Schissel 2009; Naidoo 2007; Ziguras and Law 2006). Studies have revealed that major international events, geopolitical relations, and sending countries' development trajectories can have a large impact on student migration flows (Alberts 2007), as well as on their decision making after graduation (Li and Yu 2012; Rosen and Zweig 2005). The impact of professional, societal, and personal factors on individual migrants' decision making (Hazen and Alberts 2006; Alberts and Hazen 2005), the receiving countries' immigrant policies (Guo and Jamal 2007), the home countries' recruiting policies (Wang 2009; Zweig, Fung, and Han 2008; Biao 2005), and the planned length of stay after graduation (Wadhwa et al. 2009) are discussed as factors shaping return migration flows.

In summary, early studies on brain drain assume that highly skilled migrants stay in the receiving countries instead of returning home, causing human capital loss for their countries of origin. By contrast, more recent studies on brain circulation indicate that highly skilled migrants can flow in both directions, calling the traditional brain drain perspective into question. Chinese student migrants to the US higher-education sector provide a clear case of brain circulation: not only is this clearly a circular flow, with many Chinese students now returning to China from the United States, but also, significantly, this migrant stream benefits both China and the United States.

Methodology

To investigate changing migrations trends, I use secondary data from governmental reports from the United States and China, particularly the US *Open Doors Reports* from 2001 to 2011, and China's 2009 RDCOET. In addition, I use media reports from US university newspapers, from the mainstream press in both the United States and China, and from the Chinese Service Center for Scholarly Exchange (CSCSE). I also conducted 11 in-depth interviews with Chinese students who were studying in US universities at the time of interview (from April 2010 to November 2011) to provide additional qualitative data. The sample comprised six graduate students and five undergraduate students. Interviews were conducted by phone in Mandarin and translated into English by the author. Interview questions covered the following main themes: demographic characteristics (including age, gender, family status, and citizenship), educational attainment (including degree obtained in the United States, major, and institution attended in the United States), financial issues (including funding source during study and current income source), and plans after graduation.

Changing Demographics of Chinese Students in the United States

The US higher-education sector maintains its exceptional academic reputation throughout the world. This, combined with a trend among US institutions to admit larger numbers of international students in order to expand tuition revenue, has led to an increase in the number of student migrants coming to study and obtain academic degrees in the United States. This migration trend has accelerated since the US government changed immigration policies in favor of employment-based immigration, which also benefits international students. The simultaneous economic growth of migrants' home countries has further strengthened student migrant flows.

The fastest growth of the Chinese student population in the United States started about a decade ago. From 2002 to 2005, due to the US government imposing immigration restrictions after 9/11, there was a slight decrease in Chinese student numbers. The US government's restrictive requirements and extended screening process for issuing student visas during this period led many Chinese students to look for alternative places to study, such as Australia and Canada. Since 2006, however, the Chinese student population has experienced unprecedented growth, largely due to the significant increase in Chinese undergraduate students migrating to the United States. By the year 2011, Chinese students were the largest student group in the United States by nationality, with 21.8 percent of the total international student population, representing a 23.5 percent increase over the previous year (Institute of International Education 2011b).

The composition of Chinese students in the United States is changing, however, with more and more tuition-paying undergraduate students compared to graduate students, who typically receive financial aid. The percentage of Chinese students at the graduate level declined in the past decade from 80.1 percent in 2000/01 to 48.8 percent in 2010/11, when they accounted for less than half of the Chinese student body for the first time. Meanwhile, the proportion of Chinese

EMERGING BRAIN CIRCULATION 53

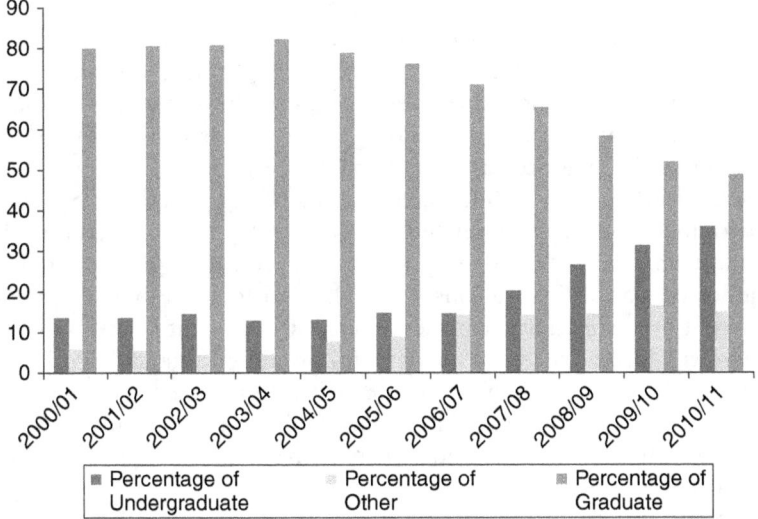

Figure 3.1 Chinese students in the United States by academic level, 2001–2011
Source: Institute of International Education (2012)

undergraduate students soared from 14.7 percent in 2006/07 to 36.2 percent in 2010/11 (figure 3.1).

The increasing wealth of Chinese families combined with recent Chinese government policies that promote student exchanges with academic institutions in developed countries, help explain the surging number of Chinese students seeking higher education abroad. In most Chinese parents' eyes, a higher-education degree guarantees their children's future, and a postgraduate degree from the Western world further secures their children's edge in the job market, no matter if their children choose to return home or to stay abroad after they graduate. This mentality is largely due to the higher reputation of academic institutions in developed countries compared with their Chinese counterparts. Thus, a postgraduate degree earned in the United States, in Chinese, "contains more gold" than one obtained from a domestic higher-education institution. As a result, after China's economic reform, going abroad and obtaining an overseas academic degree has become a journey of "gold-plating," a journey to significantly enhance one's human capital.

The newfound wealth of China's booming economy has drawn US universities' attention toward actively recruiting in China. Compared with their US-born counterparts, international students usually pay higher rates of tuition when studying in US state universities and community colleges, so recruiting internationally can significantly increase an institution's tuition revenue (Staley 2011). Many US universities contract recruiting agencies to promote themselves in big Chinese cities and sometimes give a certain number of scholarships to outstanding Chinese undergraduate students (Lewin 2008). This proactive practice has become more prevalent since the US economic downturn in 2008. According to the International Student Enrollment Survey, conducted by the Institute of International Education, when asked which foreign country or region US higher-education institutions would like to focus resources on for international student recruitment trips, 30.8 percent of respondents selected China as their top country, followed by India with 19.3 percent, and Southeast Asian countries with 19.1 percent (Institute of International Education 2011a). Thus, China is not the only country from which international students are actively recruited, but remains in a dominant position.

In addition to the recent increase in Chinese degree-seeking students, the number of Chinese nondegree seeking students in the United States has also been growing rapidly in the past decade. The Chinese government's incentive policies for scholarly exchange with developed countries have provided a major stimulus in this respect. Since 2007, when the Chinese Ministry of Education relaxed their requirements for qualified applicants and increased positions for scholarly exchange, the number of Chinese nondegree seeking students in the United States soared from 2,596 in 2006/07 to 13,268 in 2010/11, and their share among Chinese international students increased from 3.8 percent in 2006/07 to 8.4 percent in 2010/11. Even though their share is relatively lower than students at the undergraduate and graduate level, and the length of the exchange period (mostly 9–12 months) is much shorter than that for degree-seeking students (from two to more than five years), they are now an important component of the Chinese student migrant stream to the United States.

The population of Chinese Optional Practical Training (OPT) holders in the United States has experienced steady growth alongside Chinese student numbers, from 7,171 in 2006/07 to 10,484 in 2010/11. The US government allows international students enrolled in US higher-education institutions to have an up to 12-month-long OPT period per degree. For international students, the OPT program is a transition period in their immigration status from being an F-1 student to becoming an H1-B work visa holder; once they obtain full-time jobs that allow them to get work visas, they end their OPT program and become migrant workers. The length of the OPT period varies depending on the student's major, the number of H1-B visas available in that year, and the job market situation during that period. The steady increase in Chinese OPT holders can be partly explained by the increasing number of students studying in science, technology, engineering, and mathematics (STEM) fields, who are eligible to apply for a 17-month-long extension period of their OPT program, up to a total of 29 months. However, fewer job opportunities for international students in the current US job market, especially positions sponsoring H1-B worker visas, have also increased the number of OPT holders.

In summary, Chinese students are now prominent in US higher education at all educational levels, in stark contrast to a decade ago when graduate students accounted for the overwhelming majority of the Chinese international student body. This demographic change occurred largely because of the increasing wealth of Chinese families, the growing visibility of American higher-education institutions overseas, recent Chinese government policies promoting student exchange with developed countries, and the current US economic situation.

Return Migration of Chinese Students from the United States

In addition to the large and ever increasing flow of Chinese students to the United States, there is a growing trend of return migration among Chinese students. This trend has become particularly apparent since the US economic downturn. Recent studies conducted by Wadhwa et al. (2009, 3) suggest that, since the 2007–2008 financial crisis, only 10 percent of Chinese students prefer to stay in the United States permanently. This number had already been decreasing after the events of 9/11 when the United States tightened immigration policies due to security concerns. The 2009 RDCOET highlights similar trends, with the annual number of returnees back to China increasing over the past decade, from around 5,000 in 2000 to 69,200 in 2008 (Wang 2009). In August 2011, the CSCSE, a major data source on student returnees, reported that more than 393,300 Chinese students returned to China between 2006 and 2010—almost three times the number between 2001 and 2005 (CSCSE 2011). This dataset mainly tracks student returnees who need to certify the authenticity of their foreign degrees when they look for jobs, but omits returnees who do not need to use their foreign degrees for their future career in China (e.g., if they are self-employed). Thus, the real number of student returnees to China could be much larger than reported.

The major reasons for increasing return rates of Chinese overseas students relate to their career plans and family concerns for the future. One major motivation that drives Chinese overseas students to return is the uncertainty of finding a job or obtaining legal status in the United States after graduation. This fear has become a bigger issue since 2008 when economic constriction in the United States left international students facing more difficulties in finding jobs in the United States. As one undergraduate interviewee explained:

> It's totally different now...My friend told me the situation [for an accounting graduate in the job market] was much better in 2006. [At that time] you just needed one year at school to get a master's degree in accounting and then you could get a handful of job offers after you graduate. I know several friends switched their majors to accounting...from biology, physics, and others. But now, even if you have such a degree from a tier-one university, it doesn't guarantee you to have an offer by the time your OPT expires.

The challenges faced by Chinese students on the job market are compounded by language and cultural issues, as described by a graduate interviewee:

> It is hard to compete with the native-born [in the job market]. Sometimes, it is beyond the GPA you have and the number of projects you did. One of my American friends and I both applied for a position and both got a phone interview, but eventually he got the on-site interview and I got rejected right after the phone call. I asked him about the interview questions afterward and I think I performed at least no worse than him, and I have a much better resume, but he's the one who eventually got the on-site [interview], not me...The biggest barrier [to me] is not about the professional knowledge, but about language and cultural difference. Sometimes when the HR [Human Resources] started the interview with a joke, I didn't even understand why it was funny, so I can only pretend laughing, but I know most of my American colleagues can come up with better lines to keep the conversation going. These are things I can't get from school after just three-and-half years of study.

Another stimulus for return migration is worries about the US tightening policies on work visas for international migrants, especially after the economic crisis. In 2009, Congress significantly increased the visa application fee for US employers who hire more than half of their workforce as H1-B visa holders. This changing policy largely affects US high-tech industries that house the majority of highly skilled immigrants, especially Asians, as engineers. As a result, many Asian immigrants start looking for jobs in their home countries as a back-up plan, as another graduate interviewee explained:

> There is a job waiting for me in China, a well-paid one. I know it is tough for me [to find a job] here nowadays, but sometimes you have to give it a try...I heard a lot of stories from my friends about how hard it is for international students [to find a job]. No matter how well you perform in the phone interview some companies just directly hang up the phone when they hear that you don't have a green card and need H1-B sponsorship...In the job fair, some HRs don't even bother to look at your resume if they know you are an international student...It is just not fair.

On the home country side, China's prospering economy and government incentive policies play the primary role in luring highly skilled students to return (Xia 2006), even though nostalgic ties and family reasons are also major reasons for their return (Du, Wang, and Luo 2009). The Chinese government has increasingly recognized the positive economic and social contribution made by highly skilled returnees, especially returnees with US postgraduate degrees as US universities have provided many Chinese returnees with advanced research knowledge and professional skills (for example Nobel Prize winner Chen-Ning Franklin Yang and the founding president of Google China, Kai-Fu Lee). Many national and regional incentive policies have been implemented to recruit highly skilled Chinese graduates from US universities. For example, in 2008, the Chinese government implemented the *Cheung Kong Scholars Programme* to provide start-up research funding for distinguished returned scholars, with a minimum amount of one million RMB (US$170,000). In the same year, the Chinese Academy of Science implemented the *Recruitment Program of Global Experts*, which aims to motivate approximately 2,000 Chinese who work overseas in technological and scientific areas to go back to China to participate in government projects, to lead cutting-edge research in major disciplines, and to run major national labs in higher-education institutions, government-owned institutions, and regional industrial parks. Many provincial and municipal governments in China have similar recruiting policies to promote regional development (Wang 2009).

Such incentive policies and programs have already motivated many Chinese overseas students to return home. As one potential returnee said:

> I can live a decent life in the US, having a house in the suburbs, driving a Toyota, and complaining about the tax rate in my school district, but that's it...In China, I can still get the chance to be "successful"—living in a skyscraper with a view of the Nest, driving a BMW, and finding the woman I like...It is risky, but I would rather live a life with dreams.

Another potential returnee shared this perspective:

> The idea of returning really struck me when I went to my high school classmates' reunion dinner [in China]. Many of my classmates who had found jobs after attaining a bachelor's degree now earn much more than I do—cars, houses, family, everything...and I am still doing useless experiments in the lab ten hours a day and waiting for my almost impossible "green card"...I don't want to be miserable anymore...I need to go back to seize the opportunity since I am still young, since I am still willing to make a change in my life.

In addition to their career concerns, for many Chinese students family reasons are prominent in motivating their return. In Chinese tradition, if parents are alive, children are discouraged from living far from home, or in Chinese "父母在, 不远游." This attitude is especially strong among recent cohorts of Chinese student migrants in the United States, who mostly come from single-child families due to the Chinese governmental fertility policies of the 1980s. Thus, many recent cohorts of Chinese students consider going back to take care of their parents as their responsibility to the family. Such a concern is more prominent among female Chinese students. As one female potential returnee said:

> When I heard about my Dad's total paralysis on the phone, I just couldn't concentrate on anything here [in the United States]. I have to go back. I can't leave all caring work to my Mom. She has her job. She can't be there 24/7...I am the one that should support the family...I am also tired of staying in the lab running programs, tired of listening to my mom whining about why I don't have a boyfriend at 25 years old. Seeing more and more of my friends getting married and having babies just tortures me...I don't want to waste my time in the lab and in this small town...Career is not everything to me.

In summary, when considering possible return plans, Chinese student migrants usually make decisions based on their career planning and family concerns, but their decision making is also affected by the social, economic, and political contexts in both the United States and China. On the US side, the recent economic downturn, the difficult situation for international students in the job market, and the tightened immigration policies for skilled migrants all encourage the return migration of Chinese students. On the Chinese side, the recent economic boom, Chinese government incentive policies, and migrants' family ties motivate Chinese students to return home after graduation.

When Chinese overseas students contemplate their possible return, they take account of opportunities in the United States compared with their home country's prospects in the near future. Many of them consider the United States as a way station to build up their skills and social capital before they make their eventual decision of whether or not to go back to China. This approach differs significantly from the mindset held by Chinese overseas students in the 1980s and 1990s, who considered the United States as their ultimate destination. Despite their intention to return, many current students would like to spend some more time in the United States first. As one student stated:

> My final goal is still the same—to go back to China to open up my own business—just not now. If I went back now, nobody would give me any funding or resources to open a start-up company. Nobody would believe me or believe my ideas. I have to make some accomplishments [here] before I go back, so that I can tell people "See, this is what I have achieved, and what I have been good at." And that's how I can convince investors to give me funding for my career.

A similar mentality exists among Chinese scholars in the United States seeking an academic career:

> If I go back [to China] right now, nobody will care. They prefer those well-known Chinese scholars, those who have already made some accomplishment in the US...Right now, to them [Chinese education institutions], I am nobody...If you want to go back, you have to stay here to establish yourself first.

In conclusion, the number of Chinese students in the United States who intend to return to China in the future, as well as the number of highly skilled Chinese actually returning, has been growing significantly over the past decade. Factors affecting the decision making of these returnees include the social, economic, and political contexts in China and the United States, as well as the student migrants' career and family concerns. In contrast with previous cohorts, who largely preferred to stay in the United States permanently, recent Chinese student migrants typically consider the United States as a way station to build up their skills and social resources before returning to China.

Brain Circulation of Global Talent?

The recent growth in student migration flows from China to the United States and return flows from the United States to China indicate an emerging brain circulation between China and the United States that benefits both sides. For the United States, the increasing number of Chinese undergraduate students provides tuition revenue for many US universities, in addition to the large number of Chinese graduate students who contribute to the United States' academic and industrial development. For China, highly skilled returnees play important roles as key leaders in academic, economic, and political fields. These returnees are equipped with knowledge and skills from their studies in the United States, and have the cultural knowledge to succeed in China. By 2001, more than 80 percent of the Chinese Academy of Science, more than half of the Chinese Academy of Engineering, and more than three-quarter of Chinese university presidents had overseas educational experiences (Wang 2009). In 2006, the Chinese Communist Party's (CCP) official website ranked the ten most successful highly skilled returnees according to their contributions to China's economic development, and argued that "foreign educational experience is the real treasure" (Ran 2006).

These two-way migration flows of the highly skilled can reinforce one another, enabling the brain circulation of Chinese students to develop further. For example, the successful experiences of highly skilled Chinese returnees draw public attention to the advantage of possessing a foreign degree in the Chinese job market. The Chinese term "sea turtle," referring to returnees from overseas, is commonly used to describe the privileged social and economic status of these highly skilled returnees compared with domestic degree holders. The significant advantage of holding a US degree in China then stimulates more Chinese students to come to the United States seeking education, accelerating the brain circulation between China and the United States.

Concluding Remarks

This chapter investigated the migration flows of Chinese students to the United States, their possible return migration, and the circulation of student migrants between China and the United States. As a result of recent economic developments and increasing wealth in China, the number of student migrants from China to the United States has been increasing rapidly. The mindsets of Chinese students have also changed in regards to their decision making after they graduate from US universities, with higher rates of return migration of highly skilled migrants over the past decade. Both sending and receiving countries appear to benefit from this flow, with Chinese students coming to US universities for prestige degrees and contributing to the funding of US higher education, then returning to China as highly skilled professionals—a case of a win-win brain circulation between low-income and high-income countries.

Works Cited

Adams, W., ed. 1968. *The Brain Drain*. New York: Macmillan.
Alberts, H. 2007. "Beyond the Headlines: Changing Patterns in International Student Enrollment in the United States." *GeoJournal* 68: 141–53.
Alberts, H., and H. Hazen. 2005. "'There Are Always Two Voices...': International Students' Intentions to Stay in the United States or Return to their Home Countries." *International Migration* 43(3): 131–54.
Altbach, P. 1991. "Impact and Adjustment: Foreign Students in Comparative Perspective." *Higher Education* 21(3): 305–23.
Baghwati, J., and M. Partington. 1976. "Taxing the Brain Drain: A Proposal." *Challenge* 19(3): 34–8.
Beine, M., F. Docquier, and H. Rapoport. 2001. "Brain Drain and Economic Growth: Theory and Evidence." *Journal of Development Economics* 64(1): 275–89.
Biao, X. 2005. "Promoting Knowledge Exchange through Diaspora Networks (The Case of People's Republic of China)." Centre on Migration, Policy and Society (COMPAS). Available at: http://www.compas.ox.ac.uk/publications/reports-and-other-publications/diaspora-networks-china/. Accessed: June 3, 2012.
Blitz, B. 2005. "Brain Circulation: The Spanish Medical Profession and International Recruitment in The United Kingdom." *Journal of European Social Policy* 15(4): 363–79.
Breinbauer, A. 2007. "Brain Drain–Brain Circulation or...What Else Happens or Should Happen to the Brains Some Aspects of Qualified Person Mobility/Migration." IDEAS of Federal Reserve Bank of St. Louis, FIW Working Paper No.4.

Cao, X. 1996. "Debating 'Brain Drain' in the Context of Globalisation." *Compare: A Journal of Comparative and International Education* 26(3): 269–85.
Chacko, E. 2007. "From Brain Drain to Brain Gain: Reverse Migration to Bangalore and Hyderabad, India's Globalizing High Tech Cities." *GeoJournal* 68: 131–40.
Chen, T., and G. Barnett. 2000. "Research on International Student Flows from a Macro Perspective: A Network Analysis of 1985, 1989 and 1995." *Higher Education* 39: 435–53.
Chen, Y. 2007. "The Limits of Brain Circulation: Chinese Returnees and Technological Development in Beijing." Available at: http://www.cctr.ust.hk/articles/pdf/WorkingPaper15.pdf. Accessed: September 10, 2011.
Commander, S., M. Kangasniemi, and L. Winters. 2004. "The Brain Drain: Curse or Boon? A Survey of the Literature." In *Challenges to Globalization*, edited by R. Baldwin, and L. Winters, 235–72. Chicago, IL: University of Chicago Press.
CSCSE [Chinese Service Center for Scholarly Exchange]. 2011. "Open Policies Stimulate Returning Trend of Oversea Students: Highly-skilled Returnees Contribute to China's Innovation." 开放政策掀起海归回国潮留学人才领跑中国创新. August 31. Available at: http://www.cscse.edu.cn/publish/portal0/tab141/info14258.htm. Accessed: May 31, 2012.
Daugeliene, R. 2009. "Brain Circulation: Theoretical Considerations." *Inzinerine Ekonomika-Engineering Economics* 3: 49–57.
———. 2007. "The Position of Knowledge Workers in Knowledge-Based Economy: Migration Aspect." *European Integration Studies* 1: 103–12.
Du, Y., H. Wang, and Y. Luo. 2009. "The Causal Factors of Chinese Returnees: Statistics and Analysis." In *The Report on The Development of Chinese Overseas Educated Talents*, edited by H. Wang, 257–78. Beijing: China Machine Press.
Guo, S., and Z. Jamal. 2007. "Nurturing Cultural Diversity in Higher Education: A Critical Review of Selected Models." *Canadian Journal of Higher Education* 37(3): 27–49.
Hazen, H., and H. Alberts. 2006. "Visitors or Immigrants? International Students in the United States." *Population, Space and Place* 12: 201–16.
Institute of International Education. 2012. "Open Doors Report on International Students: Academic Level and Place of Origin." Available at: http://www.iie.org/en/Research-and-Publications/Open-Doors/Data/International-Students/By-Academic-Level-and-Place-of-Origin. Accessed: May 31, 2012.
———. 2011a. "International Student Enrollment Survey." Available at: http://www.iie.org/Who-We-Are/News-and-Events/Press-Center/Press-Releases/2011/~/media/Files/Corporate/Open-Doors/Special-Reports/Fall-Survey-Intl-Students-2011.ashx. Accessed: October 27, 2010.

———. 2011b. "Open Doors Report on International Students: Leading Places of Origin." Available at: http://www.iie.org/Research-and-Publications/Open-Doors/Data/International-Students/Leading-Places-of-Origin/2009-11. Accessed: May 31, 2012.

Johnson, J., and M. Regets. 1998. "International Mobility of Scientists and Engineers to the United States—Brain Drain or Brain Circulation?" 10th Issue Brief. NSF, Division of Sciences Resources Studies. Available at: http://www.nsf.gov/statistics/issuebrf/sib98316.htm. Accessed: June 3, 2012.

Kuznetsov, Y. 2006. "Diaspora Networks and the International Migration of Skills: How Countries Can Draw on Their Talent Abroad." Washington, DC: The International Bank for Reconstruction and Development.

Le, T. 2008. "Brain Drain or Brain Circulation: Evidence from OECD's International Migration and R&D Spillovers." *Scottish Journal of Political Economy* 55(5): 618–36.

Lee, J., and D. Kim. 2010. "Brain Gain or Brain Circulation? U.S. Doctoral Recipients Returning to South Korea." *Higher Education* 59: 627–43.

Lewin, T. 2008 (May 11) "Matching Newcomer to College, While Both Pay." *The New York Times*.

Li, W., and W. Yu. 2012. "Between China and the United States: Contemporary Policies and Flows of Highly Skilled Migrants." *AAPI Nexus: Policy, Practice, and Community* 10(1): 1–20.

Lowell, L., A. Findlay, and E. Stewart. 2004. "Brain Strain: Optimising Highly Skilled Migration from Developing Countries." Asylum and Migration Working Paper 3. London: Institute for Public Policy Research.

Lu, Y., L. Zong, and B. Schissel. 2009. "To Stay Or Return: Migration Intentions of Students from People's Republic of China in Saskatchewan, Canada." *International Migration and Integration* 10: 283–310.

Mahroum, S. 2005. "The International Policies of Brain Gain: A Review." *Journal of Technology Analysis & Strategic Management* 17(2): 219–30.

Meyer, J-B., and M. Brown. 1999. "Scientific Diasporas: A New Approach to the Brain Drain. Management of Social Transformation" Management of Social Transformation Discussion Paper No. 41. Available at: http://www.unesco.org/most/meyer.htm. Accessed: June 3, 2012.

Naidoo, V. 2007. "Research on the Flow of International Students to UK Universities: Determinants and Implications." *Journal of Research in International Education* 6: 287–307.

Ran, H. 2006. "China's Top Ten Most Successful Returnees: Overseas Study Experiences are True Assets" 中国十大最成功"海归": 留学经历是真正的财富. Available at: http://news.xinhuanet.com/overseas/2006-02/07/content_4147976.htm. Accessed: October 27, 2010.

Rosen, S., and D. Zweig. 2005. "Transnational Capital: Valuing Academic Returnees in a Globalizing China." In *Bridging Minds Across the Pacific: U.S.-China Educational Exchanges, 1978–2003*, edited by C. Li, 129–58. New York: Lexington Books.

Saxenian, A. 2005. "From Brain Drain to Brain Circulation: Transnational Communities and Regional Upgrading in India and China." *Studies in Comparative International Development* 40(2): 35–61.

———. 2002. "Brain Circulation: How High-skill Immigration Makes Everyone Better Off." *The Brookings Review* 20(1): 28–31.

Staley, O. 2011 (December 28). "Lure of Chinese Tuition Pushes Out Asian-Americans." *Bloomberg*. Available at: http://www.bloomberg.com/news/2011-12-28/lure-of-chinese-tuition-squeezes-out-asian-americans-at-california-schools.html. Accessed: June 3, 2012.

Stark, O. 2004. "Rethinking the Brain Drain." *World Development* 32(1): 15–22.

Stark, O., C. Helmenstein, and A. Prskawetz. 1997. "A Brain Gain with a Brain Drain." *Economics Letters* 55(2): 227–34.

Straubhaar, T. 2000. "International Mobility of the Highly Skilled: Brain Gain, Brain Drain or Brain Exchange." HWWA Discussion Paper, No. 88. Available at: http://hdl.handle.net/10419/19463. Accessed: June 3, 2012.

Tremblay, K. 2005. "Academic Mobility and Immigration." *Journal of Studies in International Education* 9(3): 196–228.

Wadhwa, V., A. Saxenian, R. Freeman, G. Gereffi, and A. Salkever. 2009. "America's Loss is the World's Gain: America's New Immigrant Entrepreneurs IV." The Kauffman Foundation. Available at: http://www.kauffman.org/research-and-policy/americas-loss-is-the-worlds-gain-americas-new-immigrant-entrepreneurs.aspx. Accessed: June 3, 2012.

Wang, H., ed. 2009. The Report of Development of Chinese Overseas Educational Talents (RDCOET). 王辉耀编. 中国留学人才发展报告, 2009, 机械工业出版社. Beijing: Mechanical and Industrial Press.

Xia, Y. 2006. *Returnees and Zhongguancun*. Beijing: China Development Publication.

Ziguras, C, and S. Law. 2006. "Recruiting International Students as Skilled Migrants: The Global 'Skills Race' as Viewed from Australia and Malaysia." *Globalisation, Societies and Education* 4(1): 59–76.

Zweig, D., C. Fung, and D. Han. 2008. "Redefining the Brain Drain: China's 'Diaspora Option.'" *Science Technology and Society* 13: 1–33.

4

"Too Many Things Pull Me Back and Forth"

Return Intentions and Transnationalism among International Students

Helen Hazen and Heike Alberts

Those with advanced education find themselves in a privileged position with respect to immigration decisions as many countries offer special opportunities for the immigration of highly skilled labor. Since the 1950s, the United States has explicitly emphasized the immigration of skilled groups, as well as offered opportunities for temporary study. Although student visas in the United States are technically fixed term, students can legally extend their visas after graduation in several ways, including optional practical training, postdoctoral positions, or work; all can potentially lead to permanent residency. Since international students' decisions have a major impact on their countries of origin as well as the United States, examining how students make the decision to stay in the United States or return home has far-reaching implications. Indeed, the potential return migration of international students has been identified as one of the most significant gaps in the literature on highly skilled migrants (Baláž and Williams 2004).

The data reported here represent the culmination of two studies we carried out at the University of Minnesota—Twin Cities, investigating international students' decisions regarding returning to their home countries. The first used focus groups to generate hypotheses regarding the factors that international students consider in deciding to return to their home countries or stay in the United States on completion of their degrees. The second employed a questionnaire to test these hypotheses with a large sample of international students at the same institution. The results of these two studies were originally published separately in the journals *Population, Space and Place* and *International Migration* (Hazen and Alberts 2006; Alberts and Hazen 2005). Here we combine these two sets of results and interpret them in the framework of transnationalism.

INTERNATIONAL STUDENT MIGRATIONS AND TRANSNATIONALISM

The 1960s and 1970s spawned an extensive literature about the movement of highly skilled migrants from low-income countries to the West—the so-called brain drain. This literature focused on the negative consequences of this migration for the countries of origin and benefits to host countries. In today's globalized world, traditional notions of brain drain are rapidly being replaced with understandings of the circulation of talent and skills (Bhandari and Blumenthal 2011; Welch and Zhen 2008; Solimano 2003; Iredale 2001; Lowell 2001). In this context, the term "brain circulation" has come into usage to describe the increasingly multidirectional nature of international flows and growing awareness that these flows may be beneficial for both sending and receiving nations (Bhandhari and Blumenthal 2011). Despite this, the dominant movement continues to be from "the less developed to the more competitive places in the world knowledge-based economy" (Meyer, Kaplan, and Charum 2002, 309).

A further development in the literature has been the idea that migrants can be embedded in both their country of origin and their host country. While often settling permanently in their new host societies, transmigrants "maintain connections, build institutions, conduct transactions, and influence local and national events in the countries from which they have emigrated" (Glick Schiller, Basch, and Szanton Blanc 1995, 48). While such connections between different countries have always existed, cheaper international travel and modern means of communication have facilitated and intensified these links (Vertovec 2004). As a consequence, transnationalism has become one of the most important analytical lenses through which migrants' practices are analyzed across the social sciences (Vertovec 2009).

Using a transnational framework implies shedding assumptions that "social life logically and automatically takes place within the nation-state framework" (Levitt 2004, unpaginated). Instead, it requires analyzing how migrants can position themselves in ways that leave them above and between nation-states. Nowadays, many migrants engage in transnational behaviors that link countries and provide them with a dual frame of reference through constantly comparing their home and host countries (Vertovec 2009, 2004). However, for academics and other highly skilled migrants, transnationalism also extends into their work, making it particularly important to interpret their experiences through the lens of transnationalism (Kim 2009; Li and Stodolska 2006; Ghosh and Wang 2003).

Processes of globalization and transnationalism are closely linked as global processes foster transnational behaviors, which, in turn, lead to or amplify globalization (Vertovec 2004). For example, while the globalization of education is one factor driving academic migrations, transnational practices, such as the transmission of knowledge, strengthen the globalization of knowledge (Gargano 2009; Vertovec 2004; Johnson and Regets 1998). One result is the emergence of global "knowledge diasporas" that link academics working in different countries (Welch and Zhen 2008). In fact, some countries have promoted the creation of formal intellectual diaspora networks in order to systematically use the skills of their citizens working abroad (Meyer and Brown 1999).

Both return migrations and the creation of knowledge diasporas are ways in which intellectual capital can circulate to the benefit of both sending and host countries. In this chapter, we focus on the first of these aspects, the potential return of international students to their home countries. We begin by considering the significance of the United States in terms of international student migrations before going on to present the findings of our studies on students' return migration intentions. We argue that transnational attitudes are common among international students, whether or not they finally elect to return to their country of origin. Furthermore, a transnational approach helps explain how international students can feel that they can benefit from, and be of benefit to, both societies—hopefully leading to a "win-win" situation for both sending and receiving countries.

International Student Migrations to the United States

The United States has been the major recipient of international students worldwide since the 1960s, with numbers growing rapidly since then. By 2003 there were an estimated 586,323 international students in the United States, equivalent to 4.6 percent of all students in the United States and an even higher proportion of graduate students and students in certain disciplines such as engineering and computer science (Institute of International Education 2004a). Despite a brief drop in international student enrollments following the events of September 11, 2001, today international student numbers are yet higher, reaching 723,277 in the 2010/11 academic year (Institute of International Education 2011).

It is widely agreed that many international students stay in the United States after graduation, although the exact proportion that stay permanently is hard to calculate. Finn (2010), in a study of science and engineering students on temporary visas, found that 60 percent of those who graduated in 1997 were still in the United States in 2007, 62 percent of 2002 graduates were still present in 2007, and 73 percent of 2006 graduates were still in the United States a year later, although stay rates varied significantly among institutions, disciplines, and by the student's country of origin. There are some indications that an increasing number of international students have been returning to their country of origin in recent years, in particular to industrializing countries like China where far-reaching economic changes have created better opportunities for returnees (Brooks and Waters 2011; *The Economist* 2011; Yatsko 1997).

To avoid the challenges of determining return rates, many return migration studies report return *intentions* rather than actual return rates. For example, Johnson and Regets (1998) report that in the early 1990s over 60 percent of foreign doctoral students planned to stay in the United States after completing their degrees. Even though migration intentions are an imperfect measure of the number of students who actually return (Baker and Finn 2003), they are a useful indicator of future migration decisions (Li et al. 1996) and provide insights into the factors that students take into account in making their decision. It has been widely argued that migration decision-making processes are complex; the level of complexity may be even greater for return migrations than the initial move abroad owing to the greater experience the migrant has to draw on after spending some time overseas (Lu, Zong, and Schissel 2009; Fischer, Martin, and Straubhaar 1997). With this in mind, some studies have investigated return intentions qualitatively in order to explore international students' intentions in depth (e.g., Butcher 2004; Zweig 1997). Beyond these few studies focused on particular countries or regions, relatively little is known about international students' decision-making processes.

Research Methods

We combine qualitative and quantitative methods to investigate international students' intentions regarding whether or not to return to their home country on completion of their degree, and how these intentions change over time. We consider three main questions: First, what initially attracts international students to the United States? Second, do international students see their stay in the United States as temporary or as a springboard toward permanent immigration, and does this intention change over time? Third, what factors do students consider in the decision of whether to return to their home countries on completion of their degree; and do these factors, or the weight assigned to each of them, vary by nationality or other characteristics, such as gender, family status, or field of study?

We began by using focus groups to generate hypotheses related to international students' migration decisions. We held six focus groups, each with students of a different nationality on the grounds that individuals from different countries might use different criteria in making migration decisions. Additionally, we had informal conversations with international students from a variety of other countries. The focus groups took place at the University of Minnesota—Twin Cities from July 2003 to May 2004 and lasted on average 90 minutes. All participants were enrolled as degree-seeking international students at the University of Minnesota at the time, the vast majority pursuing doctoral degrees. Our choice of nationalities (Chinese, Dutch, Greek, Indian, Japanese, and Tanzanian) was shaped by the goal of studying different groups, including individuals from low- and high-income countries; and countries sending large numbers of students to the United States, such as India and China (452 and 694 students at the University of Minnesota during the 2003/04 academic year), as well as countries that send relatively few (the University of Minnesota had 12 Dutch and 20 Greek students during the 2003/04 academic year) (Institute of International Education 2004b). All groups contained both male and female participants, as well as students from a variety of disciplines. We use pseudonyms for all focus group respondents in reporting results below.

In a second study, we used the themes that emerged from these focus groups to develop a questionnaire. We asked for some background information, such as nationality, age, gender, degree sought, and year of arrival in the United States. To investigate return migration decisions we compiled a list of all the reasons that focus group participants had mentioned as influencing their decision-making process (as listed in tables 4.1, 4.2, and 4.3). We then asked questionnaire respondents to indicate the extent to which they agreed with each statement.

After testing several pilot versions, we e-mailed the questionnaire to a random sample of 950 of the 3,294 international students enrolled at the University of Minnesota—Twin Cities for the 2003/04 academic year. We obtained 185 responses, a response rate of 19 percent. We found the responses to have come from a broad cross-section of the international student body, with no systematic bias by sex, continent of origin, degree level, or discipline. In analyzing our results, we looked first at the proportion of respondents who listed each response as motivating their migration decisions. We then tested hypotheses generated from the focus group findings in order to assess whether or not responses correlated with demographic categories (such as home region or gender). For instance, were women more likely than men to cite "restrictive cultural practices" as a disadvantage of the home country? We tested these hypothesized associations using chi-square tests and report the relationships that were significant at the 95 percent level.

Original Reasons for Coming to the United States

We first considered why students had initially decided to come to the United States as international students. While our focus group informants brought up a large number of factors, two stood out as the most universal: the availability of funding for graduate education and the overall quality of US higher education. Students from all focus groups agreed that funding opportunities in the United States were far better than those available in their respective home countries. Students in technical fields mentioned better research facilities as a major factor, while students in the social sciences were attracted by the breadth of courses and the potential for interdisciplinary work, plus the opportunity to pursue studies in disciplines that are marginal or nonexistent back home.

Some respondents, particularly from the three Asian focus groups, mentioned the United States' open academic atmosphere as a draw. Some of the students felt "suffocated" (Abhay and Prajwala, India) in their home countries because they were not allowed to undertake the research they wanted, or were frustrated by conservative research approaches (Jun and Jiro, Japan). As Paranjape (India) phrased it, "There are places in India that offer you physical facilities, but the mental space and the space that you really need, is that there? I don't know. I didn't find that." Chinese, Indian, and Tanzanian students also believed that a degree from a US university would improve their job prospects in their respective home countries.

While professional reasons were clearly dominant among the students who came to complete degrees in the United States, those who initially came as exchange students usually cited getting experience abroad or a "certain fascination with the US" (Jonas, the Netherlands) as the main reason for their initial visit. In our sample, all the students who had first come to the United States as exchange students were from high-income countries, perhaps giving them the luxury of international study for more than just career development goals (cf. Waters and Brooks 2010).

These focus group findings were largely confirmed by the questionnaire results. Professional justifications for coming to the United States proved to be important for the majority of respondents, with almost three-quarter reporting that "better educational opportunities in the US" had influenced their decision to come—well ahead of all other reasons (table 4.1). Some 43 percent of students felt that a US degree would improve their job opportunities back home. Citing "better educational opportunities in the US" differed significantly among home regions ($p = 0.003$), with approximately 80 percent of Africans, Asians, and Latin Americans marking this reason, compared with 61 percent of Europeans and 25 percent of North Americans (i.e., Canadians), suggesting that the level of affluence of the home region may be critical. Analyzing this hypothesis statistically, we found that those from low-income countries did indeed report educational opportunities as a motivating factor at a significantly higher rate than those from middle- or high-income countries ($p = 0.001$). Whether or not students came to the United States in order to "improve job opportunities back home" also differed significantly among regions ($p = 0.006$), with those from low-income regions more likely to mark this answer (table 4.1).

The US academic system was a further attraction for questionnaire respondents. The availability of funding in the United States was cited by 29 percent of respondents, and was strongly associated with type of degree ($p = 0.002$), with those working toward doctoral degrees most likely to mark this reason. A further 28 percent of respondents stated that "greater academic freedom in the US" was an important motivating factor. Although our focus groups had suggested that there may be regional differences with respect to the draw of academic freedom, we found no significant relationship in the survey sample.

Table 4.1 Initial motivations for coming to the United States to study

	Proportion of respondents who stated each reason (% of that group)*					
	All respondents	Africans	Asians	Europeans	North Americans	Latin Americans
Better educational opportunities in US	72	82	79	61	25	78
Desire to experience a new culture	47	27	54	47	8	44
Improve job opportunities back home	43	73	46	31	8	56
Funding opportunities in US	29	36	21	39	42	33
Greater academic freedom in US	28	36	34	31	8	6
Came with other family members	5	0	6	0	8	11

Note: Australasia is omitted from the analysis as only one respondent came from this region.
Source: Reprinted from Hazen, H., and H. Alberts. 2006. "Visitors or Immigrants? International Students in the United States." *Population, Space and Place* 12: 201–16.

Not all motivations to come to study were professional, however. Consistent with our focus group findings, the second most commonly cited reason for studying in the United States was "desire to experience a new culture," selected by 47 percent of questionnaire respondents. This reason was popular across the board, with no significant association with region, gender, or level of study. In summary, career-related and educational reasons to migrate dominated the decision to come to the United States, particularly among those from low-income countries, but the desire to experience a new culture was significant for many.

Length of Stay and Return Intentions

One of our research questions was whether international students initially saw their stay in the United States as temporary, or as a springboard toward a permanent stay from the outset. Very few survey respondents (7.5 percent) believed on arrival that they would stay permanently, the majority (67 percent) stating that they had originally intended to return to their home countries on completion of their degrees. Of those intending to return, about half wanted to get work experience in the United States before returning; most nonetheless thought that they would be home within a couple of years of graduating. Only a small minority anticipated that they would still be in the United States five years beyond graduation. The remaining quarter of respondents had had no specific ideas about length of stay on arrival in the United States. There were no significant differences among home regions or between genders in terms of these initial intentions. International students coming to the United States with the intention to immigrate permanently therefore seem to be the exception rather than the rule, although many students wanted to stay several years beyond the completion of their degrees. This is significant as, to date, few studies have examined migration decisions that could turn an originally temporary migration into permanent settlement in a host country (see also Lu, Zong, and Schissel 2009).

Irrespective of original intentions, having now completed part of their programs, the vast majority of our focus group participants described feeling torn between staying in the United States and returning to their home countries. As Xiping (China) stated, "There are always two voices. One says to go back to China, and the other says to stay here." Many students expressed the view that they no longer really knew where they belonged: "When I'm here I miss home and when I'm home I miss the things that go with being here" (Sofia, the Netherlands). While the notion of transmigration is often a positive one, with migrants occupying a position that allows them the best of both worlds, our findings suggest that a transnational life also brings with it considerable psychological stress as the individual attempts to navigate two societies, sometimes leaving them with questions over where they truly belong.

Our questionnaire responses reflected these vacillations. Of those students who had indicated a clear intention of length of stay at the outset, 36 percent stated that they had changed their minds since arriving in the United States. Of these, more than half had decided to try to lengthen their stay; about one-quarter sought to shorten it. The remainder stated that the length of their stay now depends on "other" factors, particularly career prospects (61 percent of these respondents) or family/relationship issues (28 percent).

Factors Considered in the Return Migration Decision

Our final research question focused on the factors students consider in their return intentions, and how these might vary among demographic groups. From our results, we recognize two scales that influence this decision-making process. At the scale of the individual every student has particular goals and desires that drive the decision-making process. At a broader scale, the economic, academic, political, and even cultural structures within which these decisions are embedded constrain or enable a desired course of action. At each of these scales, our respondents weighed up personal and professional reasons for wanting to stay in the United States or return home.

The Structural Framework

Professional and Economic Environments

Many students in our focus groups considered the better wages and higher economic standard of living in the United States as important advantages, and many believed that they would have better job prospects in the United States than in their home countries. In our focus groups, most students agreed that it was generally easier to find a job in the United States than in their home countries, although some pointed out that this varied by discipline or student characteristics. For example, Dao (China) noted, "If you are the top 1 percent, top 5 percent, you should definitely go back to China. If you are average among the Chinese students here, you should probably stay [in the United States]." By contrast, some students, usually from low-income countries, were actually more confident of job prospects back home than in the United States. Focus group discussions around this topic led us to hypothesize that those from Africa and poorer parts of Asia who undertake international study are more likely to be among the elite with access to good jobs back home, while potentially experiencing racial barriers to employment in the United States. For instance, in the Tanzanian focus group, Babu described how Tanzania offers a more level-playing field for getting a job:

> [The United States] is a very competitive society, so in some situations we are competed out, and we think we can fairly compete back home, and even with more advantage, you know, an added advantage with the wealth of experience and exposures from this country. And so, we see more opportunities if we go home to Tanzania than here.

The survey backed up the idea that professional opportunities and standard of living are important for encouraging the majority of students to stay in the United States, as the most commonly reported advantages of the United States were "better job/career opportunities" (reported by 64 percent of respondents) and "higher standard of living in the US" (33 percent) (table 4.2). In considering

Table 4.2 Advantages and disadvantages of the United States

	Proportion of respondents who stated each reason (% of that group)					
	Total	Africans	Asians	Europeans	North Americans	Latin Americans
Better job/career opportunities in US	64	27	55	81	83	89
Higher standard of living in US	33	0	35	34	33	50
Greater academic freedom in US	29	9	35	37	8	11
Higher quality of life in US	28	0	39	17	33	5
Family/friends in US	15	0	13	17	33	17
Partner's unwillingness to leave US	10	9	7	11	25	17
Opportunities for children in US	8	9	25	17	17	0
Political situation in US	8	9	9	8	0	11
Alienation from US culture	51	45	63	31	42	33
Different understandings of friendship in the US	31	36	33	25	8	50
Different priorities in the US	28	27	22	33	17	56
Racism in the US	27	45	32	11	25	17
US politics	21	9	16	28	67	17
Poorer quality of life in the US	21	36	14	28	42	33
Poorer working conditions in the US	16	27	12	28	17	6
Poorer standard of living in the US	6	0	7	3	8	6

Source: Adapted from Hazen, H., and H. Alberts. 2006. "Visitors or Immigrants? International Students in the United States." *Population, Space and Place* 12: 201–16.

disadvantages of the home country, "poor job/career opportunities" and "lower standard of living" were similarly reported among the top three choices (table 4.3). The regional patterns with respect to job opportunities that we had observed in focus groups—with students from low-income regions least likely to report better job prospects in the United States than back home—were also somewhat evident from the questionnaire results (table 4.2). Similarly, among the 18

Table 4.3 Advantages and disadvantages of the home country

	Proportion of respondents who stated each reason (% of that group)					
	Total	Africans	Asians	Europeans	North Americans	Latin Americans
Friends/family in home country	78	81	77	69	83	89
Feeling comfortable in home culture	44	55	47	36	28	44
Better quality of life in home country	39	73	28	50	42	56
Better professional opportunities in home country	18	55	21	8	17	6
Higher standard of living in home country	13	18	14	9	17	11
Political situation in home country	8	0	4	11	42	6
Poorer job/career opportunities in home country	50	36	38	64	67	83
Restrictive career structures in home country	30	9	37	31	0	22
Poorer standard of living in home country	21	18	20	20	0	44
Political situation in home country	20	9	25	11	8	28
Poorer quality of life in home country	18	0	21	19	17	11
Restrictive cultural practices in home country	14	0	18	8	8	11
Family expectations	7	9	8	6	0	11

Source: Adapted from Hazen, H., and H. Alberts. 2006. "Visitors or Immigrants? International Students in the United States." *Population, Space and Place* 12: 201–16.

percent of questionnaire respondents who noted that they had better professional opportunities in their home countries than in the United States (table 4.3), a strong association existed with region ($p = 0.006$), with African and Asian students noting professional opportunities as better back home at the highest rates.

Academic structures also proved to be significant in return decisions for many students. Just under one-third of respondents mentioned "greater academic freedom in US" as a reason to stay (table 4.2), while "restrictive or hierarchical career structures" was the second most popular choice among disadvantages of the home country (table 4.3). Several of our focus group participants, particularly Asian and European students, commented on the more open academic atmosphere in the United States. For instance, Ria (the Netherlands) noted that student-faculty interactions are "more relaxed" in the United States, and Taro (Japan) described them as "more straightforward." Mies (the Netherlands) observed, "I don't know if I could go back to a European university system now that I am used to a different attitude...You have a different approach to the way you want to teach and the university system works."

Overall, the vast majority of our participants believed that studying in the United States had been beneficial to their career prospects, and for most the greatest professional payback from this investment would be realized by staying in the United States to work. Indeed, in the focus groups, several students noted that there would be academic or professional obstacles to returning home. Some students in technical disciplines believed that they would not be able to apply what they had learned in the United States back home because their home countries were not as advanced in their fields, or research facilities were not as good as those in the United States. Concern among social scientists typically revolved around not being able to apply knowledge to a different cultural context. Several Japanese students were concerned about whether their US degrees would be accepted back in Japan.

The transnational position of students with respect to their jobs and skills was reinforced in focus groups in several different ways. Many students reported maintaining ties with the home country with a view to returning to work at some point in the future. May (China), for instance, states, "After [my husband's] career is well-established maybe we can move somewhere else...Maybe we can go back to China, or even somewhere else in Asia or even Europe." Other students envisaged a job that would allow them to regularly move between countries, as described by Prajwala (India),

I mean, for me it's not a question of do I want to stay here or do I want to go back? I would love to go back and be able to spend, like, seven or eight months in India and keep coming back here. Will I be able to get the kind of job that will enable me to do that, that is the question.

Ria (the Netherlands) noted that part of the need to "stay flexible" in her chosen career involves having the opportunity to move back and forth between Europe and the United States. Fun (China) described a friend of hers who, although now working in China, returns annually to the University of Minnesota to use equipment and software. Mies (the Netherlands) believed that location had actually lost some of its significance over time: "As long as you have something to do that you like, it doesn't really matter whether you're here, or in the Netherlands, or maybe even in Africa."

The Political Environment

Political structures were reported as significant to return migration decisions by a minority of students. Among questionnaire respondents, 20 percent of students—primarily Asians and Latin Americans—noted repressive or unfavorable political situations back home as discouraging a return (table 4.3). For some members of the Chinese focus group, political uncertainty, lack of reform, and corruption were seen as troubles that could be avoided by a life in the United States, as explained by Dao, "[Despite recent improvements in China] the political environment is still unclear. Superficially, China is developing quickly, but there are many uncertainties." By contrast, the United States' post-9/11 political situation was mentioned as a disadvantage of staying in the United States by 21 percent of questionnaire respondents, mostly Canadians and Europeans (table 4.2).

We also investigated the influence of the political environment in terms of government policies to encourage students studying abroad to return home. Only the Chinese focus group reported being aware of any such incentives. The Chinese described policies that actively encouraged those studying abroad to return in order to promote Westernization and globalization and import English language skills (Dao, China). The government offers returnees salaries that can compete with Western countries and provides attractive housing opportunities. Despite these efforts, according to our informants, most Chinese students still decide to stay in the United States after completing their degrees.

The Cultural Environment

While most of our study participants would stay in the United States for professional reasons, cultural factors were more often cited as a draw back to the home country. Many focus group respondents reported experiencing culture shock on arrival. Feelings of dissatisfaction or dislocation related to the migration experience were commonly projected onto the host society. Many students expressed frustration with values that they associated with the United States, particularly individualism, materialism, and competitiveness, as Stavros (Greece) describes, "It's about money [in the United States], and everybody loses... They think by working harder they'll earn more money, and maybe they'll become better people. So far we have seen the opposite." In several focus groups (China, Greece, India, and Tanzania) the participants emphasized how these individualistic values contrast with their native cultures, which were described as emphasizing cooperation and community. Even the European students, who generally expressed the lowest levels of cultural dislocation, described social relations as differing significantly between the United States and their home countries. As Sarah (UK) put it, "In America people are more concerned about standard of living and work hard to acquire things—money, material goods—whereas in Europe it's *quality* of life that counts."

This notion of *quality of life*, in contrast to the more economically focused idea of *standard of living*, was a key area of discussion in several focus groups. Students frequently brought up noneconomic characteristics of society that were described as improving quality of life. For instance, Abhay (India) describes how, "having your hair cut in India is so much more enjoyable. You get good gossip besides the haircut! And the conversation is so much livelier; it takes on all kinds of things in the world. There are all kinds of spaces and conversations that are so much easier in India than here."

In several focus groups, students observed that Americans have a different understanding of friendship from their own. Fun (China) suggests, "For Chinese it's more comfortable to share personal feelings with one another. Americans are really friendly, but it is very hard to reach their hearts." These problems are often exacerbated by language barriers, which many students felt made expressing themselves difficult. For instance, Xiping (China) explains, "Some deep conversation is very important. My English is not good enough to express myself deeply in English." Because of these cultural and linguistic differences, several focus group participants explained that they do not understand Americans, and that Americans do not understand them. As a consequence, many international students reported having primarily other foreigners as friends.

Racism in the United States was mentioned in focus groups on several occasions. Members of the Tanzanian focus group, in particular, emphasized racism as encouraging a return home. Discussions focused on feeling generally uncomfortable in US society, as summarized by Lelo, "I think, as a human being, the first thing I like in life is acceptance, and if you knock at your neighbor's door you can see in his eyes if he really accepts you." While most White students had not experienced any incidences of discrimination, several White focus group respondents described how they were uncomfortable about the direction that US politics had taken post-9/11. Over one-quarter of questionnaire respondents (and nearly half of African respondents) listed racism as a disadvantage of the United States (table 4.2).

Overall, questionnaire responses reinforced the significance of the cultural environment as a drawback to the home country. "Feeling comfortable in the home culture" and "better quality of life in home country" were the second and third most popular reasons for returning home, selected by 44 percent and 39 percent of respondents respectively (table 4.3). In addition, the top six most commonly selected choices relating to disadvantages of the United States revolved around problems with adapting to US culture, including "alienation from US culture" and "different understandings of friendship in the US" (table 4.2).

Although cultural factors typically operated as a drawback to the home country, several students in focus groups reported factors that make them feel more comfortable in the United States. Many students highlighted a stimulating international atmosphere in the United States as a positive factor. For instance, Abhay (India) reported, "I've realized that there is such a large diasporic community here... I can't quite think of cutting off from what goes on here because there have been investments in building up institutions here too." Several students pointed out that this positive international atmosphere may be true of academia than the United States more generally, however.

For several female students another appeal of US culture was its greater gender equality. Women in the Indian focus group, in particular, reported that male-female relationships are generally more egalitarian in the United States, as illustrated by Romi, "Of course I enjoy the freedom here. If I don't want to cook, I can ask my husband to cook... or I can order pizza; in India that wouldn't work." Just under 14 percent of questionnaire respondents selected "restrictive cultural practices in the home country" as a disincentive to return (table 4.3). We had hypothesized that this factor would be a stronger disincentive for women, but in analyzing questionnaire responses we found no significant difference between the number of males and females who cited this reason, nor any significant regional differences.

Individual-Scale Factors

Personal factors are clearly significant in student migration decisions, although whether their influence encourages returning home or staying in the United States depends on the student's individual circumstances. Fully 78 percent of questionnaire respondents listed "family and friends" as an advantage of returning home (table 4.3). However, 15 percent listed "family and friends," 10 percent "partner's unwillingness to leave," and 8 percent "opportunities for children" as reasons to *stay* in the United States (table 4.2). Personal factors, or the importance given to them, were often closely intertwined with cultural factors. For example, while family ties were mentioned by students of all nationalities in focus groups, the importance accorded to them seemed heavily influenced by broader cultural attitudes toward family and notions of obligation to family and community, with the Indian, Greek, and Tanzanian focus groups focusing particularly strongly on matters of family.

Our focus group discussions helped to provide the detail needed to understand the complexity of personal decisions for international students. For those respondents who had had to leave partners or children behind in their home country, the desire to return home was, unsurprisingly, strong. By contrast, three students in our focus groups were married to Americans, and so in these cases family ties worked to hold them in the United States. These students all expressed concerns over how their American partners would fare with language barriers and cultural challenges if they left the United States. When there are children in the family a return often becomes yet more difficult, even when both parents are of the same nationality. Many of our participants (even those currently without children) expressed concern that their children would not want to leave the United States once they had spent some time there, and that they themselves would think twice before moving their children once they had started school. For others, children were seen as a reason to return to the home country. Several students expressed concerns over bringing children up in the United States, often related to a belief that American society encourages less disciplined styles of childrearing, as Paranjape (India) described: "I hear children here saying 'I want this' or 'I hate you,' Oh man, you can never say that in India!" Others feared that their children would experience the same sort of identity crisis that they themselves had suffered through living between cultures.

Among Asian students the desire to be close to family members was reported not only as a cultural value, but also as a moral obligation. Participants in the Japanese focus group concurred that it is the firstborn son's obligation to take care of his parents, and it would reflect poorly on him if he did not fulfill this expectation. Not all students welcomed such obligations, however; "family expectations" were mentioned as a disadvantage of the home country by 7 percent of questionnaire respondents (table 4.3).

Our European focus group participants did not report this sense of obligation to the same degree. In addition, the relatively low cost and rapidity of travel to Europe meant that European respondents were generally satisfied with how frequently they were able to go home. Many, nonetheless, reported that they had missed important family events and were concerned about possible family emergencies, as were participants in other focus groups too. For instance, Jun (Japan) recounts, "My grandmother died last week and I couldn't go. It made me feel so bad because everybody else in the family went to the funeral." Being among family and old friends was also seen as important when the students themselves had problems, as explained by Manca (Tanzania): "People here are telling you that you are sad and that you should go and see the...what is that called?...the psychiatrist. But back home people will sit with me."

Students' willingness or ability to assimilate into a different culture varied considerably among individuals. For some, feelings of cultural difference never really disappeared, as discussed by Dao, "I am a very traditional Chinese, for me the culture is very different. I would always feel alien, no matter how good my English is, no matter how long I have been here, no matter what social status I have achieved here." As a result, many students explained that, despite their professional success, something important is missing in their lives. As Charu (India) describes, "There is a lack of family and community here. There's an emptiness here that you don't feel anywhere else in the world, a feeling of isolation." For other students, time spent moving between societies had left them with a truly transnational mindset, as Sofia (the Netherlands) explains, "Well, at least for me, since I've been back and forth like three times, and I'll probably stay here, you're kind of in between cultures." This position "in between cultures" was described by Sofia and Ria, in an exchange in the Dutch focus group, as like "walking a tightrope," balancing yourself between your two cultural positions. Several students felt that they had become so acculturated to the United States that their home cultures had now begun to seem alien, as Charu (India) described, "I have a completely different world view now. It's like having two lenses at a slightly different angle. I know what I want, and I have changed, but the people back home have not changed."

Discussion and Conclusion

Deciding whether to return to their home countries or to stay in the United States is a dilemma for most international students; many find the decision becomes more and more complex the longer they stay in the United States. The decision-making process operates at two main scales. First, the wider context constrains or enables particular migration opportunities. Factors such as the political situations, job markets, and academic structures of the home and host country influence their relative desirability, often in similar ways for most students of a particular nationality. For instance, the Chinese focus group discussed the problematic political situation in China at length, while many Indian women focused attention on gender discrimination. Individual-scale factors, unique to each student, are embedded within these broader structures, providing personal motivations for staying or leaving. For instance, whether or not a student is married and, if so, the nationality of the spouse can influence a student's decisions significantly.

At both scales—structural and individual—professional and cultural factors appear to dominate the decision-making process. Broadly speaking, professional factors typically form the strongest arguments to stay in the United States, while cultural factors often speak strongly in favor of returning to the home country. In particular, the greatest payoff from studying in the United States was reported by most students to be achieved through seeking work in the United States. Conversely, friends and family back home, as well as a more familiar cultural setting, often spoke strongly in favor of a return migration. The relative weight assigned to these different groups of factors appears to differ among nationalities as became evident in the focus groups. For instance, even though the Greeks in our focus group agreed that they would be better off professionally in the United States, the importance they attached to cultural and personal values appeared to outweigh professional concerns, and the majority favored a return to Greece. Similarly, the Tanzanian focus group strongly emphasized the importance of family and their preference for their home culture, and all students expressed a desire to return home relatively quickly. By contrast, participants in the Chinese focus group tended to emphasize broader societal constraints on their decision making, particularly the insecure political situation in China, which were reported as overriding students' personal concerns to some degree.

The relative emphasis given to structural versus individual reasons not only varies among nationalities and from person to person, but is also fluid over time. The initial decision to come to the United States to study and the decision of whether or not to return on completion of the degree are fundamentally different as most students have little firsthand experience of the United States when they arrive. In deciding to come to the United States, therefore, most students rely on a cost-benefit analysis of secondhand information, based on widely reported structural factors of the United States, such as economic and educational characteristics. Professional and educational reasons are therefore given great importance among original motivations for the move. For the return decision, by contrast, the student has the benefit of firsthand experience of the United States, and so the decision making shifts toward reasons that are more individual—structural reasons still form a framework in the background, but individual factors now influence them more heavily.

Viewing international students in a transnational framework offers several further insights. First, it is clear that many international students view their position as transnational in the sense that they consider their career and personal trajectories at a global rather than national scale. Many students reported living in a sort of limbo between home and host country, often for considerable periods of time, while weighing up their options. Instead of viewing their stay in the United States as permanent, most students reported reconsidering their migration decisions at key points. Second, most students engaged in transnational behaviors. Most students reported keeping in close contact with family and friends back home, while some also reported making an effort to try to make or sustain professional linkages in both countries, and many respondents hoped that their future jobs would allow them some degree of transnational flexibility. Finally, some students reported that they hoped to use their skills for the betterment of their home communities, suggesting that international students may, indeed, transfer skills and knowledge between home and host countries.

Whether or not our respondents elect to return to their home countries in the future, the insights gleaned here suggest that international students are likely to retain a transnational attitude. Many of our respondents reported the importance that they place on working in a stimulating international environment, and their desire to work in ways that are not constrained by national boundaries. Such attitudes may transform both home and host societies as governments and institutions strive to make conditions attractive for their intellectual elite in order to succeed in the global knowledge economy.

Works Cited

Alberts, H., and H. Hazen. 2005. "'There Are Always Two Voices...' International Students' Decisions to Stay in the U.S. or Return to their Home Countries." *International Migration* 43(3): 131–52.

Baker, J., and M. Finn. 2003. "Stay Rates of Foreign National Doctoral Students in U.S. Economics Programs." Available at: http://papers.ssrn.com/sol3/papers.cfm?abstract_id=398640. Accessed: March 3, 2005.

Baláž, V., and A. Williams. 2004. "'Been There, Done That': International Student Migration and Human Capital Transfers from the UK to Slovakia." *Population, Space and Place* 10: 217–37.

Bhandari, R., and P. Blumenthal. 2011. "Global Student Mobility and the Twenty-First Century Silk Road: National Trends and Directions." In *International Students and Global Mobility in Higher Education: National Trends and New Directions*, edited by R. Bhandari, and P. Blumenthal, 1–23. New York: Palgrave Macmillan.

Brooks, R., and J. Waters. 2011. *Student Mobilities, Migration, and the Internationalization of Higher Education*. London: Palgrave Macmillan.

Butcher, A. 2004. "Departures and Arrivals: International Students Returning to their Countries of Origin." *Asian and Pacific Migration Journal* 13(3): 275–303.

Finn, M. 2010. "Stay Rates of Foreign Doctorate Recipients from U.S. Universities, 2007." Working paper, Oak Ridge Institute for Science and Education.

Fischer, P., R. Martin, and T. Straubhaar. 1997. "Should I Stay or Should I Go?" In *International Migration, Immobility and Development*, edited by T. Hammar, G. Brochmann, K. Tomas, and T. Faist, 49–90. Oxford and New York: Berg.

Gargano, T. 2009. "(Re)Conceptualizing International Student Mobility: The Potential of Transnational Social Fields." *Journal of Studies in International Education* 13(3): 331–46.

Ghosh, S., and L. Wang. 2003. "Transnationalism and Identity: A Tale of Two Faces and Multiple Lives." *The Canadian Geographer* 47(3): 269–82.

Glick Schiller, N., L. Basch, and C. Szanton Blanc. 1995. "From Immigrant to Transmigrant: Theorizing Transnational Migration." *Anthropological Quarterly* 68(1): 48–63.

Hazen, H., and H. Alberts. 2006. "Visitors or Immigrants? International Students in the United States." *Population, Space and Place* 12: 201–16.

Institute of International Education. 2011. "Quick Facts." Available at: http://www.iie.org/Who-We-Are/News-and-Events/Press-Center/Press-Releases/2011/~/media/Files/Corporate/Open-Doors/Fast-Facts/Fast%20Facts%202011.ashx. Accessed: April 8, 2011.

———. 2004a. "Foreign Student and Total U.S. Enrollment, 2002/2003." Available at: http://opendoors.iienetwork.org/?p=35931. Accessed: August 30, 2004.

———. 2004b. "Open Doors Data Annual Census of Foreign Students 2003–04." University of Minnesota—Twin Cities Campus.

Iredale, R. 2001. "The Migration of Professionals: Theories and Typologies." *International Migration* 39(5): 7–24.

Johnson, J., and M. Regets. 1998. "International Mobility of Scientists and Engineers to the United States: Brain Drain or Brain Circulation?" *National Science Foundation Issue Brief* (NSF 98–316). Available at: http://www.nsf.gov/sbe/srs/issuebrf/sib98316.htm. Accessed: March 26, 2005.

Kim, T. 2009. "Transnational Academic Mobility, Internationalization and Interculturality in Higher Education." *Intercultural Education* 20(5): 395–405.

Levitt, P. 2004. "Transnational Migrants: When 'Home' Means More Than One Country." Available at: http://www.migrationinformation.org/feature/display.cfm?ID=261. Accessed: August 28, 2011.

Li, F., A. Findlay, A. Jowett, and R. Skeldon. 1996. "Migrating to Learn and Learning to Migrate: A Study of the Experiences and Intentions of International Student Migrants." *International Journal of Population Geography* 2: 51–67.

Li, M., and M. Stodolska. 2006. "Transnationalism, Leisure and Chinese Graduate Students in the United States." *Leisure Sciences* 28: 39–55.

Lowell, B. 2001. *International Mobility of Skilled Labour.* Geneva International Labour Office, International Migration Branch.

Lu, Y., L. Zong, and B. Schissel. 2009. "To Stay or Return: Migration Intentions of Students from People's Republic of China in Saskatchewan, Canada." *International Migration & Integration* 10: 283–310.

Meyer, J-B., D. Kaplan, and J. Charum. 2002. "Scientific Nomadism and the New Geopolitics of Knowledge." *International Social Science Journal* 53(168): 309–21.

Meyer, J-B., and M. Brown. 1999. "Scientific Diasporas: A New Approach to the Brain Drain." Paris: UNESCO-MOST Discussion Paper No. 41. Available at: www.unesco.org/most/meyer.htm. Accessed: May 5, 2012.

Solimano, A. 2003. "Globalizing Talent and Human Capital: Implications for Developing Countries." Santiago: UN. Available at: http://www

.andressolimano.com/articles/migration/Globalizing%20Human%20Capital,%20manuscript.pdf. Accessed: August 5, 2011.
The Economist. 2011. "Moving Out, On and Back." (Aug 27): 51–2.
Vertovec, S. 2009. *Transnationalism.* London: Routledge.
———. 2004. "Migrant Transnationalism and Modes of Transformation(s)." *International Migration Review* 38(3): 970–1001.
Waters, J., and R. Brooks. 2010. "Accidental Achievers? International Higher Education, Class Reproduction and Privilege in the Experiences of US Students Overseas." *British Journal of Sociology of Education* 31(2): 217–28.
Welch, A., and Z. Zhen. 2008. "Higher Education and Global Talent Flows: Brain Drain, Overseas Chinese Intellectuals, and Diasporic Knowledge Networks." *Higher Education Policy* 21: 519–37.
Yatsko, P. 1997. "Comeback Kids: China's Prodigals Come Home to Prosper in Shanghai." *Far Eastern Economic Review* 160: 70.
Zweig, D. 1997. "To Return or Not to Return: Politics vs. Economics in China's Brain Drain." *Studies in International Comparative Development* 32(1): 92–125.

5

GERMAN FACULTY IN THE UNITED STATES

RETURN MIGRATION INTENTIONS, REFORM, AND RESEARCH NETWORKS

Heike Alberts

International faculty are common in the United States, in particular in technical disciplines. They are believed to bring new perspectives in teaching and research, thus contributing to internationalization goals now prominent in US higher education (Gürüz 2011; Smetherham, Fenton, and Modood 2010). Despite their numerical importance and far-reaching impacts on the US higher-education system, international faculty's experiences, career trajectories, and migration decisions have received relatively little scholarly attention to date (Saltmarsh and Swirski 2010). In particular, not much is known about international faculty from high-income countries such as Japan and Germany (see Cheng and Yang 1998), which rank among the top five countries of origin of international scholars in the United States (Institute of International Education 2011).

While it is important to investigate international faculty's experiences in the United States, understanding their decisions to stay in the United States permanently or return to their home countries is also crucial in the context of current discussions surrounding issues of "brain circulation" and the development of international research networks. Using German faculty in the United States as an example, this study investigates three main questions: what factors do international faculty take into account in their decision of whether to return to their home countries or remain in the United States? Do their migrations to the United States represent a "brain drain" for their home country? Can brain circulation emerge even when people do not return home?

International Faculty in the United States

Foreign-born faculty come to the United States in three main ways. First, a significant proportion of international students stay in the United States after completing their degrees, many taking faculty positions and subsequently adjusting their status to permanent residency or even citizenship. Since international students are particularly common in mathematics, computer science, physics, and engineering, and earn a large percentage of the PhDs in these disciplines (Bhandari and Blumenthal 2011), these are also the disciplines in which international faculty are particularly strongly represented. Second, a large number of scientists with PhDs from overseas come to the United States for postdoctoral positions, some of whom accept faculty positions after finishing their postdocs. Third, some foreign-born academics apply directly for faculty positions in the United States, often because they cannot find good academic positions in their home countries.

Due to these different migration trajectories it is difficult to determine the exact number of international faculty in the United States as academics who adjust from one type of migration status to another might not be counted, or may be double-counted, depending on the circumstances (see Goldin, Cameron, and Belarajan 2011). Not all data sources distinguish among faculty, postdocs, researchers working in nonuniversity research institutions, and visiting researchers (see also O'Hara 2009), and there is no reliable data set for international faculty specifically. As a result, the reported numbers vary widely. In the case of German faculty—the focus of this chapter—Lossau (2004) reports 18,000 German scientists and 6,000 postdocs in the United States in the early 2000s. Remhof (2008) states that there are approximately 6,000 German PhDs in the United States. The US-based Institute of International Education (2011) registered 5,588 German scholars teaching and researching at US institutions in 2010/11, representing 4.8 percent of all international scholars in the United States (figure 5.1), but does not report how many of these scholars hold faculty positions.

It is also impossible to determine the number of Germans leaving Germany for faculty or research positions in the United States from German data. Remhof (2008) reports that among Organization for Economic Co-operation and Development (OECD) countries Germany suffers the highest loss of academics, but exact numbers are

German Faculty in the United States 91

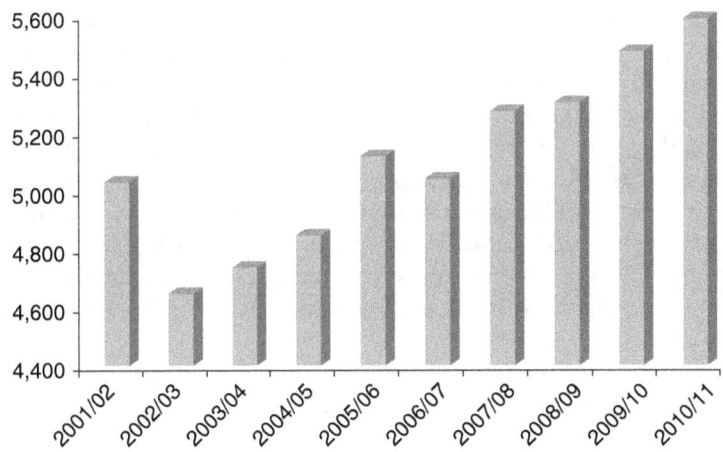

Figure 5.1 German scholars in the United States, 2001–2011
Source: Institute of International Education (2011)

not available as the German *Statistisches Bundesamt*, which publishes data about migrants, does not collect data about migrants' qualifications. Even though all people living in Germany are legally required to register with the authorities and unregister themselves when they leave the country, many academic migrants living abroad remain registered in Germany, so these data are not reliable either (Remhof 2008; see also Stiftungsverband 2002). As a result of these difficulties, all numbers have to be seen as rough estimates, but it is clear that the number of German academics working in the United States is substantial.

It is also difficult to determine stay rates of foreign scholars, although a few estimates are available. Mahroum (1998), for example, claimed that highly skilled Europeans are more likely to stay in the United States than Koreans or Japanese, but does not cite exact numbers. Based on tax records, Finn (2007) determined that 68 percent of PhD recipients from US universities in 2000 were still paying taxes in the United States in 2005. He found that there were differences according to discipline (with scientists in engineering and computer science more likely to stay than those in the social sciences and economics), as well as by nationality (with Indians and Chinese much more likely to stay than Taiwanese and Koreans) (see also Khadria 2006).

Given the positive selection of foreign academics, it is not surprising that a large percentage are employed at the most prestigious universities abroad (Mahroum 1998), attracted by the reputation of centers of academic excellence, the availability of funding, and good working conditions (see Smetherham, Fenton, and Modood 2010). In the United States, international scholars are concentrated in the most highly ranked universities; the top five institutions hosting international scholars in 2010/11 were Harvard with over 4,000, and Berkeley, Columbia, Stanford, and the University of Michigan with over 2,500 each (Institute of International Education 2011). International scholars are often found in fields in which the United States does not produce sufficient native-born graduates, such as engineering and some of the sciences, so the question of whether or not they stay permanently is not only important for their home countries but also for the United States.

The Impact on Countries of Origin

The migration of the highly skilled to other countries has been a topic of investigation for several decades. Throughout the 1960s and 1970s, many studies focused on migrations of highly skilled people from low-income to high-income countries. It was widely believed that these migrations benefited recipient countries, but deprived the countries of origin of their most talented people, representing a brain drain. Since the late 1980s, the term brain drain has gradually been replaced by terms such as "brain exchange" or brain circulation. This was partly in recognition of the fact that many movements are no longer unidirectional and permanent (Edler, Fier, and Grimpe 2011; Khoser 2007; Pellegrino 2001; Salt and Findlay 1989). Furthermore, it was revealed that these movements could represent a win-win situation for both receiving and sending nations (e.g., Bhandari and Blumenthal 2011; Brooks and Waters 2011; Pellegrino 2001; Johnson and Regets 1998; Mahroum 1998; Gaillard and Gaillard 1997). Taking this idea further, some scholars now suggest that scientific knowledge, irrespective of who produces it and where, benefits the entire world. From this perspective, the migration of the most talented scientists is a gain for all and an important characteristic of today's knowledge-driven world (Smetherham, Fenton, and Modood 2010; Cheng and Yang 1998). Thus, brain circulation occurs not only through the physical migration of people, but also via international networks that link people in different countries.

The "Exodus" of German Academics

Germany is a country with a high standard of living, strong democracy, and rich academic tradition. It is also a major player in the production of scientific knowledge. To cite just one example, Germany ranks second (after the United States) in the number of Nobel Prizes won (Gürüz 2011). Nevertheless, many highly skilled people are leaving Germany, prompting a flurry of newspaper reports with catchy headlines such as "Germany's best are leaving" and "The exodus of German scientists" (see Diehl and Dixon 2005). Most discussions focus on the United States as the most important destination country (Edler, Fier, and Grimpe 2011).

Most academic studies agree that most Germans eventually return home after a stay abroad, but reach different conclusions regarding whether this represents a serious brain drain from Germany. Many of these studies focus on postdoctoral scholars. For example, Buechtemann and Tobsch (2001) found that the majority of German postdocs judged job opportunities, access to funding and equipment, and opportunities for interdisciplinary research to be better in the United States than in Germany. However, the authors caution that many of these postdocs are working at elite US institutions, so that a comparison with less prestigious German universities is problematic. Jaschick (2011) reports that about 85 percent of German postdocs return home. He points out that many academics were actively encouraged to do their postdocs in the United States to build their resumes with international experience and improve their job prospects in Germany. Similarly, Edler, Fier, and Grimpe (2011) do not recognize a permanent brain drain of scientists as most engage in short-term international mobility; instead they report evidence of brain circulation in the form of increased transfer of knowledge across international borders.

Based on their analysis of US immigration data Diehl and Dixon (2005) concluded that, while the number of Germans moving to the United States as well as their skill level have increased since the 1990s, most of these moves are temporary. The number of Germans who adjust their status from temporary visas to permanent residency has remained stable over this period. The authors also point out that, while roughly 1,000 Germans with a doctoral degree leave Germany every year, about 20 times that number earn a doctorate, suggesting that Germany may experience what some people have termed "brain overflow."

Stiftungsverband (2002) carried out a comprehensive study of highly skilled Germans abroad, including those at nonuniversity research institutions and in nonresearch positions. This study also concluded that most highly skilled Germans eventually return, but found that those with American PhD degrees were significantly less likely to return than those with German doctoral degrees (see also Jaschik 2011). Most significantly for the present study, they found that German faculty employed at US universities described their experiences in the United States in far more positive terms than those in other places of employment. They were therefore less likely to return compared with German academics working in nonteaching positions. Revisiting the results of the Stiftungsverband (2002) study, Allmendinger and Eickmeier (2003) conclude that conditions at German universities present a serious obstacle to return for those in faculty positions. They believe that the features of the US system that allow young academics to become integrated easily and early in their careers—such as more structured PhD programs and tenure-track positions—need to be implemented to improve professional opportunities for academics in Germany. Additionally, they cite spousal hires and the availability of childcare as important areas that need reform to allow young talent to prosper in Germany.

Other studies that focus on faculty specifically have also found that those employed at universities may be more reluctant to return than those working in nonuniversity research institutions. Remhof (2008) relied on information from experts to uncover the reasons for the loss of German university personnel to the United States. He found that the lack of a tenure-track system in Germany, the burdensome bureaucracy, the strict hierarchies, and the limited freedom in terms of research topics were major considerations for German academics. He also identified several factors attracting German academics to the United States including the excellent reputation of universities, the less hierarchical structure of academia, and better support for dual-career families. These factors warrant further study. In particular, since most existing studies are based on quantitative data, qualitative data could provide a more nuanced view of the factors that German academics consider in regards to a possible return migration.

Methodology and Background

I used semistructured interviews to get in-depth information about the factors German academics consider in their decision to stay in the United States or return to Germany. A research assistant searched the websites of universities throughout the Midwestern United States for German-born faculty who had either obtained their PhD degrees in the United States and then stayed, or who had moved to the United States after completing their terminal degrees in Germany. Just under a third (15) of the 48 German professors identified in this way agreed to a telephone interview. The interviews were conducted in the language of choice of the interviewee (German or English) and lasted at least half an hour each, with some interviews morphing into lengthy discussions. We took extensive notes during the telephone interviews and expanded on them immediately after the interview to minimize the risk of information getting lost or distorted. To protect the identity of the interviewees, all names given below are pseudonyms.

The German professors interviewed for this study were employed at different types of institutions, ranging from elite research universities to smaller state universities, and worked in a wide variety of academic disciplines including biology, biophysics, business, chemistry, geography, microbiology, sociology, and psychology. One of the professors interviewed came to the United States about 40 years ago, three came in the 1980s, two in the 1990s, and the remainder in the 2000s. Four of the interviewees had obtained their PhD degrees from US universities (all from prestigious institutions, including Harvard), while eleven had moved to the United States after finishing their academic training in Germany. Several of the interviewees had not only defended their *Dissertation* (PhD) in Germany, but also their *Habilitation,* a second research degree that was obligatory in Germany until recently for a professorship (see Majcher 2002 for further information). Several had stayed in the United States after completing postdocs at prestigious universities such as Berkeley, Stanford, and UCLA. Three of the professors interviewed stated that they had had offers to return to Germany.

Factors Considered in Return Migration Decisions

At the time of the interviews, most German professors in this study did not have concrete plans to return to Germany, despite some frustrations with their experiences in the United States. Most were highly critical of some aspects of the German university system, especially in comparison to the US system. First and foremost, the vast majority believed that it was very difficult to find a good job at a German university due to the general shortage of permanent positions, as well as hiring practices that they considered problematic. While some interviewees made general comments such as: "It is easier to get a job in the US because it has more universities, more positions, and more turnover" (Herr Telschow), about half of the interviewees believed that German hiring practices specifically are the most significant problem that keeps them from returning. For instance, Herr Lahm described how, "in Germany academic jobs are often not properly advertized, so it is difficult to get in." Several voiced the idea that academic searches are not aimed at hiring the most qualified person. One professor, for example, said that many German universities want to hire people "who won't rock the boat" (Herr Schmidt). He added that there is a form of "intellectual incest," as outsiders without the necessary connections (often called "Vitamin B" as the term for "connections" is *Beziehungen* in German) do not have a chance to get hired (see also Majcher 2002). As one professor put it,

> Vitamin B is much more important in Germany. In the US connections help, but you can get a job without having connections. In the US you are hired based on your research and accomplishments, not based on who you know (Frau Elbe).

In general, there was a sense that certain people, usually senior professors, are overly influential in the hiring process. The hiring process was not perceived as open and fair, with the strong hierarchies in the German system often interpreted as the root problem.

My interviewees saw the strict hierarchies with senior professors at the top not only as an obstacle to getting hired at a German university, but also as a major disadvantage to working in the German university system. Several respondents compared senior professors to royalty—for example, two professors spoke of senior professors having "little kingdoms" (Herr Brauer and Frau Neuner), while another commented that you always have to be respectful of "your highness" (Frau Schwarz) (for an explanation of the status of senior professors, see Majcher 2002). For the German faculty interviewed for this study, the high position of senior professor has two main consequences, both of which speak strongly against working in this system. First, the senior professors often engage in a turf war, so that "more time is spent demarcating territory than getting work done" (Herr Schmidt). Second, a junior member of the department is literally an assistant to the senior professors. As one interviewee who had held such a position remarked, "It was a very unpleasant atmosphere in Germany, being an assistant to a professor. You have to walk two steps behind him and you have to carry his briefcase" (Herr Stenzel).

These hierarchical relationships usually mean that there is less collegiality than in the United States, as most of my respondents pointed out in one way or another, and very little opportunity for junior faculty members to work independently. By comparison, "In the US, people on a tenure-track position are treated as junior colleagues, but as colleagues. They are not subordinated to anybody else and can take their own decisions" (Herr Steffen).

A further major criticism was that Germany does not have a tenure-track system. My interviewees saw the strongest advantage of the US tenure-track system as allowing academics to get good positions at a young age. Many commented on the huge gap that exists in Germany between an entry-level academic (called "assistant") and a professor, with the jump between the two levels very difficult to make. For example, one interviewee explained: "In Germany you have to survive somehow for a long time before you get a decent position. Most people don't survive all these years, so they never get a chance to prove themselves in academia" (Herr Telschow). Furthermore, the vast majority of the junior positions are temporary, so there is no job security. Several respondents saw the recently created "junior professorships" in Germany as a step in the right direction, but they recognized that they are only a partial solution, as they are still only temporary positions. As one professor put it:

> The junior professorships are a good idea, but it is not enough to keep the people, because they are not like tenure-track positions. The junior professorships are only temporary, so it does not allow you to plan for life, and that is important when you are in your thirties (Herr Steffen).

The lack of job security in the junior positions was a recurring theme, with participants emphasizing that, as opposed to the United States, the German system requires young academics to change positions to move up the ladder rather than work on a career step-by-step at the same institution.

While problematic hiring practices, strong hierarchies, and a lack of tenure-track positions were the most important factors speaking against a return to Germany for many of the German academics interviewed, the related issues of lack of innovation and reform also featured prominently in the interviews. Once again, a lot of the blame was placed on the senior professors. For example, one respondent said: "In Germany it is impossible to develop something new because of the jealousy and narrow-mindedness of other professors. You have to deal with professors defending their turf. They are not interested in developing something new" (Herr Meier). Several interviewees explained that in the United States academics have true intellectual freedom, with the only limits being imposed by the need to get funding. In Germany, by contrast, research agendas are often determined by senior professors. As one particularly disgruntled respondent put it, "The greatest problem of the German system is the German professor. They are really running down the system" (Herr Meier).

More generally, the German university system was perceived as "old and crusty" (Frau Schwarz) and afraid of carrying out any real reforms. Recent reform initiatives received mixed reviews. The creation of junior professorships and a push toward making German universities more competitive globally through the so-called Excellence Initiative received some praise from interviewees, even though they expressed concern that these reforms were not far-reaching enough. Other recent developments, such as the replacement of the German *Diplom* by the bachelor's/master's system alarmed some. One professor said: "From what I hear, they seem to take the bad of the German system and combine it with the bad of the American system, so things are getting worse" (Frau Schwarz). Many people are concerned about whether the new degree programs reach the same standards as the old, and whether employers will see a bachelor's degree as sufficient.

Respondents emphasized the need for reform in not only the structure of the university, but also more generally. Many harshly criticized the amount of bureaucracy and red tape needed to carry out research. Several respondents commented that in Germany academics have to spend more time on administrative duties, restricting the time available for research. Many thought that it was difficult to navigate the system and that overly strict regulations were often an obstacle. In Germany, "All the boxes have to be checked. In the US, there is a lot more flexibility, and ways can be found around regulations" (Herr Schmidt). A professor of genetics similarly argued:

> In disciplines like gene technology there are strict limitations on what you can do in Germany. One of my American colleagues once commented that he really liked the German laws regarding genetic research. Surprised, I asked what he liked about them. He responded that the laws were so strict that most German researchers preferred to come to the US to do research (Frau Elbe).

While regulations and red tape present a major obstacle to research in Germany according to my respondents, the topic of funding was also frequently brought up. In talking about funding, most respondents clearly distinguished between senior professors and their junior colleagues. Several respondents recognized that senior professors may be financially better off than those in the United States as they have access to more funding directly from the university. Furthermore, senior professors have assistants whose responsibility is to write grant applications to bring in more money. Junior professors are much more dependent on external funding, and sometimes find that not all funding sources base their decisions on the academic merit of the proposed research. Some interviewees claimed that competition for funding was rarely fair, with "a system of elders controlling the grant system" (Herr Meier), while others were concerned that "what little money is available is not distributed to the young enthusiastic professors" (Herr Klausen). In the United States, by contrast, external funding opportunities were generally judged to be plentiful and fair. Several respondents also praised the quality of the equipment in the United States. As a result of all these factors, "In many fields it is in the United States where the cutting edge stuff is being done, not in Germany" (Frau Neuner).

It is interesting to note that the vast majority of the interviewees' comments referred to undesirable characteristics of the German university system and research issues rather than teaching when weighing up the pros and cons of a return to Germany. Even though several interviewees mentioned that the quality of teaching is generally better in the United States ("In Germany many of the lectures are just awful" [Herr Telschow]), when the topic of teaching was brought up, it was usually framed in terms of frustrations with US students. In particular, interviewees repeatedly commented on students' lack of background knowledge and skills. As one professor explained, "You see what American students missed out on in high school once they come to the university. In high school they can get around the harder subjects, so they simply don't have a good basis" (Herr Albrecht). In addition to a less-than-ideal high school education, German professors also blamed lax admission standards. "The standards here are very low; many students are ill-prepared. In Germany, the weak students are sifted out. It seems to be getting worse, with some students being practically illiterate" (Herr Vogel). Although poor standards and other issues with students were voiced as frustrations of working in the United States, not a single interviewee suggested that this was a factor that would encourage a return to Germany.

A final complex of factors speaking against a return to Germany relates to gender issues and family. All female respondents commented on how difficult it is for women to be accepted as scientists in Germany. One stated that, "it is difficult for women to get a job in the sciences in the US, but it is even more difficult in Germany. In the US women have far more rights when it comes to equality in the workplace" (Frau Schwarz). Another referred more specifically to unfair treatment: "In Germany it is often said that women are not qualified, even when it is obvious that they are. Men are given the benefit of the doubt, but women have to be outstanding before they are even considered" (Frau Elbe). While female respondents were most vocal about these issues, several male interviewees brought up similar issues, including the lack of provision for spousal hires.

More generally, several respondents had concerns about taking non-German spouses or US-born children to Germany. Some concerns focused on attitudes in Germany against foreigners in general and racial minorities specifically. For example, one male respondent stated that the "general lack of acceptance of foreigners in Germany" (Herr Meier) was an obstacle for him to move to Germany with his American wife. Similarly, a female interviewee was "not comfortable taking [her] non-White husband to Germany" (Frau Henkel). Others voiced concerns over whether their US-born children had the German language skills to make the transition successfully or would be comfortable in a different cultural environment.

Other respondents noted concerns about the social environment in the United States. Several interviewees noted "not really feeling at home here," although concrete examples of what led to these feelings were rare. Some respondents made vague statements about "disliking American culture" without specifying what exactly that meant, and several made complaints such as, "many relationships in the United States are very superficial." Several respondents felt that the United States lacked an intellectual environment outside academia: "In Germany you still have a very lively intellectual debate, and it includes a wider group of people than in the United States" (Herr Stenzel). As with teaching-related issues, these disadvantages of the United States compared to Germany were consistently worded as frustrations and disappointments, but not as factors that would lead to a return to Germany, however. This suggests that professional factors, especially those connected to hiring practices, treatment on the job, and research opportunities, are the most important factors for the majority of German academics in the United States weighing up the pros and cons of returning to Germany.

Brain Drain or Brain Circulation?

When asked about the repercussions of German academics leaving Germany, most respondents referred to the notion of the brain drain. While some respondents acknowledged that the brain drain depends on the discipline—for example, few economists leave German-speaking areas because it is more difficult for them to find a job in the United States than for natural scientists—most believed that there was a significant brain drain from Germany to other high-income countries, particularly the United States. One interviewee formulated it succinctly: "Germany produces highly-educated people for the United States" (Herr Brauer).

Opinions on how serious the brain drain is for Germany varied. Many felt that it was a serious problem. For example, one interviewee considered the impact on the German economy, "The brain drain is a huge problem as half of the PhDs go abroad, and it is usually the best who leave. Highly qualified people are Germany's most valuable capital, so it is disastrous for the economy when they leave" (Herr Steffen). Another respondent noted: "Education is the only big resource that Germany has, so nothing will be left when this goes as well" (Frau Elbe). Concern centered in particular on the fact that it is often the best in their disciplines who leave, so that Germany is losing its competitive edge. One respondent pointed to another form of brain drain occurring within Germany, however:

> Germany experiences a brain drain, both in terms of people taking jobs abroad, but also an internal brain drain as people are forced out of the system to take jobs in different positions even when they have completed a *Habilitation* [the second dissertation required at many German universities] (Herr Lahm).

While only one interviewee applied the brain drain metaphor to this internal loss of academics, many others expressed concern that many promising academics end up leaving academia because of the difficulties of securing good academic jobs.

Even though most respondents expressed concern about so many German academics leaving Germany, not all took such a bleak view. One, for example, said that "there is still enough brain in Germany, so it is not necessary to get the people back," but added that "they have to change the structure so that people want to be there. The brain drain is not a national catastrophe, but the university system is" (Herr Stenzel). Another respondent framed the out-migration of German academics in completely different terms: "The brain drain has to be seen in a global context rather than one country against another. These people are not lost to the world, they just make their contributions elsewhere, and everybody benefits from that" (Frau Henkel).

One way to reverse any potential loss, and even to benefit from academics' experiences abroad, would be if emigrants returned to Germany after working in other countries. While one interviewee stated outright that he "would not even consider going back," and added bitterly, "For starters, German universities would not even reimburse me to come for an interview" (Herr Stenzel), most would consider a return, but only if they could secure a senior position. For example, one interviewee said that, if she did not get tenure in the United States, "returning to Germany would be a highly acceptable plan B." Like several others, however, she said that she would only return for a senior position, "not one of the lower-level, temporary ones" (Frau Neuner). Several respondents agreed that the junior positions were not attractive to potential returnees. One interviewee explained:

> Once people have enjoyed the freedom in the US for a few years they no longer want to return to junior positions in Germany. I would accept somewhat worse conditions just to get back to Germany, but it would have to be a tenure-track position. I would also like to have some start-up funds and an environment that values my international experience (Herr Steffen).

This quotation illustrates that German academics abroad may be willing to make compromises to return, but are not prepared to give up the security that a tenure-track job in the United States offers. Quite apart from the fact that junior positions were seen as unattractive, several respondents believed that their chances of getting a job in Germany were better after receiving tenure in the United States and having established a strong publication record. Several respondents said that they would certainly consider a return to Germany if a top offer was made to them, but all agreed that this was unlikely.

A few interviewees stated that they felt indebted to Germany and would like to give back to the country. For example, one respondent said:

> I feel that I owe something to Germany. I enjoyed my university time in Germany very much, and obtained a great foundation that is much, much better, more general, more comprehensive than students in the United States get; more like people here get at the top ten places, so I would like to give something back (Herr Albrecht).

Most others, by contrast, did not feel in any way indebted to Germany, even though they had received a free education there. One respondent said that he did "not feel any remorse for taking [his] talent elsewhere" (Herr Stenzel); another "I do not think that I owe the German system anything. On the contrary, I feel let down by the German system because it is unable to provide its highly educated people with jobs" (Frau Elbe).

In summary, while a few respondents did not want to return to Germany, the majority would consider returning if attractive jobs became available. The vast majority believed that good jobs were scarce at the junior level and very difficult to get at the senior level. For most respondents, only a thorough reform, implementing a US-style tenure-track system that would make hiring and promotion decisions transparent and fair, would make the German university system attractive for potential returnees. The need for reform has also been highlighted by earlier studies (e.g., Allmendinger and Eickmeier 2003; Buechtemann and Tobsch 2001), as well as various initiatives. For example, a group of Germans working in the United States sent an open letter (signed by over 500 German scientists) to the German Ministry of Education, Science, Research, and Technology in 2005. The open letter was well received by the press, various organizations, and a number of politicians, and generated a plethora of responses and further initiatives (see German Scholars Organization 2011 and Initiative Zukunft Wissenschaft 2011). A group of German politicians and university presidents and other senior personnel now also organize an annual gathering of German academics in the United States. The goal of the German Academic International Network (GAIN) is to promote the return of German postdocs from the United States. They argue that now is a good time for Germans to return home as the university system is in the middle of reform and young talent is needed to push the reform forward (German Academic International Network 2012; Jaschick 2011). One of the most promising reforms is the Excellence Initiative. This initiative provides extra funds to selected German universities, some of which are used to create new positions for junior academics and provide them with more job security. There is now also some progress with spousal hiring (Jaschick 2011). Despite all these efforts to push for reform, many people argue that progress to date has been limited.

Discussion and Conclusion

With over 5,500 German scholars currently working in the United States (Institute of International Education 2011), Germany is one of the most significant source countries for international faculty in the

United States. As a country at a similar level of development as the United States and a strong democracy, migration decisions are not usually shaped by differences in standard of living or political concerns—factors that often play a large role for highly skilled migrants from low-income countries. Rather, professional reasons feature prominently in initial migrations and return decisions. Two related factors stood out as the most universal in keeping German faculty in the United States: first, interviewees saw the absence of a tenure-track system in Germany as a major deterrent, as the current system makes it difficult for junior academics to develop their own research agendas and have job security. Second, many interviewees criticized the strict hierarchies typical of German academia, which in their opinion not only have a negative impact on collegiality but also limit the career prospects of junior academics.

While a significant percentage of German faculty in the United States would consider a return to Germany, the vast majority would do so only if far-reaching reforms were implemented in the German higher-education system that address these issues. While some reforms have recently been undertaken, such as the creation of junior professorships and changes associated with the Excellence Initiative, they have not yet sufficiently addressed the fundamental disadvantages of the German system that keep German faculty in the United States.

For the United States, the major implication is that one of its major strengths is the structure of its higher-education system, including: the tenure-track system, open and fair hiring procedures, good access to equipment and funding, and last but not least a collegial and unhierarchical atmosphere. Policymakers must therefore be vigilant that financial cuts in the education sector, and the accompanying erosion of permanent positions and research funding, do not undermine this competitive advantage. If Germany and other source countries of international faculty carry out far-reaching reforms of their university systems to improve conditions, and actively support the return of academics who gained international experience, the United States will have to work harder to retain its international talent.

While a return of German faculty to Germany is highly dependent on reforms being carried out, these migrations do not necessarily translate into a "classic" brain drain where the skills of the migrants are considered lost to their home countries. As numerous scholars have pointed out, migration flows of the highly skilled have changed substantially over the last few decades. For example, many migrants visit home frequently and may stay there for extended time periods as international travel has become a lot cheaper and faster (Khoser

2007). Furthermore, modern communication technologies have made it easier to stay in touch with people at home in both personal and professional contexts. Transnational practices such as maintaining strong personal connections and collaborating with researchers in the home country can result in brain circulation, which, in turn, helps build more transnational connections (Vertovec 2009, 2002). These international connections can include so-called diaspora networks, which facilitate collaboration between the highly skilled at home and abroad (Meyer and Brown 1999). For example, Joens (2011) points out that Germans are the largest group of foreign coauthors of articles produced in global centers of knowledge production such as the United States. Seen from this global perspective, the migration of highly skilled Germans is in fact a very successful system. Indeed, German universities support the creation of international connections. For example, German universities encourage students and scholars to spend time abroad to get international experiences and build international networks to jump-start their own careers (Jaschick 2011).

Even if international research networks and other practices ensure that the out-migration of German academics is not a brain drain, this should not be an excuse for not carrying out much-needed reforms in Germany or encouraging the return of German faculty from abroad. After all, faculty contribute not only through their research, but also through their teaching of the next generation of the highly skilled.

Works Cited

Allmendinger, J., and A. Eickmaier. 2003. "Brain Drain. Ursachen für die Auswanderung akademischer Leistungseliten in die USA." *Beiträge zur Hochschulforschung* 25: 26–34.

Bhandari, R., and P. Blumenthal. 2011. "Global Student Mobility and the Twenty-First Century Silk Road: National Trends and Directions." In *International Students and Global Mobility in Higher Education. National Trends and New Directions*, edited by R. Bhandari, and P. Blumenthal, 1–23. New York: Palgrave Macmillan.

Brooks, R., and J. Waters. 2011. *Student Mobilities, Migration, and the Internationalization of Higher Education*. London: Palgrave Macmillan.

Buechtemann, C., and V. Tobsch. 2001. *Nachwuchswissenschaftler in den USA: Perspektiven der Hochschul- und Wissenschaftspolitik*. Berlin: Bundesministerium für Bildung und Forschung.

Cheng, L., and P. Yang. 1998. "Global Interaction, Global Inequality, and Migration of the Highly Trained to the United States." *International Migration Review* 32(3): 626–53.

Diehl, C., and D. Dixon. 2005. "Zieht es die Besten fort? Ausmaß und Formen der Abwanderung deutscher Hochqualifizierter in die USA." *Kölner Zeitschrift für Soziologie und Sozialpsychologie* 57(4): 714–34.

Edler, J., H. Fier, and C. Grimpe. 2011. "International Scientist Mobility and the Locus of Knowledge and Technology Transfer." *Research Policy* 40: 781–805.

Finn, M. 2007. "Stay Rates of Foreign Doctoral Recipients from US Universities." Available at: http://orise.orau.gov/files/sep/stay-rates-foreign-doctorate-recipients-2005.pdf. Accessed: August 31, 2011.

Gaillard, J., and A. Gaillard. 1997. "The International Mobility of Brains: Exodus or Circulation?" *Science, Technology & Society* 2(2): 195–228.

German Academic International Network. http://www.gain-network.org/. Accessed: April 11, 2012.

German Scholars Organization. http://www.gsonet.org/. Accessed: August 15, 2011.

Goldin, I., G. Cameron, and M. Belajaran. 2011. *Exceptional People. How Migration Shaped Our World and Will Define Our Future.* Princeton, NJ: Princeton University Press.

Gürüz, K. 2011. *Higher Education and International Student Mobility in the Global Knowledge Economy.* Albany, NY: State University of New York Press.

Initiative Zukunft Wissenschaft. http://www.zukunft-wissenschaft.de/. Accessed: August 15, 2011.

Institute of International Education. 2011. "Open Doors Report on International Educational Exchange." Available at: http://www.iie.org/Research-and-Publications/Open-Doors/Data/International-Scholars. Accessed: May 28, 2012.

Jaschik, S. 2011. "Battle for German Brains. Inside Higher Ed." Available at: http://www.insidehighered.com/news/2011/09/07/germany_woos_its_postdocs_in_the_u_s_to_come_home_with_goal_of_reforming_universities. Accessed: April 12, 2012.

Johnson, J., and M. Regets. 1998. "International Mobility of Scientists and Engineers to the United States—Brain Drain or Brain Circulation?" National Science Foundation Issue Brief 98–316. Available at: http://www.nsf.gov/sbe/srs/issuebrf/sib98316.htm. Accessed: August 4, 2012.

Jöns, H. 2011. "Transnational Academic Mobility and Gender." *Globalisation, Societies and Education* 9(2): 183–209.

Khadria, B. 2006. "Shifting Paradigms of Globalization: The Twenty-First Century Transition towards Generics in Skilled Migration from India." *International Migration* 39(5): 45–71.

Khoser, K. 2007. *International Migration: A Very Short Introduction.* Oxford: Oxford University Press.

Lossau, N. 2004. "Exodus der Besten," *Die Welt*, August 17.

Mahroum, S. 1998. "Europe and the Challenge of the Brain Drain." IPTS Report 29. Available at: http://www.jrc.ed/pages/iptsreport/vol29/english/SAT1E296.htm. Accessed: August 4, 2011.

Majcher, A. 2002. "Gender Inequality in German Academia and Strategies for Change." *German Policy Studies* 2(3): 1–34.
Meyer, J-B., and M. Brown. 1999. "Scientific Diasporas: A New Approach to the Brain Drain." Paris: UNESCO-MOST Discussion Paper No. 41 Available at: www.unesco.org/most/meyer.htm. Accessed: May 5, 2012.
O'Hara, S. 2009. "Internationalizing the Academy: The Impact of Scholar Mobility." In *Higher Education on the Move: New Developments in Global Mobility*, edited by R. Bhandari, and P. Blumenthal, 29–47. New York: Institute of International Education.
Pellegrino, A. 2001. "Trends in Latin American Skilled Migration: 'Brain Drain' or 'Brain Exchange?'" *International Migration* 39(5): 111–31.
Remhof, S. 2008. *Auswanderung von Akademikern aus Deutschland. Gründe, Auswirkungen und Gegenmaßnahmen*. Marburg: Tectum Verlag.
Salt, J., and A. Findlay. 1989. "International Migration of Highly-Skilled Manpower: Theoretical and Developmental Issues." In *The Impact of International Migration on Developing Countries*, edited by R. Appleyard, 159–80. Paris: OECD.
Saltmarsh, S., and T. Swirski. 2010. "'Pawns and Prawns': International Academics' Observations on Their Transition to Working in an Australian University." *Journal of Higher Education Policy and Management* 32(3): 291–301.
Smetherham, C., S. Fenton, and T. Modood. 2010. "How Global is the UK Academic Labour Market?" *Globalisation, Societies and Education* 8(3): 411–28.
Stiftungsverband für die deutsche Wissenschaft. 2002. "Brain Drain-Brain Gain. Eine Untersuchung über internationale Berufskarrieren." Available at: http://www.stifterverband.org/publikationen_und_podcasts/positionen _dokumentationen/braindrain_braingain_2002.pdf. Accessed: September 1, 2012.
Vertovec, S. 2009. *Transnationalism*. London and New York: Routledge.
———. 2002. "Transnational Networks and Skilled Labour Migration." Paper given at the conference: Ladenburger Diskurs "Migration" Gottlieb Daimler- und Karl Benz-Stiftung, Ladenburg, February 14–15.

2
Diversity

6

INTERNATIONAL FACULTY:

A SOURCE OF DIVERSITY

Rebecca Theobald

Individuals described as "international" or "foreign-born" faculty have long made significant contributions to American higher education. Since the 1990s, the professoriate has become less dominated by White native-born males, with almost a quarter of faculty in colleges and universities identified as foreign-born. At many institutions, international faculty now constitute a more significant source of diversity than do American-born minorities of color. A study of international faculty interactions in geography departments offers one perspective on the important contributions international faculty members make to diversity on campuses across the United States, and what issues arise for them and their employers as they step into a new academic setting.

CONTRIBUTIONS OF INTERNATIONAL FACULTY

International faculty contribute to American higher education in several ways, depending on the context. In isolated and homogenous institutions, international faculty provide links to the outside world, particularly for first-generation college students (CIES 2004). In multicultural and cosmopolitan settings, foreign-born faculty can serve as role models to other immigrants. International colleagues also widen perspectives on research and give voice to globalization in higher education. Diversification of the faculty alters institutions over the long term as international faculty, native-born minorities, and women mentor students and younger academics, affect institutional governance, and ask different types of research questions (Subedi 2006; Walsh 2006; Pulido 2002; Welsh 1997; Katz and Monk 1993).

In the last 20 years, reports have addressed the United States' dependency on foreign-born scientists as international graduate students obtain significant numbers of places in research university programs (Regets 2007; Committee on Education and the Workforce 2003; Selfa et al. 1997). As the president of the National Academy of Engineering put it, "The United States has been skimming the best and brightest from around the world" (Wulf 2006, 1). Educators, government officials, and employers note that with greater global competition scientists and engineers will become scarce and the pool of native-born individuals will be insufficient to compensate for this deficit. In other words, the United States is dependent on continuing to attract foreign talent.

Most studies show that highly skilled immigrants contribute positively to the economic growth of the United States, although considerable discussion about immigrants taking jobs from American citizens continues (Hall et al. 2011; Regets 2007; Chellaraj, Maskus, and Mattoo 2006, 2005). The contradictions of this situation result in foreign-born faculty being welcomed for the talent and productivity they contribute to the US economy, but looked at warily for their effects on the labor force, mirroring discussions about the position of immigrants in society as a whole. Whether education's main objective is to provide individuals with "knowledge, understanding and skills necessary to play a full, informed role in their society...[or] one that situates the needs of education more directly within national economic strategy" (Walsh 1998, 96), monetary and emotional investment in higher education ensures that the role of international faculty will be a continuing topic of discussion.

Faculty Diversity in the United States

The increased diversity of people on campuses reflects changing immigration patterns to the United States and growth within higher-education institutions during the latter half of the twentieth century. Faculty composition has altered over the last several decades, with fewer new faculty identifying as White, native-born males (Finkelstein, Seal, and Schuster 1998), and a sizeable percentage of younger faculty being non-US born (Magner 1996). While some of these changes reflect long-term increases in the non-White population of the United States, others result from direct challenges to existing systems of admissions and promotion (Perry 2007; Simpson 2004; Gunther 1980). For example, many institutions crafted deliberate policies of inclusion and recruitment for students and faculty, such as encouraging thematic hiring (academic positions, often interdisciplinary and created across academic units, likely to generate a diverse applicant pool), appointing administrators charged with increasing diversity, publishing statistics regarding race and ethnicity of students and faculty, and creating web resources for diverse populations (Office of Institutional Research 2011; University of Washington 2011; Vincent 2011; Gutmann and Daniels 2007; Gleeson 2006; Brus et al. 2003). Building on traditions of scholars who cross borders and offer services where they are rewarded monetarily or intellectually (Gürüz 2011), administrators incorporate these faculty recruitment and retention strategies into creating world-class universities, recognizing that labels of ethnicity and citizenship should not determine expectations regarding research and teaching (eChinaCities 2011, Stromquist 2007). As a result, the competitive environment for highly desirable faculty is strong in both high- and low-income countries (Haupt, Krieger, and Lange 2011; Campaign for Berkeley 2007; *The Economist* 2005; Van Damme 2002).

According to the *Open Doors* reports published by the Institute of International Education, the number of foreign scholars entering the United States increased steadily from 1995/96 through 2001/02. In 2003/04, 3,110 fewer foreign scholars came to the United States reflecting a backlash from the September 11 attacks (Gardner and Witherell 2005, 2003; Witherell 2004), although that trend has now reversed (figure 6.1). The latest numbers, for 2010/11, show 115,313

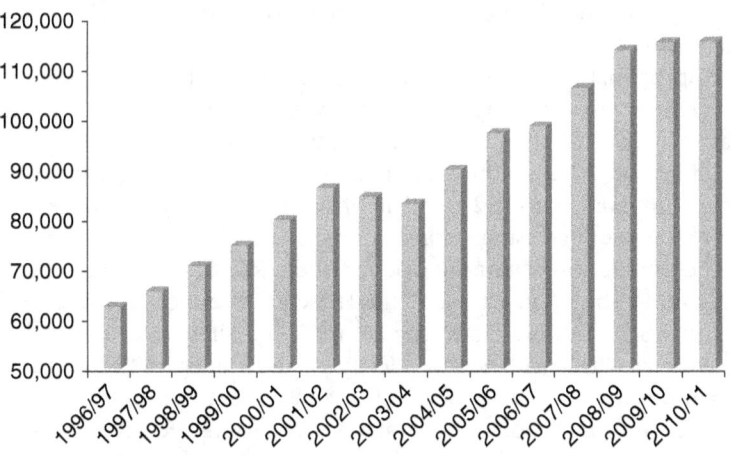

Figure 6.1 Total number of international scholars in the United States, 1996/97–2010/11

Sources: Institute of International Education (2011, 2006, 2003)

Table 6.1 Full-time instructional faculty in degree-granting institutions by selected faculty status, gender, and race/ethnicity

	Total US faculty	With tenure	On tenure track	US population
Number	728,977	326,562	159,689	308,745,538
Gender	%	%	%	%
Men	57.0	66.1	51.7	49.2
Women	43.0	33.9	48.3	50.8
Race/Ethnicity				
White, non-Hispanic	75.6	81.7	68.7	72.4
Black, non-Hispanic	5.4	4.4	6.4	12.6
Hispanic	3.8	3.1	4.0	16.3
Asian/Pacific Islander	8.2	7.9	10.9	5.0
American Indian/Alaskan Native	0.5	0.4	0.4	0.9
Race/ethnicity unknown	2.2	1.3	2.7	6.2*
Nonresident alien	4.2	1.2	7.0	12.2**

Sources: US Census Bureau 2011; US Department of Education 2010; US Census Bureau 2009.

Notes: *Some other race (Categories from the US Census Bureau and the US Department of Education are not always consistent. The Department of Education uses "Race/ethnicity unknown" and the Census Bureau uses "Some other race.")

***US Census Bureau 2009* (The closest figure for the "Nonresident alien category" from the Census Bureau to match the Department of Education is from 2009 rather than from 2011.)

international scholars teaching or conducting research at US campuses (Institute of International Education 2011), a slight increase from 2009/10.

Approximately 4.2 percent of all full-time faculty members at institutions surveyed through the Integrated Postsecondary Education Data System in Fall 2009 were nonresident aliens (US Department of Education 2010). Nonresident aliens constitute 7 percent of all faculty, compared with 1.2 percent of tenured faculty, indicating that new hires are increasingly foreign-born, reflecting the demographics of the population obtaining doctoral degrees. They are also increasingly non-White (table 6.1). While these are the most comprehensive national statistics available, the nonresident alien category excludes individuals with permanent residency status (holders of "green cards") and immigrants who have become citizens, so determining an accurate number of foreign-born faculty at US institutions requires finesse.

The greater diversity of faculty on campus, including larger numbers of women, foreign-born individuals, and American minorities of color, reflect more accurately the diverse populations they serve on many campuses. However, some express concern that foreign-born scholars now represent a disproportionate number of researchers and faculty, particularly in science, technology, engineering, and mathematics (STEM) fields. For example, between 1990 and 2000, "The share of US [science and engineering] occupations filled by scientists or engineers who were born abroad increased... at the doctorate level from 24 to 38 percent" (National Science Board 2003, 9). In 2004, 27.5 percent of doctoral degrees were granted to nonresident aliens, concentrated in science and engineering, with just under a third of doctorates granted to nonresident aliens in social sciences, education, health, or humanities (Hill and Green 2007).

Institutions are therefore often confronted with the reality that the pool of prepared, non-White individuals is heavily populated by foreign-born scholars (Mamiseishvili and Rosser 2010; Sabharwal and Corley 2009; Lin and Gao 2008). Between 2001 and 2009, for instance, the number of STEM degrees conferred on nonresident aliens increased by 25.8 percent while the number of degrees granted to Native Americans, African Americans, Asian Americans, and Hispanics increased an average of just 14.6 percent (US Department of Education 2011). Native-born minorities remain underrepresented in tenure-track positions and at research universities (Mahtani 2004; Garcia 2000), suggesting that more should be done to educate, mentor, and recruit American minorities of color (Tapia 2007). Insights into professors' challenges due to gender or minority status have assisted administrators in recognizing and addressing institutional barriers to success for these populations (Price et al. 2005; Xie and Shauman 2003; Garcia 2000). Foreign-born faculty also profit from these analyses, but higher-education personnel throughout the United States would still benefit from a greater awareness of the challenges faced by immigrant faculty, including occupational discrimination, personal prejudice, and cultural adjustment (Manrique and Manrique 1999).

One challenge that is unique to international faculty is the obstacles that they encounter related to their immigration status. Complicated visa requirements or travel restrictions may constrain professional and personal contacts. Because of these challenges, foreign-born scholars and students at higher-education institutions have reported canceling visits to their home countries or for overseas research as they were uncertain whether they could return to the United States (Lowell 2003). Furthermore, lack of US citizenship can also limit opportunities for research funding. Individuals without permanent resident status, and the institutions hosting them, must therefore be vigilant regarding regulations pertaining to their situation (Springer et al. 2009).

In this chapter, I discuss issues related to diversity and retention that are prominent in regards to international faculty members as well as native-born minorities. Using early-career foreign-born geography faculty as an example, I explore the experiences of international faculty in the United States. Furthermore, I investigate departmental and institutional concerns regarding diversity as articulated by geography department chairs and academic deans in order to obtain a better understanding of how international faculty contribute to diversity on US campuses.

Methodology

I focused on early-career geography faculty to identify the various factors contributing to career success or failure of foreign-born faculty in higher education. Building on research conducted through the Geography Faculty Development Alliance (Solem and Foote 2004), I developed an on-line survey of foreign-born early-career faculty (n=103) teaching in geography departments in the United States (Theobald 2007). To gain a better understanding of institutional perspectives on international faculty, I also interviewed 30 department chairs and 10 academic deans; 5 chairs and 1 dean were foreign-born.

Geography's four areas of study—physical, human, environment-society relations, and geospatial technology—span a wide spectrum of higher education, providing a good case study for examining issues related to international faculty. Furthermore, the Association of American Geographers (AAG) has addressed equity and faculty development issues (Foote 2010; Foote and Palmer 2005; Solem and Ray 2005; Lawson 2004), including recommendations that departments increase the numbers of women and minorities (Diversity Task Force 2006). Acknowledging friction between concepts of diversity and internationalization, 2007 AAG president Kavita Pandit—herself a foreign-born faculty member working in the United States—stated that hiring international faculty was not a substitute for supporting and hiring American minorities of color (Solis and Darden 2007; also chapter 7 of this book).

Experiences of Foreign-Born Faculty

Experiences of early-career foreign-born academic geographers differed compared to both native-born faculty and their longer-serving counterparts. In my study of foreign-born geographers, over 70 percent had received doctoral degrees at research universities in the United States or Canada. The majority worked in geography departments at research universities, with about a third employed at master's-level institutions. However, early-career foreign-born faculty were more likely to be women, more were engaged in geospatial technologies, and more were born in Asian countries than international faculty holding more advanced positions in the professoriate (Theobald 2009). These trends reflect similar tendencies seen throughout academia for both scholars and students immigrating to the United States (National Center for Education Statistics 2005; see also Lin, Pearce, and Wang 2009). The changing demographics of international faculty indicate the need for different responses from institutions than those undertaken when most international faculty were White men from European countries. In open-ended comments from survey respondents, foreign-born faculty observed that day-to-day interactions can be draining, as one is often considered the "other":

> Being typically regarded, whether negatively or positively, as a foreigner, despite obtaining US citizenship and living in the US for decades prevents me from feeling really part of a community, irrespective of the transience involved in academic settings. Culturally, it is also awkward to have to explain often one's identity, which suggests that there is a normal US identity, often assumed to be Anglo, White, Christian, male-like (European male).

Personal stresses are difficult to alleviate without family support and cultural accommodations:

> Having family in another country that you cannot see as frequently or rely on regularly for support in the balancing act of teaching/research/service and personal life is the single greatest stress I face as a foreign academic in the United States. As a female professor with small children who lives in the US and aging parents who live abroad, the stresses of combining professional and family life that affect all academics are compounded by gender and the global span of our family (Canadian female).

Despite these challenges, some respondents are not only happy to be working in the United States, but grateful for the opportunity to live a safe and fulfilling life:

> I have never felt like I was an outsider in the US. In fact, I feel more secure and more at home here than I would in my own country where

the political environment is highly volatile. Some of the best people I met in the course of my long years of personal and professional life have been Americans. They have gone out of their way to resolve my problems whether they are of a personal or professional nature. While I definitely miss the cultural milieu of my country, I feel no significant loss of identity (African male).

These comments illustrate varied viewpoints of foreign-born faculty, indicating why invoking general solutions to challenges requires creativity and attentiveness. Therefore, departments and institutions should focus on early-career mentoring to meet the diverse needs of all new professors, while continuing to recognize the particular issues challenging foreign-born faculty (see chapter 10 of this book).

Departmental and Institutional Concerns

Achieving a meaningful career in academia is a complex process, including acculturation to one's department and discipline, which is likely more difficult for international faculty than for native-born faculty. While programs such as Fulbright Scholar-in-Residence explicitly acknowledge the importance of providing opportunities for visiting international faculty to interact with colleagues in professional and personal circumstances (CIES 2008), most foreign-born faculty accepting tenure-track positions are expected to adapt to their new institution with little regard for their familiarity with American undergraduate and graduate education, which can be bewildering to foreign-born scholars. Devoting resources to help faculty meet immigration requirements and supporting them during the adjustment period makes the transition more effective for both individual and institution, particularly at locations that have not hosted substantial populations of foreign-born faculty. More generally, significant variations exist among different types of institutions, such as those located in rural and urban areas, large universities and small colleges, and institutions espousing a particular religious or secular approach to learning (Thelin 2004). These characteristics of place interact, affecting the conditions under which faculty are expected to teach, research, and live.

The institution, department, and community affect recruitment and retention of early-career foreign-born faculty. During interviews, administrators acknowledged challenges of minority and foreign-born faculty in adjusting to their new communities:

The idea is not just to get the best faculty, but you also want to retain the faculty...recognizing that [city] is not New York...and so there are all these other complications that arise as the fact is that you oftentimes want to be near a large metropolitan area that offers restaurants and children's activities...If you are in a small town in say Indiana, for instance, or North Carolina...then it's much harder to find ethnic communities or diversity (dean, baccalaureate institution).

Administrators did not see limitations of funding or cosmopolitanism as excuses for lack of diversity, but considered them challenges that need to be overcome. As the previous quotation shows, the problem for institutions in less attractive places is not only recruiting international faculty but also retaining them, although this issue is not limited to international faculty:

We haven't had trouble attracting people to the job search, but keeping them has been a problem...There are some specific problems related to internationals, but the main issues relate to all faculty in general (department chair, master's university).

The characteristics of the institution and diversity of the community's population can trump other qualities when applicants weigh up job opportunities and consider whether to establish permanent roots. Generally speaking, administrators at large universities assumed that foreign-born faculty would have networks of compatriots to guide them in adjusting, while those in more isolated locations recognized the need to provide substantive institutional assistance for individuals who might be the sole ethnic minority in the community.

If you go to [small town] and that's your first job, this is a serious issue...I've trained international students whose first jobs were in tiny little places. Then they had major adjustment periods to the sort of cultural landscape that they found themselves in (department chair, research university).

Institutional Diversity

Department chairs and deans stressed that diversity was a substantial, and sometimes bothersome, issue. Furthermore, different institutions define diversity and related concepts in different ways. On one campus, diversity and internationalization—including the desire to recruit foreign-born faculty—may be two distinct goals, on another internationalization may be a subset of diversity, and on a third there may be little discussion about either concept. In some institutions "diversity" is changing to "multiculturalism" and includes age, ethnicity, race, country of origin, differently abled, and sexual orientation (Manrique and Manrique 1999). In these settings, some administrators consider departments diverse if professors received doctoral training from a variety of institutions, originate from different parts of the country or the world, live in multiple socioeconomic circumstances, and inhabit varied characteristics informing their perceptions of daily life.

When asked how their institutions view diversity, most interviewees initially interpreted the term as relating to externally visible markers. "They track minorities. But somebody from the Bahamas is counted, because they are Black. It's all about race" (department chair, baccalaureate institution). Chairs indicated that diversity meant that underrepresented groups had to be increased—in the United States usually African Americans, Hispanics, Native Americans, and sometimes Asian Americans—among the ranks of faculty and students. However, there is no uniform way of counting individuals. For example, one institution's policy to diversify faculty mentions specifically only faculty of color and women, not international faculty (Office of Diversity and Equity 2001). In another case, a department chair at a master's university notes: "My understanding has been that a foreign-born Asian or whatever doesn't count toward diversity."

Many deans reported that diversity often ended up being largely a process of checking boxes, missing a huge opportunity to substantively broaden their institution's outlook and perspective.

> The easy way out is to check boxes...so you get so many Blacks, so many Hispanics, so many whatever. But...there is more difficulty to having it really diversified...It's easy to think that you have succeeded if you check all those boxes, but you have left out kids from [small town], because you are not diversifying in other ways also...The definition that means everything to everybody ends up meaning nothing to nobody...We need to have some boxes and feelings that you made some progress, but you shouldn't just stop at the boxes...In other words, you can't just say I have ten Blacks, ten Hispanics, ten Asians if all of them think like the White...You want to diversify in a broader sense: socioeconomic, gender, and so on. And so I think having more people from different cultures is a way to introduce diversity because you are going to see what the world is going to get into (dean, baccalaureate institution).

Despite these complications, administrators at all levels asserted that foreign-born faculty can support diversity goals. A source of frustration was the fact that White international faculty are often ignored as a source of diversity. "The political science department has just hired a Russian woman. Now, when they fill out their forms, it looks as though they hired a White woman, but we are operating from very different places, and the fact that she's a Russian national adds a whole new dimension to their department" (department chair, research university). Other interviewees expressed frustration that not even foreign-born professors of color would be counted.

> Currently if you are a foreign national and don't have a "green card," they don't count for diversity...I have a wonderful gentleman who was born in Nigeria. Wonderful lecturer, students love him. He's had nothing but problems getting a "green card." And as far as the university is concerned, he's foreign faculty, doesn't count for any diversity as defined by the college (dean, research university).
>
> The law says that diverse means that you're a United States citizen and a person of color, so that therefore internationals don't actually count. The affirmative action people are even frustrated with it because all these numbers are only tracked by those who self-identify. So if you're a Chinese national who has a "green card," or an H1 visa, and you self-identify as Chinese on your affirmative action form...we can count that. But if you didn't self-identify because you actually read the affirmative action form and it said Americans, and you marked nothing, well, then you don't count (department chair, master's university).

How diversity is defined often does not make sense to administrators who are attempting to bring in new perspectives to their campuses, incorporate different types of individuals into the faculty ranks, and satisfy legal and political requirements:

> The university defines people [as] international formally by their visa status. Right now, I don't have a "green card." I am working on an H1-B visa. So I am considered definitely international. When I get [a] "green card" I think I will still be foreign. But if I become [an] American citizen, the university cannot, by law, classify me as international. Then I would be American. But informally I would be international (department chair, master's university).

In addition to the question of how the institution classifies people, self-identification also plays a role. Therefore some deans wondered whether it is actually useful or necessary to track foreign-born faculty beyond those who have visas. In summary, international faculty and administrators observed that there are multiple contradictions in how diversity is measured and addressed at their institutions.

In academic settings, diversity is most often shaped through institutional policies and hiring practices. Most universities and colleges have policies stating that women and minorities are encouraged to apply (Ketchum 2007). Some institutions have extended those statements through more proactive pushes for minority faculty, as *Inside Higher Education* reported has occurred at Colgate University in rural New York State.

> Traditionally...there has been a broad consensus (even if no formal policy exists) that the top factor to consider in a faculty hire is excellence in teaching and research, followed by match of candidates with the subfield specialties needed, then followed by diversity concerns...Colgate has a hard time holding on to minority professors...[The dean] has asked departments to flop the second and third criteria. Excellence will stay on top, but diversity would generally trump subfield choice (Jaschik 2007, 1).

When asked about the nature and numbers of international faculty applicants, 19 of 30 chairs agreed that the percentage of international applicants has continued to rise, with one-third to two-thirds of those in applicant pools being foreign-born. The most dramatic increase in foreign-born applicants in geography departments was for technical jobs associated with geospatial technology, with primarily Asian-born individuals applying for those positions. The percentage of foreign-born applicants differed based on location and type of institution. For example, large research universities in major cities receive more international applicants than small institutions in rural areas. Positions at associate institutions seldom attracted foreign-born applicants.

While institutional policies can be strongly supportive of hiring a diverse faculty body, applicant pools often make it hard to reach these goals. While chairs reported large pools of qualified international applicants, most felt that the number of American minorities was too small to reach the diversity goals set. Several chairs commented that their deans did not grasp the composition of the available pool of applicants and expressed frustration when asked to diversify their departments. "The number of African Americans or Latinos that apply has just been miniscule. There are very few PhDs who are ethnic minorities" (department chair, research university). Many, therefore, considered expectations to hire domestic minorities to be completely unrealistic:

> Like anyplace else, talking about diversity and making it happen are not the same thing. We are getting ready to hire a physical geographer,

and my dean came to me and said, "you know, it would be great if you could hire an African American woman for this position" and I replied that I only knew one of those and she seemed happy in her job. There just isn't the understanding during these discussions that the pool of people to choose from is not out there (department chair, research university).

However, some studies have challenged the idea that there are insufficient prospective faculty of color, suggesting that in spite of statements supporting diversity, actions during the recruiting process as well as psychosocial and behavioral dimensions of diversity on campus constrain native minorities (Tuitt, Danowitz Sagaria, and Sotello Viernes Turner 2007, Hurtado et al. 1999).

The tensions set up by conflicting diversity goals can even lead to unrest among colleagues, although admittedly this is not a common occurrence. Nonetheless, disputes have been reported between African American and African professors on historically Black campuses (Ngwainmbi 2006; Wilson 2001). One dean observed that some African Americans felt that hiring Africans was not contributing to diversity, instead signaling a "cop-out" on the part of the university. It is unclear how this issue might evolve as American minorities increase in hiring pools and institutions incorporate fewer non-White males in decision-making positions (Myers and Turner 2004; Johnsrud and Sadao 1998). The only consensus on diversity—from different types of institutions in different parts of the United States—was that a narrow definition of diversity, restricted to American minorities of color, does not reflect the variety of perspectives administrators seek on college and university campuses.

Discussion: Balancing Faculty and Institutional Needs

Foreign-born professors play an increasingly important role in American higher-education institutions, both in terms of sheer numbers and through their interactions and activities. The majority of deans agreed that international faculty members contribute to teaching and research missions of the institution, are regularly considered for open positions, and are treated no differently than other faculty members. Foreign-born faculty, often perceived as high achievers, were considered by some respondents to have similar adjustment issues to native-born faculty, and sometimes were perceived as facing fewer difficulties adjusting to small, homogeneous, rural communities than did American minorities of color. However, there was less agreement over whether international faculty receive adequate mentoring or are provided with sufficient personal and professional resources. Nonetheless, deans and chairs indicated that early-career faculty development in the form of orientation, mentoring, teaching and learning programs, and resources are priorities on their campuses.

Officially, every department chair indicated that they would like to have a variety of viewpoints and backgrounds represented by faculty within their departments. Although personnel management and evaluating research agendas might be more complicated as a result, chairs recognize the positive aspects of departments reflecting a diversity of perspectives beyond the ubiquitous White male. However, hiring diverse faculty is much more difficult in practice. Department chairs approached the concept of diversity from a variety of directions, noting that the notion of "diversity" differs among institutions, under reporting laws for government or accrediting bodies, and by departmental procedure. A few chairs identified conflicts on campuses between foreign-born faculty and American minorities of color, but most said there was no conflict, possibly in part because there were so few applicants of African American, Hispanic, or Native American origin. As more American minorities inch into the hiring pool, and processes of globalization maintain a global circulation of talent, a more open conversation about hiring practices and applicant pools will be required.

Chairs acknowledged that they need to be clear about expectations and requirements so that international faculty members receive appropriate signals, even if they might be considered overly obvious for native-born Americans. While mentoring relationships could meet this need, chairs also recognized that not every personal relationship blossoms into something useful, and that foreign-born faculty, particularly those who have not had experience with mentors in graduate school, might not be sure how to approach someone at a higher-status level. Individual attention to all new faculty seems the best way to overcome obstacles and prevent cultural misunderstandings.

Works Cited

Brus, C., S. Buckley, C. Colvin, J. Coulter, P. Jones, P. Kutzko, W. Welburn, and C. Westerhaus. 2003. *Diversity Administration Review Report: Recommendations.* Iowa City, IA: University of Iowa.

Campaign for Berkeley. 2007. "The Hewlett Challenge: Faculty of Distinction." Berkeley, CA: University of California, Berkeley. Available at: http://hewlettchallenge.berkeley.edu/. Accessed: July 15, 2011.

Chellaraj, G., K. Maskus, and A. Mattoo. 2006. "Skilled Immigrants, Higher Education, and U.S. Innovation." In *International Migration, Remittances and the Brain Drain*, edited by C. Ozden, and M. Schiff, 245–60. Washington, DC: The World Bank and Palgrave Macmillan.

———. 2005. "The Contribution of Skilled Immigration and International Graduate Students to U.S. Innovation." World Bank Policy Research Working Paper 3588. Washington, DC: The World Bank.

Committee on Education and the Workforce. 2003 (December 17). "International Studies in Higher Education Act." Washington, DC: United States House of Representatives. Available at: http://edworkforce.house.gov/issues/108th/education/highereducation/intbillsummary.htm. Accessed: June 6, 2012.

Council for International Exchange of Scholars (CIES). 2008. *Fulbright Scholar Program: Guidelines for Scholar-in-Residence Proposals 2009–2010*. Washington, DC: US Department of State.

———. 2004. *Fulbright Scholar Program Annual Report 2003*. Washington, DC: US Department of State.

eChinaCities.com. 2011 (March 25). "Shenzhen University to Recruit Top Professors at Any Price." *Shenzhen in Pulse*. Available at: http://www.echinacities.com/shenzhen/city-in-pulse/shenzhen-university-to-recruit-top-professors-at-any-price.html. Accessed: July 1, 2011.

Finkelstein, M., R. Seal, and J. Schuster. 1998. *The New Academic Generation: A Profession in Transformation*. Baltimore, MD: The Johns Hopkins University Press.

Foote, K. 2010. "Supporting International Faculty in U.S. Geography." *AAG Newsletter* 45(8): 3.

Foote, K., and J. Palmer. 2005. "The Geography Faculty Development Alliance." Boulder, CO: University of Colorado. (http://www.colorado.edu/geography/gfda/gfda.html).

Garcia, M., ed. 2000. *Succeeding in an Academic Career: A Guide for Faculty of Color*. Westport, CT: Greenwood Press Reference Collection.

Gardner, D., and S. Witherell. 2005. "U.S. Sees Slowing Decline in International Student Enrollment in 2004/05." New York: Institute of International Education. Available at: http://opendoors.iienetwork.org/?p=69736. Accessed: June 6, 2012.

———. 2003. "International Student Enrollment Growth Slows in 2002/2003. Large Gains from Leading Countries Offset Numerous Decreases." New York: Institute of International Education. Available at: http://opendoors.iienetwork.org/?p=36523. Accessed: June 6, 2012.

Gleeson, T. 2006. *Faculty Hiring Initiatives in the College of Arts and Sciences*. Memo, November 4. Available at: http://www.colorado.edu/ArtsSciences/overview/docs/Hiring.pdf. Accessed: June 6, 2012.

Gunther, G., ed. 1980. "University of California Regents v. Bakke." In *Cases and Materials on Constitutional Law*, 10th edition., 804–34. Mineola, NY: The Foundation Press.

Gürüz, K. 2011. *Higher Education and International Student Mobility in the Global Knowledge Economy*, 2nd edition. Albany, NY: State University of New York Press.

Gutmann, A., and R. Daniels. 2007 (December 4). "Progress Report on Minority Equity." *Almanac Supplement* 54(14). Philadelphia, PA: University of Pennsylvania.

Hall, M., A. Singer, G. DeJong, and D. Roempke Graefe. 2011. *The Geography of Immigrant Skills: Educational Profiles of Metropolitan Areas*. Washington, DC: Metropolitan Policy Program at Brookings.

Haupt, A., T. Krieger, and T. Lange. 2011. "Competition for the International Pool of Talent: Education Policy and Student Mobility." Working Paper Series, Number 2011-02. Paderborn, Germany: Center for International Economics, Paderborn University, March 2011. Available at: http://groups.uni-paderborn.de/fiwi/RePEc/pdf/wpaper/WP35.pdf . Accessed: July 1, 2011.

Hill, S., and M. Green. 2007. "S&E Degrees, by Race/Ethnicity of Recipients: 1995-2004." Arlington, VA: National Science Foundation, Division of Science Resource Statistics.

Hurtado, S., J. Milem, A. Clayton-Pedersen, and W. Allen. 1999. "Enacting Diverse Learning Environments: Improving the Climate for Racial/Ethnic Diversity in Higher Education." *ASHE-ERIC Higher Education Report*, 26(8). Washington, DC: The George Washington University, Graduate School of Education and Human Development.

Institute of International Education. 2011. "Open Doors 2011: Report on International Educational Exchange." New York: Institute of International Education. Available at: http://www.iie.org/en/research-and-publications/~/media/Files/Corporate/Open-Doors/Open-Doors-2011-Briefing-Presentation.ashx. Accessed: March 18, 2012.

———. 2006. "Open Doors 2006." New York: Institute of International Education. Available at: http://opendoors.iienetwork.org/?p=89233. Accessed: February 1, 2007.

———. 2003. "International Scholars State by State, 1993/94-2002/03." Open Doors. New York: Institute of International Education. Available at: http://opendoors.iienetwork.org/?p=37196. Accessed: April 12, 2003.

Jaschik, S. 2007. "New Approach to Diversity." *Inside Higher Ed*. Available at: http://www.insidehighered.com/news/2007/04/20/colgate. Accessed: April 20, 2007.

Johnsrud, L., and K. Sadao. 1998. "The Common Experience of 'Otherness': Ethnic and Racial Minority Faculty." *The Review of Higher Education* 21(4): 315-42.

Katz, C., and J. Monk. 1993. *Full Circles: Geographies of Women over the Life Course*. London: Routledge.

Ketchum, J., ed. 2007. "Jobs in Geography." *AAG Newsletter* 46(2). June: 16-21.

Lawson, V. 2004. "Healthy Departments, Healthy Discipline." *AAG Newsletter*. September: 3-4.

Lin, Z., R. Pearce, and W. Wang. 2009. "Imported Talents: Demographic Characteristics, Achievement and Job Satisfaction of Foreign Born Full Time Faculty in Four-Year American Colleges." *Higher Education* 57(6): 703–21.

Lin, Z., and Y. Gao. 2008. "Behind the Advanced American Higher Education System: A Comparative Study of Refereed Journal Articles Published by Native and Foreign Born Faculty Members." *Journal of Higher Education* CNKI:SUN:HIGH.0.2008-07-008.

Lowell, O. 2003. "Homeland Insecurity: Champaign-Urbana's International Community Shaken by New INS Rules." *CounterPunch*. Available at: http://www.counterpunch.org/lowell02082003.html. Accessed: June 17, 2007.

Magner, D. 1996. "New Generation of Professors Is Changing the Face of Academe." *The Chronicle of Higher Education*. February 2: 17.

Mahtani, M. 2004. "Mapping Race and Gender in the Academy: The Experiences of Women of Colour Faculty and Graduate Students in Britain, the US and Canada." *Journal of Geography in Higher Education* 28(1): 91–9.

Mamiseishvili, K., and V. Rosser. 2010. "International and Citizen Faculty in the United States: An Examination of their Productivity at Research Universities." *Research in Higher Education* 51(1): 88–107.

Manrique, C., and G. Manrique. 1999. *The Multicultural or Immigrant Faculty in American Society*. Mellen Studies in Education. Lewiston, New York: The Edwin Mellen Press.

Myers, S., and C. Turner. 2004. "The Effects of Ph.D. Supply on Minority Faculty Representation." *The American Economic Review* 94(2): 296–301.

National Center for Education Statistics. 2005. *Digest of Education Statistics Tables and Figures*. Washington, DC: United States Department of Education. Available at: http://nces.ed.gov/programs/digest/d05_tf.asp. Accessed: August 1, 2006.

National Science Board. 2003. *The Science and Engineering Workforce: Realizing America's Potential*. Washington, DC: National Science Foundation.

Ngwainmbi, E. 2006. "The Struggles of Foreign-Born Faculty." *Diverse Education*, June 29. Available at: http://diverseeducation.com/article/6031/. Accessed: 8/1/06.

Office of Diversity and Equity. 2001. "Faculty Diversity Action Plan." Boulder, CO: University of Colorado at Boulder.

Office of Institutional Research. 2011. "2010–11 Diversity Report." Denver, CO: University of Colorado System.

Perry, B. 2007. *The Michigan Affirmative Action Cases*. Lawrence, KS: University Press of Kansas.

Price, E., A. Gozu, D. Kern, N. Powe, G. Wand, S. Golden, and L. Cooper. 2005. "The Role of Cultural Diversity Climate in Recruitment, Promotion, and Retention of Faculty in Academic Medicine." *Journal of General Internal Medicine* 20: 565–71.

Pulido, L. 2002. "Reflections on a White Discipline." *The Professional Geographer* 54(1): 42–9.

Regets, M. 2007. *Research Issues in the International Migration of Highly Skilled Workers: A Perspective with Data from the United States.* Washington, DC: National Science Foundation Division of Science Resources Statistics.

Sabharwal, M., and E. Corley. 2009. "Faculty Job Satisfaction across Gender and Discipline." *The Social Science Journal* 46: 539–56.

Selfa, L., N. Suter, S. Koch, S. Myers, R. Johnson, D. Zahs, B. Kuhr, and S. Abraham. 1997. *1993 National Study of Postsecondary Faculty (NSOPF-93).* Washington, DC: US Department of Education, National Center for Education Statistics.

Simpson, S. 2004. *Texas Higher Education Lacks Racial Diversity, Report Finds: Civil Rights Groups and Law Faculty Urge "Blend It, Don't End It?"* Washington, DC: The Leadership Conference on Civil and Human Rights/The Leadership Conference Education Fund, June 24. Available at: http://www.civilrights.org/press/2004/texas-higher-education-lacks-racial-diversity-report-finds.html. Accessed: July 1, 2011.

Solem, M., and K. Foote. 2004. "Concerns, Attitudes, and Abilities of Early Career Geography Faculty." *Annals of the Association of American Geographers* 94(4): 889–912.

Solem, M., and W. Ray. 2005. *Gauging Disciplinary Support for Internationalization: A Survey of Geographers.* Washington, DC: Association of American Geographers.

Solis, P., and J. Darden, organizers. 2007. "The AAG Diversity Task Force: Final Report and Recommendations for the Association and for Geography Departments as Agents of Change." Panel Session. San Francisco: Association of American Geographers Annual Meeting, April 17–21.

Springer, S., M. Wailes, S. Marlay, and L. Schafer. 2009. "Institutional Policies and Practices Concerning Permanent Residency." NAFSA Resource Library, Washington, DC: NAFSA: Association for International Educators. Available at: http://www.nafsa.org/resourcelibrary/default.aspx?id=16118. Accessed: July 15, 2011.

Stromquist, Nelly P. 2007. "Internationalization as a Response to Globalization: Radical Shifts in University Environments." *Higher Education* 53(1): 81–105.

Subedi, B. 2006. "Theorizing a 'Halfie' Researcher's Identity in Transnational Fieldwork." *International Journal of Qualitative Studies in Education* 19(5): 573–93.

Tapia, R. 2007. "True Diversity Doesn't Come From Abroad." *The Chronicle of Higher Education*, September 28. Available at: http://chronicle.com/article/True-Diversity-Doesn-t-Come/20812. Accessed: June 12, 2011.

The Economist. 2005. "The Brains Business: A Survey of Higher Education." September 10: 3–22.

Thelin, J. 2004. *A History of American Higher Education.* Baltimore, MD: The Johns Hopkins University Press.

Theobald, R. 2009. "New Faces in Academic Places: Gender and the Experiences of Early-Career, Foreign-Born, and Native-Born Geographers." *Journal of Geographical Science* 57: 7–32.

———. 2007. "Foreign-Born Early-Career Faculty in American Higher Education: The Case of the Discipline of Geography." PhD Dissertation, University of Colorado at Boulder.

Tuitt, F., M. Danowitz Sagaria, and C. Sotello ViernesTurner. 2007. "Signals and Strategies in Hiring Faculty of Color." In *Higher Education: Handbook of Theory and Research*, edited by J. Smart, 22: 497–535.

United States Census Bureau. 2011. "Overview of Race and Hispanic Origin: 2010." Washington, DC: U.S. Department of Commerce. Available at: http://www.census.gov/prod/cen2010/briefs/c2010br-02.pdf. Accessed: June 30, 2011.

United States Census Bureau. 2009. Table 1.1 Population by Sex, Age, Nativity, and U.S. Citizenship Status: 2009. "Characteristics of the Foreign-Born Population by Nativity and U.S. Citizenship Status." Washington, DC: U.S. Department of Commerce. Available at: http://www.census.gov/population/www/socdemo/foreign/cps2009.html#cit. Accessed: July 6, 2011.

United States Department of Education. 2011. "Postsecondary Awards in Science, Technology, Engineering, and Mathematics, by State: 2001 and 2009." Washington, DC: National Center for Education Statistics. Available at: http://nces.ed.gov/pubsearch/pubsinfo.asp?pubid=2011226. Accessed: July 1, 2011.

———. 2010. Table 260. "Full-Time Instructional Faculty in Degree-Granting Institutions, By Race/Ethnicity, Sex, and Academic Rank: Fall 2005, Fall 2007, and Fall 2009." Digest of Education Statistics 2010. Washington, DC: National Center for Education Statistics. Available at: http://nces.ed.gov/programs/digest/d10/tables/dt10_260.asp. Accessed: July 1, 2011.

University of Washington. 2011. "Diversity Webpage." Seattle, WA: University of Washington. Available at: http://www.washington.edu/diversity/index.shtml. Accessed: July 1, 2011.

Van Damme, D. 2002. "Outlooks for the International Higher Education Community in Constructing the Global Knowledge Society." Paper presented at the First Global Forum on International Quality Assurance, Accreditation and the Recognition of Qualifications in Higher Education, United Nations Educational, Scientific and Cultural Organization. Paris, France, October 17–18.

Vincent, G. 2011. "Division of Diversity and Community Engagement: 2010–2011 Impact Report." Austin, TX: The University of Texas at Austin.

Walsh, K. 2006. "'Dad Says I'm Tied to a Shooting Star!' Grounding (Research on) British Expatriate Belonging." *Area* 38(3): 268–78.
Walsh, M. 1998. *State Policy Update: Colorado.* Washington, DC: Education Week.
Welsh, A. 1997. "The Peripatetic Professor: The Internationalisation of the Academic Profession." *Higher Education* 34: 323–45.
Wilson, R. 2001. "A Battle Over Race, Nationality, and Control at a Black University: At Virginia State U., Black Americans and Black Africans Each See Bias from the Other Side." *The Chronicle of Higher Education.* July 27: A8.
Witherell, S. 2004. "Open Doors: Report on International Educational Exchange." Washington, DC: Institute of International Education.
Wulf, W. 2006. "Foreign-Born Researchers are Key to U.S. Prosperity and Security." *In Focus.* Winter/Spring: 1.
Xie, Y., and K. Shauman. 2003. *Women in Science: Career Processes and Outcomes.* Cambridge, MA: Harvard University Press.

7

INTERNATIONAL STUDENTS AND DIVERSITY

CHALLENGES AND OPPORTUNITIES FOR CAMPUS INTERNATIONALIZATION

Kavita Pandit

In the face of heightened competition for globally mobile students over the past decade, the recruitment of international students has taken an unprecedented center stage in US universities. It has been spurred partially by the recognition that international students are valuable intellectual and economic assets and that there is now fierce worldwide competition for these students. However, the interest in increasing international student numbers goes beyond this. From the point of view of academics and educators, international students provide opportunities for domestic students to engage with those coming from different cultures, which, in turn, allow them to shed stereotypes, explore new perspectives, and gain intercultural skills. Not surprisingly, more and more American institutions are beginning to incorporate international students as part of their "comprehensive internationalization strategies" (ACE 2011). A comprehensive internationalization strategy views internationalization as a process that is deeply intertwined with the teaching, research, and outreach missions of the university, rather than just as a set of discrete activities like study abroad and international student recruitment (Hudzik 2011). Bringing international students to the campus is seen as integral to the university's mission to prepare students to live and work in a diverse and intercultural environment (Pandit 2009; Bevis 2002).

The lofty ideals of international students as catalysts of campus diversity and internationalization often face barriers on the ground, however. On most campuses there is only limited mingling of international students with domestic students, creating few opportunities for either group to gain cross-cultural experiences (Teekens 2000). International students often arrive with their own stereotypes and prejudices about Americans, particularly US minorities. These attitudes often remain unexamined, even as international students are assigned to teach undergraduate students—a potent recipe for cultural miscommunication and conflict. Furthermore, institutional structures often separate the various offices that work with international students. Discussions of internationalization are often separate from those related to domestic diversity, with the result that international diversity and domestic diversity are sometimes seen to be in competition. Given the current focus on international student recruitment, then, there is an urgent need to examine the challenges and opportunities inherent in increasing international diversity and meeting the idealized goals of building an internationalized campus.

This chapter poses and responds to a number of questions that include: how can we create opportunities for meaningful social interactions between international and domestic students? What are we doing to help socialize international students to diversity within the United States and to help them challenge their own stereotypes? And, how can we ensure that our institutional strategies are designed to address these pressing issues that are vital to advancing campus internationalization?

Background: International Students and Diversity on US Campuses

Although international students have long had a presence in American universities, it was only in the post–World War II era that US universities began thinking about them as a distinct group. The establishment of the Fulbright Program in 1946, in particular, was pivotal in drawing attention to the role of international students and international exchanges as valuable tools in the country's effort to increase its influence around the world. The idea was that by living and studying in the United States international students would develop an appreciation for its society and values and be more inclined to be sympathetic toward the United States when they assumed leadership positions in their home countries. Whereas in the first quarter of the twentieth century, the management of international cultural exchanges was largely handled by private nonprofit agencies such as the YWCA, by mid-century universities began to take a serious look at their direct responsibility toward international students and their adjustment needs. The foreign student advisor quickly became a ubiquitous presence on US campuses, working to orient and ease international students into the American classroom, campus, and society (Bevis and Lucas 2007).

As numbers of international students in the United States continued to grow in subsequent decades, a number of studies (e.g., Helms 1978; Sanders and Ward 1970) documented the challenges that they faced in adapting to study and life in the United States. Problems such as social withdrawal, depression, academic difficulty, and loss of self-esteem began to be documented (Bevis and Lucas 2007). The growing awareness created by the civil rights movements at this time also helped focus attention on discrimination encountered by international students, and research on cross-cultural communication expanded dramatically (Brown 2009; Graham 1992). On campus, the focus was not only on integrating international students but also on appropriate intercultural training for staff that work with internationals—programs that are now commonplace at large universities (Andrade 2006; Peterson et al. 1999).

Whereas for most of the prior half century, the United States could count on being the preferred destination of internationally mobile students, the 1990s brought in an era of intensified global competition for these students. A number of countries, led by Australia, began to regard international students not only as intellectual capital but also as a source of revenue. According to some, this heightened focus on recruitment occurred at the same time as higher education itself was being transformed from being a public good to an internationally traded commodity (Altbach 2006). US universities, many for the first time in their history, have now begun actively recruiting international students.

Regardless of their primary motivation for international student recruitment, universities are making a concerted effort to situate these efforts within a broader campus internationalization strategy (ACE 2011; Hudzik 2011). This is because of an awareness that international students can serve as powerful catalysts of campus internationalization since they provide most US students with their first contact with another culture (Pandit and Alderman 2004). By living and studying alongside international students, domestic students are in a position to gain a broader perspective of the world themselves and develop intercultural communications skills that are critical to both a broad-based education as well as competitiveness in today's job market. One of the most extraordinary opportunities afforded by campuses with diverse international populations is an environment in which students can interact with persons with very different backgrounds, life experiences, and perspectives. International students provide a mirror through which US-born students can view the world, the United States, and themselves from a very different perspective. Thus, instead of being a liability to be overcome, the diversity of international students can be an asset to advance learning opportunities for all students. Herein lies the true value of an internationally diverse campus.

Interactions between International and Domestic Students

The translation of international diversity into intercultural learning demands that there be meaningful interactions between domestic and international students. Studies in Australia, one of the countries that have been most aggressive in international student recruitment, found that domestic students expected international students to adjust to them and not vice versa, something that was disappointing to some international students (Marginson 2002; Smart, Volet, and Ang 2000). American undergraduate students likewise report reluctance to engage with international students, partly because of nervousness about their ability to be understood (Pandit and Alderman 2004). However, the problem is often in both directions, with international students often finding it more comfortable to remain within their growing co-ethnic communities than making the effort to build connections beyond them (Jenkins and Rubin 1993). Thielen and Limbird (1992) suggest that there are often instances of international students deliberately avoiding contact with Americans because of concern that their values may change in a way that is not appreciated in their home countries.

Engendering meaningful interactions between international and US-born students therefore requires deliberate action and programming. Pandit and Alderman (2004) provide one example of this: the international student interview exercise assigned in their introductory geography class. The exercise required students in the class (who were overwhelmingly US-born) to write a short paper on cultural differences based on information they obtained through an interview with an international student. Although domestic students initially reported considerable trepidation in having to approach and spend time with a stranger from another country, they were extremely positive about it at the conclusion of the term and reported that the exercise had helped them shed some long-held stereotypes and develop new friendships. A very similar approach is reflected in "language partners" programs used by many schools. These programs partner international students who are interested in improving their English proficiency with US-born students who volunteer to be language partners. The international student and his/her language partner make time to engage socially. These interactions provide opportunities not only for the international student to practice their English, but also often for the pair of students to develop a cultural understanding and forge deep friendships.

Student affairs staff also have an important role to play in this regard. Orientation programs for new international students could be enhanced by having domestic students serve as peer mentors or buddies. International students from specific countries, in turn, could serve as peer mentors in predeparture orientations for US-born students planning to study abroad in that country. For example, at my own institution—the University of Georgia—we organize a "Welcome-Bon Voyage" reception each semester that brings together students from the university who will be studying abroad at one of our international partner institutions with international students from our partner universities studying at the University of Georgia. It is amazing to see the connections form as the US-born students seek out international students from the institutions to which they will be traveling to learn more. Similarly, Peterson et al. (1999) discuss their positive experiences in holding intercultural communication workshops that bring together domestic and international students. Their workshop sessions are designed such that students discuss everyday issues such as friendship, gender relations, and classroom expectations. Because the focus is on issues that all participants encounter in their lives, they found that students engaged in the conversation as individuals rather than as spokespersons for their particular ethnic or nationality group. Having established this communication, participants begin viewing themselves through the eyes of others. These are only a few of the many examples of creative programming that can be put in place to create meaningful interactions between international and domestic students (see Leask 2009).

Bringing together students from diverse backgrounds is just the first step in a longer journey. If the conversations and discussions that ensue are to lead to dialogue and understanding, it is vital that domestic students are developmentally prepared to engage (Bennett and Salonen 2007). Bennett and Bennett's Intercultural Sensitivity Model provides a valuable guide for all those who work with students (2004). The model suggests that, over time, individuals progress from an initial "ethnocentric" stage, where they tend to deny, resist, or minimize cultural differences, to an "ethnorelative" stage in which they see culture as a resource and learn to adapt to and appreciate differences. Our efforts to bring together international and domestic students must, therefore, be matched with the appropriate interventions to move students from the earlier to the latter stage.

Embarking on such a project can often meet unanticipated structural challenges within a university. Campus-level support services tend to focus on supporting and protecting international students, while academic and "developmental" services are seen as the responsibility of the academic department/program (Thielen and Limbird 1992, 123). However, efforts to prepare students for intercultural engagement and then introduce appropriate activities that foster interaction require a dialogue between international student services staff and academic advising staff. International student services, in turn, are often decentralized, with admissions offices, immigration and visa offices, and international student life supporting various aspects of an international student's needs. Here, too, a stronger collaboration is necessary to ensure that the various offices work in coordination.

Hudzik (2011) notes that, while there is no magic solution to institutional barriers; institutional commitment, leadership, and persistence can go a long way toward surmounting them. Regular coordination and conversation between the various groups working with international and US-born students can give rise to joint initiatives to advance interactions between students. Involving faculty in these initiatives is particularly important because it is they who have regular contact with international and domestic students in the classroom and laboratory. They have the ability to incorporate academic projects and assignments that advance interchange, peer learning, and collaboration between international and domestic students (Pandit and Alderman 2004). Institutional start-up or incubator funds can play an important role in getting these efforts rolling, and, as Hudzik (2011) observes, success can then beget success.

Addressing International Students' Attitudes toward US Minorities

A persistent assumption underlying many of the writings in the area of international students and campus diversity is that international students are the providers of intercultural perspectives and that domestic students are the consumers. Studies of intolerance and stereotyping in reference to international students, therefore, overwhelmingly focus on the negative attitudes that they encounter (e.g., Lee and Rice 2007; Hanassab 2006; Plakans 1997). While this literature has been important in highlighting problems faced by international students and proposing strategies to address them, it has not given similar attention to the reverse problem, specifically the negative attitudes that international students themselves may harbor toward subgroups of Americans.

This is problematic, given that there is evidence that many international students come to the United States with their own preset opinions and attitudes, particularly with respect to race. For instance, Talbot, Geelhoed, and Ninggal (1999), surveying Asian students about their attitudes toward African Americans, found that the former arrived in the United States with negative attitudes of African Americans based largely on media portrayals and anecdotal information from friends and family. They noted that their finding was consistent with that of unpublished 1992 data from Chambers and Lewis that found that Asian students reported a lower comfort level toward African Americans than did students from Europe and Latin America.

What makes these observations even more problematic is that many international students serve as graduate teaching assistants in the university, in a position of authority over a diverse group of undergraduate students. For example, Jenkins and Rubin (1993) found that Chinese international teaching assistants scored significantly lower ethnic tolerance scores than their American counterparts. Jenkins and Rubin then compared how the Chinese and American teaching assistants evaluated a mathematics quiz taken by a culturally diverse group of undergraduates when the teaching assistants had knowledge of the race/ethnicity of the test-taker. They found that the international teaching assistants with lower ethnic tolerance scores generally gave all students lower grades on the test. No such effect was found for American teaching assistants. While the researchers were not able to tease out whether the international teaching assistants were engaging in ethnically biased grading, there was sufficient evidence that they had lower ethnic tolerance scores and that their grading norms were indeed different.

Further concerns are raised by Fels (1993), who examined this issue from the perspective of the students. He interviewed a number of African American students to gauge their feelings toward foreign students and international student exchanges in general. Recurring comments made by his respondents included that international students are afraid of African Americans and shun/avoid them, that international students hold negative stereotypes of African Americans based on media portrayals, and that international students are not really interested in the everyday problems of Americans. What was also of concern was that, as a consequence of their negative perceptions of and interactions with international students, the African American students expressed reservations about studying abroad, fearing that they would face similar discrimination. Based on these findings, Fels (1993) challenges the notion that the presence of international students on US campuses is a "win-win" proposition, and argues that there are hidden costs associated with recruiting large numbers of international students, costs that are disproportionately borne by African American students.

What these studies collectively highlight is that it is not just US-born students that need preparation to benefit from intercultural exchange. International students likewise need programs that are designed to help them learn about diversity in America and to confront prejudices that they themselves may hold. Particularly urgent is the need to incorporate diversity programming in the training of international teaching assistants, addressing not just race and ethnicity, but issues of gender and sexual orientation as well. A rising number of international students come from societies where issues of gender and sexuality are not openly discussed and behavior that deviates from the norm is illegal or grounds for social ostracism. The importance of this extends beyond the need to address issues of fairness in teaching. Given that a significant proportion of our international students will go on to settle permanently in the United States, programs such as these will allow them to understand the history of civil rights in the United States and develop a feeling for the importance placed on diversity in the United States today.

Developing such programming provides a way for international education offices and multicultural affairs/diversity offices to partner with one another and surmount what has been a historic divide between these two areas. In most universities, international education has been focused on a series of activities such as expanding study abroad, recruiting international students, and developing international partnerships and programming. Multicultural education, in contrast, has academic roots and goals, including the development of courses, curricular programs, and pedagogy focused on understanding racial, ethnic, and other types of cultural diversity within the United States.

Whereas in recent years, international education has become a core institutional priority in many universities, multicultural education, according to many in the field, continues to operate at the periphery of the university (Olson, Evans, and Shoenberg 2007; Peterson et al. 1999). There has been much interest in recent years in finding common ground between international and multicultural education, and the development of programming to orient international students to domestic diversity is an outstanding example of a project that meets common goals.

Conclusions

The growing numbers of international students in American universities are bringing a new element of diversity to our campuses. Their presence has the potential to advance intercultural learning of our domestic students and provide momentum to internationalization efforts. Yet, the reality on most campuses is that intermingling between domestic and international students is fairly limited and, when it occurs, students are often unprepared to handle cultural differences. Given this, expanding the international student population may not lead to the positive intercultural outcomes that are touted as reasons for ratcheting up international student recruitment. We also need to recognize that many international students have grown up in ethnic and racially homogenous countries, or contexts in which ethnic and/or gender discrimination may be more overt, and therefore carry their own prejudices with them to the United States. Unexamined, these stereotypes can lead to a domestic backlash against international cultural exchange. Productive engagement with these issues will require greater coordination and collaboration between all the administrative offices that work with international students and diversity issues.

Toward this end it is critical that we design and support programming that pushes domestic and international students out of their co-ethnic comfort zones and allows them to learn from one another. It is our responsibility as educators and administrators to help them recognize and confront their own biases and educate them about diversity in the United States. Finally, we need to forge stronger collaborations and partnerships between the various campus offices with responsibility for international students and diversity issues. The sort of programming and initiatives necessary require close coordination between student services, international education offices, and offices of multicultural education, among others. With the right types of partnerships and programming we will be able to match the rising presence of international students with an increase in intercultural exchange and vibrancy on campus.

References

Altbach, P. 2006. *International Higher Education: Reflections on Policy and Practice.* Chestnut Hill, MA: Boston College Center for International Higher Education.

American Council on Education [ACE]. 2011. *Strength through Global Leadership and Engagement: U.S. Higher Education in the 21st Century.* Report of the Blue Ribbon Panel on Global Engagement. Washington, DC: American Council on Education.

Andrade, M. 2006. "International Students in English-Speaking Universities: Adjustment Factors." *Journal of Research in International Education* 5: 131–54.

Bennett, J., and M. Bennett. 2004. "Developing Intercultural Sensitivity." In *Handbook of Intercultural Training,* 3rd edition, edited by D. Landis, J. Bennett, and M. Bennett. Thousand Oaks, CA: Sage.

Bennett, J., and R. Salonen. 2007 (March/April). "Intercultural Communication and the New American Campus." *Change*: 46–50.

Bevis, T. 2002. "At a Glance: International Students in the United States." *International Educator* 11(3): 12–17.

Bevis, T., and C. Lucas. 2007. *International Students in American Colleges and Universities: A History.* New York: Palgrave.

Brown, L. 2009. "A Failure of Communication on the Cross-Cultural Campus." *Journal of Studies in International Education* 13(4): 439–54.

Chambers, T., and J. Lewis. 1992. [A Study of International Students' Comfort with Black Americans]. Unpublished raw data.

Fels, M. 1993. "Assumptions of African-American Students about International Education Exchange." Paper presented at the Speech Communication Association Convention, Miami, Florida, November 20.

Graham, J. 1992. "Bias-Free Teaching as a Topic in a Course for International Teaching Assistants." *TESOL Quarterly* 26(3): 585–9.

Hanassab, S. 2006. "Diversity, International Students, and Perceived Discrimination: Implications for Educators and Counselors." *Journal of Studies in International Education* 10(2): 157–72.

Helms, A. 1978. "Cultures in Conflict: Arab Students in American Universities." Paper presented at Annual Meeting of the Southwestern Anthropological Association, San Francisco, California, March 23–25.

Hudzik, J. 2011. *Comprehensive Internationalization: From Concept to Action.* Washington, DC: NAFSA.

Jenkins, S., and D. Rubin. 1993. "International Teaching Assistants and Minority Students: The Two Sides of Cultural Diversity in American Higher Education." *The Journal of Graduate Teaching Assistant Development* 1(1): 17–24.

Leask, B. 2009. "Using Formal and Informal Curricula to Improve Interactions between Home and International Students." *Journal of Studies in International Education* 13(20): 205–21.
Lee, J., and C. Rice. 2007. "Welcome to America? International Student Perceptions of Discrimination." *Higher Education* 53: 381–409.
Marginson, S. 2002. "The Phenomenal Rise of International Degrees Down Under." *Change* 34(3): 34–44.
Olson, C., R. Evans, and R. Shoenberg. 2007. *At Home in the World: Bridging the Gap between International and Multicultural Education.* Washington, DC: American Council on Education.
Pandit, K. 2009. "Leading Internationalization." *Annals of the Association of American Geographers* 99(4): 645–56.
Pandit, K., and D. Alderman. 2004. "Border Crossings in the Classroom: The International Student Interview as a Strategy for Promoting Intercultural Understanding." *The Journal of Geography* 103: 127–36.
Peterson, D., P. Briggs, L. Dreasher, D. Horner, and T. Nelson. 1999. "Contributions of International Students and Programs to Campus Diversity." *New Directions for Student Services* 86: 67–77.
Plakans, B. 1997. "Undergraduates' Experiences with Attitudes toward International Teaching Assistants." *TESOL Quarterly* 31(1): 95–119.
Sanders, I., and J. Ward. 1970. *Bridges to Understanding: International Programs of American Colleges and Universities.* New York: McGraw Hill.
Smart, D., S. Volet, and G. Ang. 2000. *Fostering Social Cohesion in Universities: Bridging the Cultural Divide.* Canberra: Australian Education International.
Talbot, D., R. Geelhoed, and M. Tajudin Hj. Ninggal. 1999. "A Qualitative Study of Asian International Students' Attitudes toward African Americans." *NASPA Journal* 36(3): 210–21.
Teekens, H. 2000. "Teaching and Learning in the International Classroom." In *Internationalization at Home: A Position Paper*, edited by P. Crowther, M. Joris, M. Otten, B. Nilsson, H. Teekens, and B. Wachter, 29–34. Amsterdam: European Association for International Education.
Thielen, T., and M. Limbird. 1992. "Integrating Foreign Students into the University Community." In *Working with International Students and Scholars on American Campuses,* edited by D. McIntire, and P. Willer, 119–35. Washington, DC: National Association of Student Personnel Administrators, Inc.

3
CHALLENGES AND SUPPORT

8

SUCCEEDING ABROAD:

INTERNATIONAL STUDENTS IN THE UNITED STATES

Alisa Eland and Kay Thomas

The United States has a long history of hosting international students (Bevis and Lucas 2007), and currently receives the highest number of international students of any country in the world. With the exception of a few years, the number of international students in the United States has steadily increased since the 1950s (Chow and Bhandari 2010), a trend that is likely to continue. Colleges and universities in the United States recruit internationally for many reasons. They want to obtain the best and the brightest students, increase diversity in the student body and in the classroom, help their programs gain a more global perspective, foster educational exchanges with specific institutions in other countries, and sometimes also gain economic benefit as international students are frequently charged a higher-tuition rate than local students. Recruiting international students is seen as a key strategy for creating a global institution and interculturally competent students, faculty, and staff (Leask 2009).

Faculty typically recognize the important contributions that international students make to their classes and departments. Many international students are highly qualified academically, and therefore much sought after by departments. In addition, simply having international students may increase a department's ranking. International students also provide important international perspectives, which increase the overall learning experience for all students, and help prepare domestic students for the world of work (Trice 2003). International students and alumni can also provide their departments with connections to academic institutions, government agencies, and corporations for collaborations and other opportunities (Trice 2003).

While faculty and university administrators understand and value the benefits of international enrollees, they do not always know how to support international students and help them to be successful. To help international students succeed, it is important to understand what distinguishes them from domestic students (Thomas and Althen 1989), the challenges they face, and what approaches and resources would help them. By learning about how education systems differ among countries, faculty and staff can put their own educational assumptions into perspective (Andersen and Powell 1991), become familiar with the differing experiences and expectations about education that international students often bring, and be in a better position to assist international students.

This chapter investigates the challenges international students face at US higher-education institutions and how faculty, advisers, and other student service professionals can help international students to succeed. It is based on our many years of experience working in the international student service office of a major research university with thousands of international students (Alisa 28 years, Kay over 40 years), as well as our research about international students and our own teaching experiences. We contextualize our personal insights within the literature on international students. We begin by providing a broad overview of the common challenges faced by international students that are observed by those working with international students in an advising and/or counseling capacity. We then consider how US higher education poses a unique array of challenges to international students, and conclude by exploring how faculty and staff working with international students can address these place-specific factors.

Overview of Academic and Nonacademic Challenges

In order to understand the complexity of the international student experience in the United States, it is helpful to provide a brief overview of the variety of academic and nonacademic challenges they face. International students have to meet the same admission standards as other students, so they are intellectually and academically prepared. However, other challenges can interfere with their ability to succeed, including those common to all students as well as some that are unique to being international. These challenges range from academic issues to cultural differences, from personal to logistical matters.

Many challenges that international students face are due to being in an education system that differs from the system in their home country. Most bring different experiences and expectations regarding classroom dynamics, academic writing style, the role of the instructor, and course content. If English is not their native language, the level and amount of required reading, writing, and speaking in class may be daunting. With many requirements, responsibilities, and activities competing for their attention, concentrating on studies can be difficult. Students must have strong motivation to do the hard work that it takes to succeed. Pressure to excel from self, home, or a sponsor can motivate some students, but can contribute to a feeling of being overwhelmed for others. Some of the more serious academic consequences that may result from these pressures include failing classes, being suspended for inadequate academic performance, and even accusations of academic dishonesty.

Nonacademic challenges include cultural, personal, social, and legal matters. Living in a different culture means adjusting to many new things all at once, including language, climate, transportation, a new living situation, food, managing money, and being away from family and friends at home. Because of extensive Internet use and media exposure, many international students come to the United States believing that they know a lot about US culture. However, that does not necessarily mean that these students fully understand and are prepared for the realities of US campus life. Many students are away from their families for the first time and must learn how to deal with finding a residence, cooking and caring for themselves, and learning how to navigate the new environment and how to manage their time. Some students do not yet have the life skills to live independently, such as getting enough sleep, eating nutritious meals, and getting along with roommates. Undergraduate students, in particular, may have had their schedules and activities managed by their parents before coming to the United States, while graduate students may not have had to juggle as many responsibilities in their home countries. This can lead to not feeling well physically or emotionally, which ultimately can affect students' ability to be successful in their studies. Compounding these problems, many students also experience loneliness, isolation, and uncertainty about how to make friends because they are away from family and friends at home and they are not sure how to connect with US students.

Students in their late teens and twenties are still forming their identities and this can lead to questions about self. They may feel that their personality characteristics and what they value is changing as a result of being in a new place and having new experiences. Others may find that they either do not like, or do not perform well, in the field their family wants them to study. How this might affect their identity within their family can be a concern to them. Some international students will explore and question their sexual identity. Students from a family system or culture in which there is little or no acceptance of being gay, lesbian, bisexual, or transgender, may find that the new opportunities that the United States provides for more openly exploring sexuality may lead to shifts in their perception of self. How these changes will be accepted at home or by other students of their nationality studying in the United States may be of serious concern to them.

While international students may in many ways experience more freedom in the United States than in their home countries, they are also restricted in ways that US students are not due to their nonresident visa status. They must abide by US government regulations that proscribe the number of credits they must take each semester and the number of years they can remain in a degree program, whether or not they can work, how many hours they can work, whether they can travel, how stable they must remain financially, and what opportunities exist for their spouses and children. Students with government or private financial sponsorship must follow their sponsor's policies governing their choice of major and courses, course load, grades required, and ability to get a job. Other legal issues international students may encounter are not directly linked to their legal status, but to their unfamiliarity with US laws; landlord or roommate problems and driving violations are some of the most common issues encountered in this respect. It is important that international students know how and where to get legal advice if these issues come up.

Health problems reported by international students are similar to those of US students, including headaches, stomach disturbances, colds and flu, depression, anxiety, and difficulty sleeping, but many international students face additional challenges in accessing care for their health conditions. Many are not aware that they have health insurance or what it covers, even when this information has been given at orientation. Students who are not used to a privatized medical system may feel especially concerned about how much they may have to pay for particular procedures or how to access care via a health insurance system. Some do not know where to go when they are sick or injured, are not comfortable going to a clinic or hospital in the United States, or simply do not trust Western medicine. This may result in not seeking medical attention before the ailment gets serious, and can lead to students missing classes.

A small number of international students face far more serious nonacademic problems, including being a victim of crime (such as identity theft, credit card theft, robbery, or violence), addictions (e.g., alcohol, drugs, or gaming), having suicidal thoughts, or experiencing life-threatening injuries and illnesses. Because they may have a different view of or experience with the police or the legal system, or in order to avoid embarrassment, they may be hesitant to seek help. And without the social support network that they have grown up with back home, these very serious situations can become even more devastating, with significant implications for the student's ability to succeed.

This initial overview highlights some of the broad range of adjustment challenges that are commonly seen by those individuals who work in advising and counseling capacities with international students. We argue that it is critical for all faculty and staff who work with international students across campus to be aware of these issues in order to be able to pick up on warning signs of potential problems and provide an opportunity for them to help ease their students' transition into their new setting.

International Students in the US Education System

While many of the issues mentioned above apply to international students studying in a wide variety of countries, there are several aspects of the US education system in particular that pose particular challenges for international students. Education systems vary in some key ways that affect a student's experience, including pedagogical approaches, classroom expectations and dynamics, communication, roles and relationships in the academic setting, academic freedom, and academic honesty and conduct. We, therefore, now turn to discussing what is distinctive about the US education system, why it is challenging for some international students, and how faculty and staff in US institutions can help international students deal with these challenges.

Education systems evolve out of the history and culture of a particular country, giving each system a unique character and mode of operation. Both students and instructors in US classrooms bring culturally based rules and expectations about education and classroom behavior (Ward 2001; Andersen and Powell 1991). It is important for international students to understand what is expected of them in the US education system as they must be able to adjust their expectations and behaviors in order to be successful in the US context. Likewise it is important for faculty and staff to learn how education systems in other countries may differ from those in the United States so that they can be more effective in helping international students succeed.

Classroom Culture

One particularly important distinction between different classroom cultures relates to the contrast between cultures that tend to emphasize collectivism and those that are more individualistic. Ting-Toomey (1999), drawing on Triandis's work (1995, as cited in Ting-Toomey 1999, 67), provides a useful summary of collectivism versus individualism:

> *Individualism* refers to the broad value tendencies of a culture in emphasizing the importance of individual identity over group identity, individual rights over group rights, and individual needs over group needs. Individualism promotes self-efficiency, individual responsibilities, and personal autonomy. In contrast, *collectivism* refers to the broad value tendencies of a culture in emphasizing the "we" identity over the "I" identity, group rights over individual rights, and in-group-oriented needs over individual wants and desires. Collectivism promotes relational interdependence, in-group harmony, and in-group collaborative spirit.

In a classroom context, collectivism is reflected in a style of learning where students are expected to listen, understand, and memorize the knowledge that the instructor provides, generating a shared understanding of the world. Individualism, by contrast, generates a style of learning where knowledge is open to question and critical thinking is highly valued. Related to these ideas, "power distance" explains how people feel and relate to power and hierarchy (Hofstede 1980). In a classroom in a high-power-distance culture, teachers are the sole initiators of activities as their role is to transfer wisdom and knowledge to students who are obedient and show respect toward them. In low-power-distance cultures, teachers still transfer knowledge but respect and encourage their students' independence; as such, students are expected to speak up in class and can contradict their teachers (Knight n.d.).

These cultural dimensions translate into two contrasting pedagogical approaches: the teacher-centered approach and learner-centered approach (Eland, Smithee, and Greenblatt 2009). The teacher-centered approach, also called the "discipleship model" (Badke 2003), is found in cultures that are more collectivist and that have higher power distance. The goal of education is for the teacher to pass knowledge to the students. The student's role is to receive and memorize what the teacher conveys. Students do not question the instructor or raise contrasting views because that would disrupt the harmony of the group or classroom. The contrasting learner-centered approach is found in more individualistic cultures that have lower power distance. Here, the student plays a more active role in the learning process. Students learn from teachers, but students also contribute their own knowledge, ideas, and experiences to the learning process. Students are evaluated by professors, but they also have the opportunity to evaluate their professors. These and additional differences between the two approaches are summarized in table 8.1.

In the United States, which is an individualistic, low-power-distance culture, the learner-centered approach is dominant. Badke (2003) offers some explanations for how this developed: the dominant culture in the United States was founded and influenced by people who came from other countries and who consciously created a new culture that was different from the ones they left. Since they left their home countries to start a new life, they tended to be independent thinkers and challenge traditional knowledge systems and ways of life; what was new was valued. This independent, questioning spirit influenced education in the United States. Students are expected to think critically about what they are learning, and to question the experts and traditional ways of thinking. Practical application of knowledge is also greatly valued, so students must apply theories, models, and knowledge to real-world situations. For students coming from teacher-centered systems of learning, this difference can represent a significant culture shock, requiring them to "relearn" how to succeed in an academic setting.

These profound differences not only require a major adjustment on the part of many international students, but can even put them in danger of violating academic conventions in the United States. Every culture has standards about academic conduct and academic honesty, but the rules vary across cultures, as do the consequences for breaking them. Because the United States is a strongly individualistic culture, great value is placed on the rights and responsibilities of the individual. As a consequence, academic rules and US laws protect

Table 8.1 Comparison of teacher- and learner-centered pedagogical approaches

Aspect	Teacher-centered approach	Learner-centered approach
Preferred teaching methods	Lecture	Lecture, discussion in large and small groups, application of theory
Instructor's role	Direct the learning process, be source of knowledge, clarify and interpret written texts and other information	Present content, facilitate learning process and dialogue, demonstrate analytical skills
Learner's role	Listen to lectures, take notes, read assigned texts, memorize content, demonstrate memorization through tests and written papers	Listen, take notes, read, think critically about content, express perspectives in class, participate in dialog, demonstrate understanding, be able to learn independently
Who directs learning process	Instructor	Instructor and student
Use of the computer and Internet	Considered only as an adjunct to the lecture	Can be an intrinsic part of achieving the course objectives, and used by the professor to engage the students in further exploration of the topic as well as out-of-class discussion topics
Learning mode	Top down, i.e. instructor imparts knowledge to students	Cooperative, participatory, interactive between instructor and learner
Evaluation methods	Written and oral exams	Written and oral exams, presentations, class participation, papers, quizzes, group projects, demonstration of skills (e.g., in lab), classmates' evaluations
Who conducts evaluation	Instructors evaluate students	Instructors evaluate students, students evaluate instructors, classmates evaluate each other
Desired outcomes	Memorize information, absorb knowledge	Gain knowledge, apply concepts to new situations, use critical analysis skills

Source: Adapted from Eland, A., M. Smithee, and S. Greenblatt. 2009. *U.S. Classroom Culture*. U.S. Culture Series, Washington, DC: NAFSA, Association of International Educators.

the individual's right to own his or her words, ideas, and products, as exemplified by the strong stance taken on US campuses against plagiarism. For some international students, by contrast, rote memorization and the repeating of a senior scholar's work is an expected part of the learning process and so the concept of plagiarism may be confusing. As a result, they may not understand the exact rules or the seriousness of breaking them in the United States, leading to potential infractions. It is therefore imperative that international students are told specifically what is considered academic dishonesty in the United States, how seriously it is taken, what the consequences are for plagiarism, and how to cite sources accurately to avoid the problem. Faculty can play a significant role in this respect by outlining their expectations clearly in the syllabus or on assignments and providing resources such as citation guidelines or publication style manuals.

Classroom dynamics can also be influenced by individualism-collectivism and power distance. Broadly speaking, students from individualistic cultures like the United States are encouraged to be active participants in class, engaging in debate and asking questions; overall, they are more willing to "stand out." This is in stark contrast to students from collectivist cultures, as typified by most Asian countries, where students are trained to "fit in" and avoid drawing attention to themselves (Ward 2001). As Ward (2001, unpaginated) notes:

> Collectivism is strongly related to power distance [PD], and those students who are from high PD cultures are also less likely to question and debate. This is generally seen as an inappropriate challenge to the teacher, which may result in loss of face. Students from high power distance cultures are more strongly motivated to show respect to teachers and to maintain formal and distant relationships with them. It is not difficult to see that these differences in cultural values can lead to misperceptions across cultural groups. From one perspective, quiet but attentive collectivist students may be perceived as uninterested or withdrawn by individualist teachers. From another viewpoint, the relatively frequent interruptions to lectures by individualist students may be seen as rude and unmannered by their collectivist classmates.

In order to be successful in the US classroom, international students from collectivist cultures have to learn to be more like their more talkative classmates, even though they may be uncomfortable with or even shocked at how much students participate in class. A variety of pedagogic techniques may assist international students in making this transition. For instance, giving students time to think about an answer before calling on them, or allowing them time to discuss their ideas in small groups before presenting to the class as a whole can often help a student used to a collectivist classroom style ease into greater participation. If class participation is graded, it is important to explain specifically what is expected.

Also related to individualism, students in the United States have a great deal of freedom to choose or change their field of study, courses, and research topics and design (Eland, Smithee, and Greenblatt 2009). By contrast, many other countries have education systems with more rigid academic programs without as much choice or flexibility. International students typically like the freedom in the United States but many find it hard to make academic decisions on their own because they have not had the opportunity previously (Eland 2001). Instead, they may be more familiar with relying on academic advisers and instructors to make decisions for them. Faculty and staff can help these students by explaining that decisions are the student's responsibility, but coaching them through the decision-making process.

Sometimes international students are also unprepared for and confused by what they consider very informal behavior on the part of instructors. Instructors in the United States often go by their first names, wear casual clothing including jeans, and joke with their students. Such behaviors are inconsistent with behaviors of faculty in high-power-distance cultures, where higher levels of formality may be an expression of respect between student and instructor. Students from high-power-distance cultures may even expect disinterest or disapproval on the part of faculty, leading to confusion over the meaning of friendly behavior. While it is important that instructors convey warmth to help the student feel at ease, it is also important that instructors explain their role in recognition that international students may not be used to US conventions.

The emphasis placed on planning ahead and adhering to schedules that is common in the United States is also not necessarily shared by people from other countries (Althen 2003). In some countries, time is more fluid. Being on time to classes and appointments and meeting deadlines is not strictly enforced. But an international student who brings a more relaxed approach to time to a US classroom will likely find that the instructor is not happy with chronic lateness, may not accept work that is turned in after the deadline, and may lower the student's grade due to these issues. Again, simply explaining expectations and consequences for not complying in advance is one important way in which instructors can help international students to make this transition.

Communication Challenges

Although international students who are nonnative English speakers have to show a high level of English proficiency to be admitted to US colleges and universities, some students are still not adequately prepared for the large quantity and difficulty of reading materials, the amount and style of writing, the difficulty of listening comprehension in class, the challenge of contributing to in-class discussions and presentations (Gebhard 2010), and cultural differences in communication. If English proficiency is insufficient, advisers should refer international students to English support courses and help them design a course load each semester that gives them adequate time to deal with English difficulties (Charles and Stewart 1991). Faculty and staff can also help nonnative speakers by speaking more slowly and avoiding idioms, writing information and instructions down for students, and allowing students more time on exams when they first arrive.

Communication problems are not limited to spoken and written language, however. The meaning of gestures can also vary significantly across cultures, leading to potential confusion. For example, shaking your head from side to side does not mean "no" in every culture (Taras and Rowney 2007). In different contexts, it could mean "no," "yes," "I understand," or "I am listening to you." For instructors and staff, trying to get students to clarify their meaning verbally may help. This may require considerable patience, allowing for some pauses and silence. Although silence can make Westerners feel uncomfortable, "in Asia long pauses in conversation are interpreted as signs of respect and satisfaction" (Taras and Rowney 2007, 71).

Another important distinction in communication styles is between "low-context" and "high-context" communication (Hall 1976). In cultures with low-context communication, meaning is usually expressed verbally and in a direct and straightforward manner. The message is expected to be persuasive and easily decoded by the listener (Ting-Toomey 1999). In high-context communication, by contrast, meaning is best "conveyed through the context (e.g., social roles or positions) and the nonverbal channels (e.g., pauses, silence, tone of voice) of the verbal message" (Ting-Toomey 1999, 100), with "the receiver.... assum[ing] the responsibility to infer the hidden or contextual meanings of the message" (Ting-Toomey 1999, 101). In the US academic setting, low-context communication is the norm. Professors are expected to deliver information in a clear and straightforward manner and students are expected to ask the professor directly if help or clarification is needed. For students who grew up high-context cultures, where it may even be considered rude for someone of lower status to address a higher-status individual directly, speaking up in class or seeking help from a professor may be daunting. Once again, faculty and staff can help students make the transition by clarifying their expectation of communication and inviting students to state their perspectives and ask questions.

Teamwork is another context in which communication may pose a significant challenge. Cross-cultural teamwork is a common methodology in US classrooms, and provides many potential benefits. The members of cross-cultural teams come from diverse backgrounds so they bring a broader range of assumptions, perspectives, and ideas to the task (Nemeth 1985), and come up with more creative solutions than homogeneous groups (Taras and Rowney 2007). However, if cross-cultural teams are not managed well, difficulties can arise from communication, status, and cultural differences (Taras and Rowney 2007). For example, students who are more fluent in English are likely to dominate discussions; international students may also speak less than US students due to differences in communication styles, causing others to perceive them as less prepared. As a result, "regardless of their skills and qualifications, group members who are less fluent in the language may be attributed with lower expertise and perceived as less knowledgeable of the subject" (Taras and Rowney 2007, 72). To facilitate teamwork with cross-cultural teams, additional efforts should be made to ensure that all participants have an opportunity to contribute ideas, even if some ideas appear unconventional, and that everyone understands all ideas on the table. Native speakers may need to be encouraged to avoid slang and dominating the proceedings, but can play a valuable role in proofreading final drafts (Taras and Rowney 2007).

Coping with Adversity

A further area in which international student expectations may differ significantly from those of US students relates to how students deal with adversity. In particular, international students may be more hesitant than domestic students to seek personal counseling due to cultural ideas about who one approaches for help and what it means if someone needs counseling. In some cultures, problems are only dealt with within the family or with close friends. There may be stigma and shame associated with seeking help from a professional (Lovett

2009). So some students will either seek help from family or take a "nonaction" approach, letting nature run its course (Lovett 2009).

As such, many international students could be helped by discussion of what kind of issues they can talk to counselors about and what they can expect from counseling. Faculty and international student advisers should work collaboratively to ensure that international students understand the resources available on campus to deal with issues that arise. International students can also make connections and get social support through buddy programs that match international students with domestic students, skills training (e.g., academic or career skills workshops or groups), and cultural exchange programs (Yeh and Inose 2003). Counseling center staff can also partner with other campus offices to encourage international students to join student organizations and other groups to help them develop a feeling of connection, which has been shown to correlate with less acculturative stress (Yeh and Inose 2003, 26).

When faculty and staff are working with international students who are experiencing serious situations, whether academic, personal, or legal, they should recognize the limits of their ability to help and refer students to specialists on campus. When making referrals to other campus resources it is important to remember that it might be uncomfortable for the student, so care should be taken to build trust with the student and to smooth the way for them to get to the next office, for instance, by calling ahead and providing the student with the specific name of a contact (Charles and Stewart 1991). Faculty have to be particularly aware of the possible stigma of such words as disability, mental health, depression, counseling, and therapy. If resistance or shame is detected, a referral to an adviser in the international student office or to a doctor at the health service instead of to a counselor might be an alternative.

What International Students Need to Know

As we have already outlined, one key facet of international student success is ensuring that students are made aware of some of the potential challenges they may face in adapting to the US education system. Here we expand on some of these factors that, due to culture differences, may not be obvious to international students. These tips can be presented at orientation, but would be more effectively presented later, after students have started classes.

International students need to plan realistic schedules. Many will need help doing this because what was realistic in their home countries was likely different. For example, in many countries, undergraduates may successfully take 25 credits per semester because the classes require less work. Students need to understand that in the United States, for every hour in class, they should plan to spend 2 to 3 hours outside of class studying and doing homework. The academic adviser can explain what is a realistic course load (taking into account the minimum required by immigration regulations).

International students may also need to be told that going to all of their classes every day is critical, as regular class attendance at the university level is not essential in all countries. Even if the instructor does not keep track of attendance, the content that is discussed in class is usually included in tests and other requirements and classes move quickly. Class syllabi should be designed to help students know what is expected and what is included in grading.

Before they begin classes, international students need to learn that academic institutions in the United States take academic honesty very seriously, and that following the rules is essential to being academically successful. They need to hear that it is their responsibility to know, understand, and follow the academic conduct rules at their institution (Eland, Smithee, and Greenblatt 2009). Sometimes students, both United States and international, truly do not know the rules and accidentally plagiarize or cheat in other ways. They need to know that even accidental cheating can and likely will have serious consequences. It is recommended that they be provided with the institution's policy on academic integrity, specific examples of what is considered cheating, likely consequences of cheating, and most importantly resources for making sure that they are correctly citing sources and abiding by all other rules regarding academic honesty.

As emphasized earlier, class discussion is an important part of learning in the US classroom. Even if they are not accustomed to speaking up in class, international students need to develop the skills and confidence to participate. In small group work, the student can ask participants to speak more slowly. International students can also observe US students and try imitating their behavior (Gebhard 2010). They need to know that it is their responsibility to talk to instructors and teaching assistants if they are having trouble speaking up in class, understanding the material, or have questions about the class.

International students may not be used to seeking help because in many cultures (especially collectivist cultures) help is offered, one need not ask for it. In addition to coming to understand that it is their responsibility to ask for help, they also need to learn about the variety of resources available on campus. It is important to explain what services are provided at each of the offices, such as writing centers, tutors, and counseling.

Students need to remember the basics of healthy living if they want to be able to give optimal effort and focus to their studies. They need to get enough sleep every night, especially before exams, eat nutritious food, get exercise, and take time for rest and rejuvenation. Developing a daily practice such as meditation, prayer or yoga—even if for only a few minutes a day—can help relieve stress and focus the mind.

Making friends with US students can seem difficult because US students are so busy. But feeling connected on campus helps ensure academic success (Doss Bowman 2011). A good way for international students to meet both US and international students is to get involved in activities such as study groups, sports, and hobbies (Leder and Forgasz 2004). It is helpful for students to know about university- or college-sponsored social events, clubs, and workshops that help students connect with each other (Doss Bowman 2011).

Experience and research show that international students do have the inner resources to deal with the difficulties they encounter during their studies in the United States. It is helpful to remind them that they probably already have personal approaches and strategies to help them manage difficulties that can help them here. It might also help for them to hear what veteran international students have recommended (Eland, Smithee, and Greenblatt 2009), including keeping a positive attitude, being willing to try things that are uncomfortable or unfamiliar, keeping a sense of humor, and being able to laugh about mistakes (Gebhard 2010). It is also important for students to think about the challenges they have faced and how far they have come (Gebhard 2010).

International students may also be empowered by hearing that equal access to education and equal opportunity are guiding principles of the US education system (Althen 2003). Some international students will come from education systems that are more exclusive and do not strive for such diversity so it can be unfamiliar and perplexing. Difference may take many forms and there may even be productive overlap between the challenges facing international students and other minority groups such as those with disabilities or "othered" because of their sexuality. For instance, at the University of Minnesota, including a statement about diversity at international student orientation has contributed to an increased number of international students who are gay, lesbian, bisexual, or questioning their identity coming to the international student office seeking support and resources.

Conclusion

US colleges and universities strive for diversity within the student body, faculty, and staff. International students provide one important aspect of this diverse community. As Lipson (2008, 25) notes:

> Pluralism is a fact of life in North American universities and a fundamental value shared by students, faculty, and the wider society. Tolerance for others is expected. Teachers and students here come in all shapes and sizes. They are citizens of all nations, members of all races and religions, men and women, gay and straight, old and young.

In maximizing the opportunities provided by a diverse student body, US institutions of higher education must also acknowledge their responsibility to strive to enable all their students to succeed. International students experience a variety of unique challenges in this respect and universities and colleges must explore a variety of ways to foster success within this group.

International students have the ability to succeed at US colleges and universities, but face many challenges, both academic and nonacademic. In particular, the classroom culture in which the student is now working may be very different from that back home, potentially leading to confusion and feelings of dislocation. Communication problems only increase the challenge of adapting to this new setting, particularly for nonnative English speakers. International students need to learn what is expected of them, as it is often different from their home country institutions, and they need to know where to turn for help. Faculty and staff can ease their adjustment by learning what is different and challenging for international students about the US education system, and then tailoring their support and intervention accordingly.

Works Cited

Althen, G. 2003. *American Ways.* Yarmouth, ME: Intercultural Press.

Andersen, J., and R. Powell. 1991. "Intercultural Communication and the Classroom." In *Intercultural Communication: A Reader,* 6th edition, edited by L. Samovar, and R. Porter, 208–14. Belmont, CA: Wadsworth.

Badke, W. 2003. *Beyond the Answer Sheet: Academic Success for International Students.* New York: iUniverse.
Bevis, T., and C. Lucas. 2007. *International Students in American Colleges and Universities: A History.* New York: Palgrave Macmillan.
Charles, H., and M. Stewart. 1991. "Academic Advising of International Students." *Journal of Multicultural Counseling and Development* 19(4): 173–81.
Chow, P., and R. Bhandari. 2010. *Open Doors 2010 Report on International Educational Exchange.* New York: Institute of International Education.
Doss Bowman, K. 2011. "Helping International Students Thrive on U.S. Campuses." *International Educator* September-October.
Eland, A. 2001. "Intersection of Academics and Culture: The Academic Experience of International Graduate Students." Unpublished PhD Dissertation. University of Minnesota.
Eland, A., M. Smithee, and S. Greenblatt. 2009. *U.S. Classroom Culture.* U.S. Culture Series, Washington, DC: NAFSA, Association of International Educators.
Gebhard, J. 2010. *What Do International Students Think and Feel? Adapting to U.S. College Life and Culture.* Ann Arbor, MI: University of Michigan Press.
Hall, E. 1976. *Beyond Culture.* New York: Doubleday.
Hofstede, G. 1980. *Culture Consequences.* Beverly Hills, CA: Sage.
Knight, A. No date. "Power Distance in the Classroom." Available at: http://culturallyteaching.com/2009/06/10/power-distance-in-the-classroom/. Accessed: January 16, 2012.
Leask, B. 2009. "Using Formal and Informal Curricula to Improve Interactions between Home and International Students." *Journal of Studies in International Education* 13(2): 205–21.
Leder, G., and H. Forgasz. 2004. "Australian and International Mature Students: The Daily Challenges." *Higher Education Research and Development* 23(2): 183–98.
Lipson, C. 2008. *Succeeding as an International Student in the United States and Canada.* Chicago, IL: The University of Chicago Press.
Lovett, N. 2009. "Cross-Cultural Influences on the Help-Seeking Behaviors of Adolescent Females." Available at: http://proceedings.com.au/isana2009/PDF/paper_Lovett.pdf. Accessed: June 5, 2012.
Nemeth, C. 1985. "Dissent, Group Process, and Creativity." *Advances in Group Process* 2: 57–75.
Taras, V., and J. Rowney. 2007. "Effects of Cultural Diversity on In-Class Communication and Student Project Team Dynamics: Creating Synergy in the Diverse Classroom." *International Studies in Educational Administration* 35(2): 66–81.
Thomas, K., and G. Althen. 1989. "Counseling Foreign Students." In *Counseling across Cultures*, 3rd edition, edited by P. Pedersen, J. Draguns, W. Lonner, and J. Trimble. Honolulu, HI: University of Hawaii Press.

Ting-Toomey, S. 1999. *Communicating Across Cultures.* New York: Guilford Press.
Triandis, H. 1995. *Individualism and Collectivism.* Boulder, CO: Westview Press.
Trice, A. 2003. "Faculty Perceptions of Graduate International Students: The Benefits and Challenges." *Journal of Studies in International Education* 7(4): 379–403.
Ward, C. 2001. "The Impact of International Students on Domestic Students and Host Institutions." Available at: http://www.educationcounts.govt.nz/publications/international/the_impact_of_international_students_on_domestic_students_and_host_institutions. Accessed: June 5, 2012.
Yeh, C., and M. Inose. 2003. "International Students' Reported English Fluency, Support Satisfaction, and Social Connectiveness as Predictors of Acculturative Stress." *Counseling Psychology Quarterly* 16(1): 15–28.

9

AFRICAN STUDENTS IN THE US HIGHER-EDUCATION SYSTEM

A WINDOW OF OPPORTUNITIES AND CHALLENGES

Jane Irungu

In recent years higher education has become a global commodity traded across countries and cultures. Students are now traveling more frequently across borders in search of opportunities to study outside their countries of origin. The United States remains one of the top five destinations for foreign students seeking higher education abroad. Each year higher-education institutions in the United States enroll over half a million international students. African students represent approximately 5 percent of these international enrollees. A total of 37,062 students from African nations studied in the United States in 2009/10 and 36,890 in 2010/11 (Institute of International Education 2012). Nigeria and Kenya are among the top 25 sending countries to the United States.

International students are recruited mostly for their contribution to campus diversity and their ability to bring in tuition dollars. Administrators agree that there is real value in having international students on campus, and the US government acknowledges that the presence of international students infuses billions of dollars into the US economy in tuition fees and living expenses (Irungu 2011). In fact, international education—recruitment and matriculation—is the fifth largest service industry in the United States (Institute of International Education 2008).

Nations around the world, those from Africa included, hold the US higher-education system in high esteem. African students' mobility to the West continues to grow, in part due to overstretched higher-education systems (Chow 2011) that are unable to accommodate the demand for higher education in Africa. The soaring numbers can also be accounted for by the perception that higher education in the West is more advanced and comparatively better in some educational areas than are colleges and universities in Africa and other low-income regions. Perceived higher quality of higher education, the availability of a broad range of areas of study, and established academic and student affairs support services are major reasons for students' mobility to the US and European countries (Institute of International Education 2008). For some, scholarship opportunities in athletics are a further attraction (Lee and Opio 2011).

This chapter focuses on the experiences of African students in US universities and how administrators and faculty might ease the transition for African students in the United States. Although there are a significant number of studies on international students, the continued demand for higher education in North America by African nationals warrants focus on the experiences of African students specifically. After arriving from their home countries, international students undergo orientation sessions, whose goal is to help the students integrate into their new academic and social environment. These programs, while helpful, usually overlook the uniqueness of students' countries of origin, lived experiences, and the degree of separation between home culture and American culture. Students' experiences are varied and unique, yet many orientation programs, student services, and other internationally focused support systems do not have culture- or region-specific programs during orientation. Programs lump all international students together as one homogeneous group in terms of social, cultural, academic, and personal needs. Research that distinctly focuses on international students from Africa is very limited, so a solid basis for such targeted programs is lacking. More specificity would be helpful in the creation of targeted transitional and recurring academic and personal support programs for international students from Africa.

I have had the opportunity to engage in conversations with many African students during my 14 years of working with international students as an instructor, academic advisor, and administrator charged with a portfolio that includes underrepresented populations, their retention, and successful graduation. In this chapter, I use information from my own personal communications with students as well as data from other studies on African students to illustrate some of the key opportunities and constraints facing this group (all names used below are pseudonyms). It is my hope that this chapter will help readers understand African students' experiences in the US higher-education system, and offer a frame of reference as faculty and administrators teach, train, and guide students for success and the realization of their own American dreams.

Reasons for Coming to the United States

The perception that studying in America is a window of opportunity is a great motivation for many prospective students. Many Africans believe the United States is one of the most fascinating and richest countries in the world, and that chances for upward mobility are high in this land of abundance. As Pipher (2002, xxv) notes:

> America was freedom, the land of opportunity, and the Promised Land. And the dreams of our ancestors are the dreams of our Kurdish, Vietnamese, Sudanese, Afghani, and other new-comers today. Gold Mountain is Silicon Valley. The land of milk and honey is our land of Coke and French fries. America is where streets are lined with compact discs and SUVs. We have free schools and free people. Everybody has a dream in America.

In this vein, many students from Africa view coming to America as an opportunity to make a positive difference in their lives and those of their families. They envision freedom and success, as noted by Nabisu from Tunisia:

> For me it was more about freedom, it was about a dream, it was more about understanding what life in America is about because I was intrigued about the movies, commercials, and all the history and stuff—for me it was more about freedom—it is a bigger country and many people from all over the world come here to start a life here. There is more opportunity than in many other countries. You get a better financial life. I would like to have a good financial base some day (personal communication 2006).

Nabisu's sentiment emphasizes the value placed on education by most students and their families—that education is "an investment in the family's human capital with the expected result of increasing net family earning" (Arthur 2000, 22). Higher education is the proven route to upward social and economic mobility, particularly if it is from an America institution (Okoth, 2003). African students who study in the United States and other Western countries are, thus, considered to have a wider range of opportunities, and even guaranteed job placement, when they return home. As Juma described:

> If you have a degree from the US...in [country X] the employer won't care from what university. They say "oh you are from the US it is good," the employer won't care, that is the stereotype...because it is the US, the big country, so if you have a college degree from somewhere else like a big country like the US that will be much better for you to get [a job] in my country (personal communication 2006).

Education from an American institution is viewed with pride, not only by immediate and extended families, but also by entire villages, communities, and governments.

Suffice it to say that African students, as well as a lot of other international students, come to study in America with great expectations and untested dreams. They envision successful and fulfilling college experiences at some of the best and most advanced universities in the world as the start to a great future. In spite of these high hopes, many international students from Africa experience significant social, academic, and personal adjustment and adaptation challenges and barriers that threaten their American dream of a high-quality education.

Adjustment Challenges

Adjustment to the host society is one of the most pressing issues for international students. Whereas studies that focus on African students are limited, there are studies that deal with international students' adjustment and adaptation in general. For example, Brown (2008), Chapdelaine and Alextich (2004), Lacina (2002), and Wilton and Constantine (2003) discuss issues surrounding sociocultural shock, one of the most common transitional issues for many students. Other helpful research includes studies on psychological and emotional distress (e.g., Westin 2007; Constantine, Okazaki, and Utsey 2004; Ying 2002; Zhai 2002; Al-Sharideh and Goe 1998); academic challenges (Jung and McCroskey 2004; Tomich, McWhirter, and Darcy 2003; Ying 2003, 2002; Senyshyn, Warford, and Zhan 2000; Dee and Henkin 1999; Dillion and Swann 1997; Furnham 1997); loneliness and alienation (Trice 2007; Klomegah 2006); prejudice and discrimination (Bonazzo and Wong 2007; Lee 2007; Lee and Rice 2007; Poyrazli and Lopez 2007); and a lack of belonging that translates into feelings of loss, powerlessness, and low self-esteem (Poyrazli and Lopez 2007; Frey and Roysircar 2006). These experiences are seen as common to international students in US colleges and universities. In this section, I outline the issues that I consider to be most significant for African students: social integration, academic integration, psychological adjustments, and financial hardship.

Social Integration

Trying to fit into a new culture, new norms, and new ways of doing things is challenging for any student (Chapdelaine and Alextich 2004); it is particularly challenging for students whose culture is significantly removed from the culture of the host country. Students who come to study in the United States from Africa, Asia, and the Middle East find it much more difficult to assimilate into American culture than do students from Europe and Canada, owing to the greater differences and separation of the cultures (Lee and Rice 2007; Poyrazli and Grahame 2007; Alazzi and Chiodo 2006; Poyrazli and Kavanaugh 2006; Constantine et al. 2005; Poyrazli et al. 2002). Students from Africa often find the cultural gap overwhelming. The transitional process can be challenging and can create barriers to a fulfilling and successful experience.

Whether coming for educational purposes, work, visiting, or to relocate permanently, Africans have been migrating to the United States in greater numbers in recent years (Brettell and DeBerjeois 2004; Gordon 2004; Okoth 2003; Pipher 2002; Arthur 2000). There is very little written about their personal and social integration, but there is evidence that Africans struggle to fit in in an environment with a history of slavery and prejudice against individuals of African descent. The impact of this history continues to affect African students to this day. African students report being perceived as "foreigners" or "outsiders" (Lee and Opio 2011). Many students feel discriminated against because of their race, ethnicity, culture, and continent of origin. The feeling that they do not belong increases their detachment from the host environment and this can cause severe homesickness. Even among athletes, who are often celebrated for their achievement on the field and become celebrities, the feeling of being outsiders is prevalent (Lee and Opio 2011), and it is often still hard for students to make friends. As one student athlete noted:

> Of course it's obvious once you open your mouth and speak, people will tell you are not from here...People will judge either way...you look different, you speak different, you have different features. [I] am not sure if it's a natural reaction from the differences. Sometime you

might feel like you [are] being judged but people will take the easy route out even if they don't understand you or get what you say. They just want to move on I guess (cited in Lee and Opio 2011, 637).

There are many barriers to integration, but one of the major barriers is discrimination. The feeling of being accepted by the host society is important to African students. Being accepted as part of the community by domestic students, faculty, and the broader community within and around the campus or country eases the feeling of being foreign and new. Individuals from Africa come from communities based on extended families that make up villages. Their societies are typically collective and communal, and therefore being accepted as a member of a larger group—in this case the university population—is very important. As one student from Tanzania explains:

This is a very different culture compared to our own culture...We grew up in a very different society, where I know who is my uncle, who is my auntie, who is my niece, who is my everybody...[Back home] we live in extended relations, we participate in everybody's events, they come to our events, and so we have each other's memories. That's the thing I miss in coming to this country (Alberts and Hazen 2004, unpublished raw data).

This lack of "group membership" in the new environment can be isolating, leaving students feeling unwelcome, doubting their status in the group. Lee (2007), Lee and Rice (2007), and Poyrazli and Grahame (2007) report the prevalence of stereotypical assumptions and prejudice directed at international students from Africa and elsewhere because of their foreign roots, race, ethnicity, and skin color. Students perceive a nonsupportive, discriminatory environment when they experience hostile attitudes, cultural intolerance, and an unwelcoming atmosphere, as explained by a Kenyan student in a study examining the cultural adjustment of African students:

It's frustrating to know that people think less of you because of the color of your skin. I belong on this campus just as much as anybody else and I get mad when people treat me like I don't belong here (cited in Constantine et al. 2005, 62).

Students from Africa have even reported discrimination from faculty, evidenced by prejudicial language, and a lack of support and guidance in educational pursuits (Blake 2006). Constantine et al. (2005, 61) quote a student from Nigeria who recounts how a teaching assistant had used a racial slur (the "N" word) to describe her:

> I was so shocked he said this in front of [other students], that I couldn't say anything and just left the session. I ended up dropping the class because I couldn't go back to face the professor and the other students.

Beoku-Betts (2004) reports another case where female African students studying science reported that faculty doubted their abilities as graduate students and some students were forced to take remedial classes without any proof that they needed that kind of support. The author attributes this negative perception of African students to "third world marginality," "a notion that stems from colonial and post-colonial legacies that perceive Africa not quite as progressive as the developed countries" (Beoku-Betts 2004, 124). The perception of being a "third-world student" is something African students in America have to deal with whether they meet academic expectations or not:

> I remember when the grades came out. One professor came up to me and said, "Oh, for a person who comes from the Third World, you've done pretty good." So it was like no matter what, I was always viewed as a Third World person, you know (cited in Beoku-Betts 2004, 124).

Lee (2007) identifies this nonacceptance as neo-racism, a form of racism that centers on discrimination and exclusion of those from low-income countries because of their culture. Lee (2007, 389) notes:

> Neo-racism finds refuge in popular understandings of "human nature" and appeals to "common sense" nationalist instincts, but ultimately gives new energy to principles of exclusion and nationalism. Discrimination becomes, seemingly, justified by cultural difference or national origin rather than by physical characteristics alone and can thus disarm the fight against racism by appealing to "natural" tendencies to preserve group cultural identity—in this case the dominant group.

In higher education, this kind of discrimination manifests itself in, "less than objective academic evaluations, losing or not being able to obtain financial aid, negative remarks from faculty or fellow students, and barriers to forming interpersonal relations in the host society" (Lee 2007, 390).

Discrimination also creates barriers in interpersonal relationships and to acculturation into a host society. Negotiating life in a foreign country where one's presence and cultural background are either not welcome or are questioned can very easily affect foreign students' efforts and performance in the classroom. This can negatively affect academic performance and cause students to doubt their own abilities; consciously or unconsciously, they internalize the negative perceptions about them and this can be detrimental to their self-esteem. In such cases, some students will isolate themselves and will not seek academic guidance, leaving them academic loners. Such students need to be encouraged to interact with other students and with faculty and staff. Students who work collaboratively with others in and outside the classroom have better learning outcomes, and a more successful university experience than students who are less engaged (Kuh 2003).

There is another less talked about discrimination against African students. Black Africans are often "judged under the same false stereotype as African-Americans including images that portray Black males as violent, unintelligent and disrespectful" (Lee and Opio 2011, 631). Using color—black, brown, white—to describe ethnicity or community affiliation or representation of culture is often confusing to African students who come from communities where race is not at the top of the list when it comes to important issues affecting society. The color of one's skin as an identifier of ethnicity, intelligence, personal attributes, or community membership is uncommon in many African societies where tribe membership and nationhood is far more significant than race. For most African students marking a box that identifies them as "foreign" and also as Black, White, Multiracial, or otherwise can be a confusing experience and its effects should not be underestimated. With this categorization, students start feeling perturbed by a prescribed identity that does not truly describe who they are. They feel misrepresented yet have no way of questioning or changing policies that are already in place. These experiences have been shown to undermine academic success, even for the most qualified and celebrated African students (Lee and Opio 2011).

Academic Integration

When international students enroll in foreign institutions of higher learning, they often find themselves in an unfamiliar, competitive, and challenging academic environment. Most have no idea that the educational culture and academic expectations of the host country often differ significantly from what they are used to in their home countries (Bevis 2006; Tatar 2005). In their examination of barriers to adjustment and the needs of international students, researchers have detailed the frustrations with the academic experience that many international students experience: differences in classroom culture, language difficulties in oral and written communication, and sometimes the anxiety of trying to adopt new learning styles (Poyrazli and Grahame 2007; Lacina 2002).

Language barriers are a common challenge for African students. With over 2,000 languages spoken in Africa, most African students are proficient in more than one language, with English frequently a second, third, or even fourth language. Although instruction in most African high schools, especially in Anglo-Africa, is in English, African students still tend to have some difficulties in oral and written English. This is a common occurrence in the acquisition of any foreign language. Interference from native languages can slow organizational structures of sentences and/or meaning of words in the target language. Difficulties with the English language may also be due to differences in accent, pronunciation, slang, and use of specialized English words. All these have a negative effect on oral and written assignments (Zhai 2002), and can cause apprehension in use of the language by students (Jung and McCroskey 2004).

For African students, interference from tribal languages in pronunciation and tone is evident in their "African accents." African students are usually aware that their accents sound foreign, or are made aware of them when people react with surprise when they speak. Some students have reported being discriminated against because of pronunciation, tone, and lexical differences in spoken language. Negative perceptions and prejudice related to language have even been reported as coming from faculty members (Beoku-Betts 2004). This experience of "otherness" in accent can create uneasiness and unwillingness to openly participate in classroom discussions. As one student notes: "When I speak in class, some of the other students laugh at my accent. As a result, I just keep to myself, even though I may have something to say" (cited in Blake 2006). Lack of participation in the classroom is a particular barrier to success in US higher education because of its emphasis on collaborative learning styles and student participation. Perceptions of discrimination because of language can create barriers to collaborative and participatory learning, inhibit social self-efficacy, and cause acculturative stress and even severe psychological problems (Constantine et al. 2005).

Supporting students' efforts in polishing their written and oral English can be a great step toward student success. This can eliminate the self-conscious bias that comes with having a foreign accent. To support students' efforts instructors should avoid calling attention to the accent and try to diversify their methods for student participation, for example by encouraging students to write on the board or through organizing electronic discussions.

The other common academic integration challenge involves pedagogical styles. Students from Africa are used to systems that emphasize reproduction of knowledge for testing purposes. Teachers instruct and prepare students to take national examinations that determine the next step in admissions to upper-level classes, trade schools, colleges, and universities. Teaching to tests creates a culture of rote memorization and verbatim reproduction of knowledge. When students enroll in the US system that is more decentralized in terms of curriculum, policy, and learning outcomes, students have to relearn how to be creative, critical in their writing styles, and original in their presentation of knowledge. Thus, many international students who come to the United States find it challenging to cope with pedagogical approaches and skills that emphasize critical thinking, analyzing, synthesizing, making judgments, questioning, debating, and persuading (Lee 2007; Westin 2007; Robertson, Line, and Thomas 2000). This difference in pedagogical cultures can have particularly severe repercussions in the context of plagiarism. The culture of note taking without critique can lead to a habit of reproducing materials as presented. Students trained in this style of learning are at a risk of forgetting to acknowledge sources when they write, and plagiarism cases are more common among students who come from such academic backgrounds (Chen and Van Ullen 2011). Students may, therefore, need help with understanding appropriate use of academic scholarship, the value of creativity, and respect for intellectual property.

Psychological Adjustment

Trying to adjust, adapt, or assimilate to a new environment is challenging. Students have to adjust to new sociocultural norms, intercultural interactions, educational systems, food, weather patterns, prejudice, discrimination, negative stereotypes about who they are and where they come from, and a lot more. The resulting culture shock can be overwhelming, resulting in psychological stress, and sometimes even mental illness. African students may be especially vulnerable in this respect as there is a cultural bias against sharing their problems with other students or seeking mental health counseling. Moore and Constantine (2005) explain that this may be due to the fact that students from Africa seek support from family and friends more often than they do from people that they have no close relationship with. They also tend to choose forbearance over sharing or asking for help, as one Tanzanian student observes: "People tell you 'go for counseling, go for that,' you know, it is that kind of system. It's a very different society. In our society we have the system of solving our own problems, life's frustrations and such" (Alberts and Hazen 2004, unpublished raw data). This approach is sometimes described as coping collectively, a behavior that is "determined by the context of relationships with significant others and stems from concerns about others' well-being" (Moore and Constantine 2005, 341). In addition, many students worry about causing distress to family members back home, who may be going through challenges of their own.

African students come from countries where health services for psychological stress and other mental health issues are not as well developed as in the West. There is therefore a lack of familiarity with seeking help from mental health professionals. In some African countries, mental illness is viewed with suspicion and fear. It is taboo in some communities to associate with "mad" people, and those who exhibit signs of psychotic behavior or depression may be ostracized by their communities. Instead of viewing mental illness as a health challenge, students from Africa tend to suffer in silence, with potentially severe implications for the well-being of the student.

Academic advisors in US colleges and universities are trained to assist students in understanding when it might be wise to seek help from a counselor, why it is okay to do so, and how treatment is correlated with success. This is why it is so vital to have developmental advising for students on a regular basis—not only to check on their grades and academic plans, but also to talk about their acclimation to the campus.

Financial Hardships

Difficulties are not limited to cultural and academic issues. The issue of finances is particularly important for African students, mainly because of the expectation that students studying abroad will help out with family and community obligations via remittances. Often, families do not understand the financial strain that a foreign student is under in trying to meet the cost of education, food, shelter, and other contingencies in their host country. It is a common belief that once a student is in America, money will no longer be an issue. According to most African cultures, the relative who has more is expected to share with others in the family—an expectation that can create incredible pressures. To meet family expectations, some students have had to drop out of school and find work outside campus. Working outside campus without legal authorization can turn into an immigration minefield and even result in deportation. It would be helpful if recruiters were more candid about the strain of financial obligations, particularly for students enrolling without an established source of financial support, to make students aware that coming to America with limited funding often leads to serious problems.

Meeting the Challenges

Supporting African students in the United States requires an understanding of cultural differences between African students and their US counterparts, and an appreciation of cultural diversity among African students themselves. Several recommendations could help to support African students, so that they can have a rewarding, less stressful, and more satisfying experience on US campuses.

Making students aware of the challenges they may face could go a long way toward easing acculturation challenges. Providing tailored orientation programs would be a significant step in this regard. Orientation programs should be tailored to African students and presented by staff who are familiar with African cultures as well as socioeconomic and political trends. African students tend to open up to people who display an understanding of and respect for their cultures and their continent instead of making judgments and questioning their experiences. The programs should focus on issues that range from seemingly easy topics such as where to get hair done for women or how to open a bank account and write checks, to more complicated issues of how students can gradually learn to appreciate US culture without abandoning their own culture.

Creating opportunities for making friends and establishing social networks could also prove a significant benefit for many African students. International affairs offices, campus activities offices, and faculty and student leaders should encourage social interaction between international students and their American counterparts. It would be helpful to have other African students already on campus welcome incoming students during orientation and subsequent months, in order to help new students to establish a broader network of social support. Starting with students with whom they share cultural similarities, and then broadening their circle to include domestic and other international students would provide a promising approach for those newly arrived. Many students also appreciate being put in touch with students from their respective home countries who are already in the United States so that they have somebody they can communicate with prior to arriving on campus. Once they arrive on campus, the friendship can be a firm starting point for the incoming student.

Providing networking opportunities may also help ease feelings of isolation. A strong sense of social support through community engagement with other African immigrants is an often untapped resource for African students. Africans are typically very community oriented and tend to gravitate toward other Africans, irrespective of country of origin. Staff and other students could arrange meeting opportunities to facilitate these interactions. This can be a step toward establishing community and family away from home—a very important aspect of African culture.

Racial discrimination remains a challenging topic; it should not be tolerated on university campuses and students should not be encouraged to "tough it out" or "persevere." Instead, international students should be encouraged to share challenges or negative experiences with advisors, counselors, or other staff. Professional development seminars for faculty and staff on how to interact with and support students from Africa would be helpful. There should also be educational forums and open dialog on assumptions and stereotypes about Africa. Dismantling stereotypes through meaningful interactions could alleviate psychological distress for students. Allowing African students to share about themselves and their culture can also boost their self-esteem and give them a voice to define themselves instead of being defined by others.

Support for enhancing language skills in English is a great way of integrating students academically. Although some African students feel that they are proficient in English, speech classes that allow them to interact with domestic students would enhance their understanding of nuances and other forms of speech used in the host environment. Understanding the host language in context can boost students' confidence and allow for better academic integration both inside and outside the classroom.

Finally, due to the financial difficulties experienced by many African students, universities should establish more scholarship opportunities for students from Africa. Funders need to recognize that students from Africa are often expected to send remittances to assist immediate and extended family, putting additional financial pressures on African students beyond those faced by most students.

Conclusion

The United States continues to be the preferred destination for students who want to study abroad. Opportunities for a quality education that could lead to well-paid jobs in their home countries continue to attract students to America. African students are no exception, and come to the United States with high expectations of standard of living and educational opportunities. However, many students are unprepared for the serious adjustment problems that they face once they arrive. Social, academic, and personal issues can create unpleasant experiences that both inhibit learning and slow adjustment to the host society. While African students share many problems with international students from other countries, the large gap between their native cultures and US culture, as well as the prejudice and discrimination they may encounter in the United States, make adjustment particularly challenging for them. In order to help African students, university administrators and faculty must endeavor to understand the specific social and academic needs of African students and develop programs that are tailored toward their specific needs.

Orientation programs should take African students' cultural backgrounds into consideration and offer targeted advice to address the issues that are particularly difficult for these students. Furthermore, there should be ongoing programs, at least throughout the first year of enrollment, to address adjustment issues that arise and provide continuing support. Since many African students do not have a lot of funds available—and indeed are often expected to send remittances home—offering more scholarships would provide relief from financial pressures that interfere with academic success. Finally, there should be an effort by universities and US educational centers in Africa to provide more comprehensive information about the realities of studying in the United States. It is often not mentioned that studying in the United States requires a lot of hard work amid significant social, academic, and personal adjustment issues. If students arrive in the United States with more realistic expectations and receive more targeted support once they arrive, the United States could truly become the land of opportunity for them.

Works Cited

Alazzi, K., and J. Chiodo. 2006. "Uncovering Problems and Identifying Coping Strategies of Middle Eastern University Students." *International Education* 35(2): 65–81.

Alberts, H., and H. Hazen. 2004. [Tanzanian Focus Group Transcript.] Unpublished raw data.

Al-Sharideh, K., and W. Goe. 1998. "Ethnic Communities within the University: An Examination of Factors Influencing the Personal Adjustment of International Students." *Research in Higher Education* 39(6): 699–725.

Arthur, J. 2000. "Invisible Sojourners: African Immigrant Diaspora in the United States." Westport, CT: Praeger Publishers.

Beoku-Betts, J. 2004. "African Women Pursuing Graduate Studies in the Sciences: Racism, Gender Bias, and Third World Marginality." *NWSA Journal* 16(1): 116–35.

Bevis, T. 2006. "International Students." In *Understanding College Students Sub-Populations: A Guide for Students Affairs Professional*, edited by L. Gohn and G. Albin, 267–93. NASPA: Student Affairs Administrators in Higher Education.

Blake, A. 2006. "The Experiences and Adjustment Problems of Africans at a Historically Black Institution." *College Student Journal* 40(4): 808–13.

Bonazzo, C., and Y. Wong. 2007. "Japanese International Female Students' Experience of Discrimination, Prejudice, and Stereotypes." *College Student Journal* 41(3): 631–9.

Brettell, C., and P. deBerjeois. 2004. "Anthropology and the Study of Immigrant Women." In *Migration, Globalization, and Ethnic Relations: An Interdisciplinary Approach*, edited by M. Mobasher, and M. Sadri, 323–38. New Jersey: Pearson, Prentice Hall.

Brown, L. 2008. "The Incidence of Study-Related Stress in International Students in the Initial Stage of the International Sojourn." *Journal of Studies in International Education* 12(1): 5–27.

Chapdelaine, R., and L. Alexitch. 2004. "Social Skills Difficulty: Model of Culture Shock for International Graduate Students." *Journal of College Student Development* 45(2): 167–84.

Chen, Y., and M. Van Ullen. 2011. "Helping International Students Succeed Academically through Research Process and Plagiarism Workshops." *College and Research Libraries* 72(3): 209–35.

Chow, P. 2011. "What International Students Think about U.S. Higher Education: Attitudes and Perceptions of Prospective Students in Africa, Asia, Europe and Latin America." New York: Institute of International Education. Available at: http://www.iie.org/en/Research-and-Publications/Publications-and-Reports/IIE-Bookstore. Accessed: February 23, 2012.

Constantine, M., G. Anderson, L. Berkel, L. Caldwell, and S. Utsey. 2005. "Examining the Cultural Adjustment Experiences of African

International College Students: A Qualitative Analysis." *Journal of Counseling Psychology* 52(1): 57–66.

Constantine, M., S. Okazaki, and S. Utsey. 2004. "Self-Concealment, Social Self-Efficacy, Acculturative Stress, and Depression in African, Asian, and Latin American International College Students." *The American Journal of Orthopsychiatry* 74(3): 230–41.

Dee, R., and A. Henkin. 1999. "Challenges to Adjustment to College Life in the United States: Experiences of Korean Students." *International Education* 29(1): 54–70.

Dillion, R., and J. Swann. 1997. "Studying in America: Assessing How Uncertainty Reduction and Communication Satisfaction Influence International Students' Adjustment to U.S. Campus Life." Paper presented at the Annual Meeting of the National Communication Association, Chicago, November 19–23.

Frey, L., and G. Roysircar. 2006. "South Asian and East Asian International Students' Perceived Prejudice, Acculturation, and Frequency of Help Resource Utilization." *Journal of Multicultural Counseling and Development* 34(4): 208–22.

Furnham, A. 1997. "The Experience of Being an Overseas Student." In *Overseas Students in Higher Education: Issues in Teaching and Learning*, edited by D. McNamara, and R. Harris, 13–29. New York: Routledge.

Gordon, A. 2004. "The New Diaspora: African Immigrants to the United States." In *Migration, Globalization, and Ethnic Relations: An Interdisciplinary Approach*, edited by M. Mobasher, and M. Sadri. New Jersey: Pearson, Prentice Hall

Institute of International Education. 2012. "International Students in the U.S." Available at: http://www.iie.org/Research-and-Publications/Open-Doors. Accessed: May 22, 2012.

———. 2008. "International Students' Enrollment in U.S. Rebounds." Available at: http://opendoors.iienetwork.org/?p=113743. Accessed: February 14, 2008.

Irungu, J. 2011. *Engaging College Students for Success: International Students in U.S. Higher Education Institutions*. Saarbrücken: LAP-Lambert Academic Publishing.

Jung, H., and J. McCroskey. 2004. "Communication Apprehension in a First Language and Self-Perceived Competence as Predictors of Communication Apprehension in a Second Language: A Study of Speakers of English as a Second Language." *Communications Quarterly* 52(2): 170–81.

Klomegah, R. 2006. "Social Factors Relating to Alienation Experienced by International Students in the United States." *College Student Journal* 40(2): 303–15.

Kuh, G. 2003. "What We're Learning about Student Engagement from NSSE: Benchmarks for Effective Educational Practices." *Change* 35(2): 24–32.

Lacina, J. 2002. "Preparing International Students for a Successful Social Experience in Higher Education." In *Internationalizing Higher Education:*

Building Vital Programs on Campuses: New Direction for Higher Education, edited by B. Speck, and B. Carmical, 117. San Francisco, CA: Jossey-Bass.
Lee, J. 2007. "Neo-Racism towards International Students: A Critical Need for Change." *About Campus* 11(6): 28–30.
Lee, J., and C. Rice. 2007. "Welcome to America? International Student Perceptions of Discrimination." *Higher Education* 53(3): 381–409.
Lee, J., and T. Opio. 2011. "Coming to America: Challenges and Difficulties Faced by African Student Athletes." *Sport, Education and Society* 16(5): 629–44.
Moore, J., and M. Constantine. 2005. "Development and Initial Validation of the Collectivistic Coping Styles Measure with African, Asian, and Latin American International Students." *Journal of Mental Health Counseling* 27(4): 329–47.
Okoth, K. 2003. "Kenya: What Role for Diaspora Development?" Migration Information Source. Available at: http://www.migrationinformation.org/feature/display.cfm?ID=150. Accessed: April 22, 2012.
Poyrazli, S., C. Arbona, A. Nora, R. McPherson, and S. Pisecco. 2002. "Relation between Assertiveness, Academic Self-Efficacy, and Psychosocial Adjustment among International Graduate Students." *Journal of College Student Development* 4(5): 632–42.
Poyrazli, S., and K. Grahame. 2007. "Barriers to Adjustment: Needs of International Students within a Semi-Urban Campus Community." *Journal of Instructional Psychology* 34(1): 28–45.
Poyrazli, S., and M. Lopez. 2007. "An Exploratory Study of Perceived Discrimination and Homesickness: A Comparison of International Students and American Students." *The Journal of Psychology* 141(3): 263–80.
Poyrazli, S., and P. Kavanaugh. 2006. "Marital Status, Ethnicity, Academic Achievement and Adjustment Strains: The Case of Graduate International Students." *College Student Journal* 40(4): 767–80.
Pipher, M. 2002. *The Middle of Everywhere: The World's Refugees Come to Our Town*. Orlando, FL: Harcourt Inc.
Robertson, M., S. Line, and J. Thomas. 2000. "International Students, Learning Environment and Perceptions: A Case Study Using the Delphi Technique." *Higher Education Research and Development* 19(1): 89–102.
Senyshyn, R., M. Warford, and J. Zhan. 2000. "Issues of Adjustment to Higher Education: International Students' Perspectives." *International Education* 30(1): 17–35.
Tatar, S. 2005. "Classroom Participation by International Students: The Case of Turkish Graduate Students." *Journal of Studies in International Education* 9(4): 337–55.
Tomich, P., J. McWhirter, and M. Darcy. 2003. "The Personality and International Students' Adaptation Experience." *International Education* 33(1): 22–39.
Trice, A. 2007. "Faculty Perspectives Regarding Graduate International Students' Isolation from Host National Students." *International Education Journal* 8(1): 108–17.

Westin, D. 2007. "Social Support during the Academic Transition of International Students in Ph.D. Programs." Unpublished Doctoral Dissertation. Virginia: Virginia Commonwealth University.

Wilton, L., and M. Constantine. 2003. "Length of Residence, Cultural Adjustment Difficulties, and Psychological Distress Symptoms in Asian and Latin American International College Students." *Journal of College Counseling* 6(2): 177–87.

Ying, Y. 2003. "Academic Achievement and Quality of Overseas Study among Taiwanese Students in the United States." *College Student Journal* 37(3): 470–80.

Ying, Y. 2002. "Formation of Cross-Cultural Relationships of Taiwanese International Students in the United States." *Journal of Community Psychology* 30(1): 45–55.

Zhai, L. 2002. "Studying International Students: Adjustment and Social Support." Office of Institutional Research, San Diego Community College District. [ERIC Document no. ED 474481].

10

Supporting and Mentoring International Faculty:

Issues and Strategies

Ken Foote

This chapter focuses on strategies for supporting and mentoring foreign-born scholars and scientists pursuing careers in US colleges and universities. Foreign-born or international scholars account for an increasing proportion of the US professoriate, but little has been written about their experiences, the cultural and legal challenges they are confronted with, the advantages they offer, and the policy and institutional changes that might be implemented to support them (Germain-Rutherford and Kerr 2009; Theobald 2009; Alberts 2008; Collins 2008; Manrique and Manrique 1999). Some challenges are difficult to surmount, but others can be addressed quite readily given adequate awareness of the issues involved.

US faculty and administrators are the audience I have in mind for this chapter, for two reasons. First, among the many challenges international faculty face, many involve negotiating new—or at least different—roles and responsibilities with US colleagues in US institutions. Unquestioned assumptions about research and teaching responsibilities, advising, service and "how things get done" can create hidden barriers and preconceptions that can sometimes block or undermine communication. Second, research indicates that support offered to international faculty by their US peers and administrators can go a long way to helping international faculty adjust and thrive in US institutions. As Theobald (2007, iii) notes in her study of foreign-born early-career faculty, "The department chair is identified as a highly influential factor affecting an early-career faculty member's progress, as chairs are responsible not only for encouraging faculty development, but also for setting the tenor and tone of department culture." Peers and other administrators can also be the source of help if they are aware of some of the issues addressed in this chapter and this book.

My own interest in improving support for international faculty began well over a decade ago. Since 2002, I have organized workshops for early-career geography instructors as part of the Geography Faculty Development Alliance (GFDA) and Enhancing Departments and Graduate Education in Geography (EDGE) projects (EDGE 2012; GFDA 2012; Foote 2010; Foote and Solem 2009; Solem and Foote 2009). These workshops were designed to address a number of the most stressful issues faced by faculty in the first few years of their careers, such as time management, course planning, and publishing. Research has shown that help with these topics can reduce stress and increase productivity among early-career faculty and help them succeed professionally (Solem, Foote, and Monk 2009; Boice 2000, 1992; Menges 1999; Fink 1984).

As soon as I had begun these workshops I noticed that the international faculty participating in these workshops sometimes reported different experiences from their domestic counterparts (Solem and Foote 2004). These differences revolved around their legal and citizenship status, how curricula and courses are organized in US universities, who is in charge and how decisions are made within their institution, and challenges of sustaining personal and family lives far away from their home countries and communities. During focus group discussions held at the workshops, it was not unusual for international faculty to express a sense of isolation. They felt they had to face a wide range of challenging career issues related to their difference, without getting much help and support from colleagues or their institutions. Yet, at the same time, many international faculty recognized that their status also offered benefits. In particular, they saw their international experiences and perspectives as a resource in their teaching, research, and service. As I discuss these points below, I include quotations from early-career geographers who agreed to be interviewed in focus groups during GFDA workshops held between 2005 and 2007.

When I began to research these issues with colleagues, we found that very little attention focused on international faculty in US colleges and universities (Foote et al. 2008). Some research, especially in the area of educational policy, has concentrated on international students who come to the United States for undergraduate and graduate degrees. But if these students stay and enter the professoriate, attention seems to fade. As we noted, "Little is known about the experiences of foreign-born academics in the US. They are a hidden minority on many US campuses and few statistics are compiled about their needs, accomplishments, or problems" (Foote et al. 2008, 167).

The Importance of Better Support

The invisibility of these issues is surprising given the increasing numbers of international faculty members in American colleges and universities in recent years and the role they may play in US higher education in coming decades. A National Science Foundation (2000) report a decade ago found that approximately 20 percent of US science and engineering faculty were foreign-born and that this proportion was growing. Some disciplines, like geography, already have higher proportions. According to data from 2005, approximately 32 percent of geography faculty in the United States are foreign-born (Association of American Geographers 2006). So, perhaps the most important reason for supporting international faculty is that they will be vital to sustaining and improving the quality of American higher education in coming decades as the demographics of higher education change to reflect its growing globalization. If foreign-born faculty lack the support they need to succeed they may become marginalized and leave the professoriate. This would be a tremendous loss of intellectual and scientific talent at a time when the globalization of higher education is making competition for high-quality faculty ever keener.

Debate about maintaining the quality and competitiveness of the academic workforce is one of the few areas in which issues of better support for international faculty are being raised (Richardson, McBey, and McKenna 2006). This is especially in the context of whether US institutions have the vision needed to maintain or advance their positions in the changing landscape of world universities, in which the global competition for academic "knowledge workers" seems to be increasing (Dillon 2004). Unless US universities are able to do more to support international faculty, they may find their choices limited in searching for the best job candidates, particularly since changing immigration and security procedures since the 9/11 terrorist attacks have made it more difficult to recruit students and faculty internationally.

Another reason to pay closer attention to the needs of international faculty is that current migration patterns are different from those of the past. The United States benefited tremendously from a large number of scientists and scholars who fled Europe before and during World War II as a result of the Holocaust and political repression (Fleming and Bailyn 1969). In the 1960s and 1970s, the growth of academic opportunities in the United States attracted another wave of scientists, especially from Britain and its Commonwealth. The migration that is going on today is not only larger in scope, but also more varied. The earlier waves of academic migrants, apart from nationality, were relatively homogenous in terms of gender and in respect to their educational, social, and cultural backgrounds. Today's migrants come from all over the world, from far different educational systems and traditions, and include more women than in the past. Simply relying on the status quo and assuming that these migrants will manage as well as previous waves may not be enough to convince them to stay in the United States. Different responses and more concerted efforts at the disciplinary or institutional levels may be needed to address the needs of international faculty; in this respect, professional development opportunities and support tailored to the needs of particular groups are critical.

Finally, international faculty can help to support efforts by many US colleges and universities to increase diversity and cultivate multiculturalism among their faculty and students. These efforts have picked up momentum in recent years for a variety of reasons, and the experiences, perspectives, and contacts international faculty bring to their institutions can be great assets (Moody 2004; Robison 2003). This is equally true of efforts to increase international experiences for college students through study abroad and exchange programs since international faculty can be instrumental in developing and expanding these programs.

Apart from these issues, international faculty have received little research attention, though there have been a few studies. These have mostly focused on: (1) ethnographic and case studies of the experiences of these faculty; or (2) statistical summaries of international faculty in different universities and disciplines. The case studies touch on issues of cross-cultural transition, workplace discrimination, and ways in which these new faculty offer shifting perspectives on established fields of knowledge (Chapman and Pyvis 2006; Collins 2006; Richardson, McBey and McKenna 2006; Subedi 2006; Cooper and Stevens 2002; Pulido 2002; Vargas 2002; García 2000; Bystydzienski and Resnik 1994; Solomon 1985). These studies highlight issues similar to those faced by minorities and women in academic appointments. Additional research has focused on disparities in the ways international faculty are treated by colleagues and institutions and some of the anxieties these faculty sometimes face in relation to language, cultural values, political beliefs, educational expectations, and legal status (Germain-Rutherford and Kerr 2009; Scheyvens, Wild, and Overton 2003; Abel 2002; Lim and Herrera-Sobek 2000; National Association of State Universities and Land Grant Colleges 2000); these concerns mirror issues identified in other research on the international migration of nonacademic professionals (Iredale 2001; Meyer 2001; Mills 1994; Tichenor 1994).

Key Issues in Providing Better Support

Given the diversity of scholars coming to the United States, it is hard to make sweeping recommendations to "do this" or "do that." The issues I outline below crosscut and intersect individual lives and careers at all sorts of angles depending on age, place of residence, gender, institution type, sexuality, nation of origin, length of time in the United States, and many other factors. Nonetheless, I have tried to outline some of the major topics and ranked them tentatively in terms of importance.

Visas, Immigration, and Related Paperwork

Visas and the paperwork required for immigration are certainly among the most important issues affecting international faculty when they first take positions in the United States. More than a minor inconvenience, visa and citizenship issues can consume time and money and leave faculty in limbo with respect to their citizenship and travel options for extended periods of time. US immigration laws offer two primary ways for hiring faculty, either as priority workers "able to demonstrate extraordinary ability in the sciences, arts, education, business, or athletics through sustained national or international acclaim," or as "outstanding professors and researchers" who are better qualified than any US citizens or permanent resident for a particular position (USCIS 2012). The documentation the US Citizenship and Immigration Service (USCIS) requires to meet these prerequisites can be extensive; furthermore, under US law, there is a limit set on the number of permanent visas that can be issued each year. These limits can create long delays for many migrants.

Given the importance of these issues, it is striking how much variation exists in helping international faculty with their visas and citizenship petitions. Some universities have staff that help faculty through the whole process and cover all or part of the costs. Others offer no support and expect the faculty themselves to shoulder the cost and responsibility. One GFDA participant recounted: "My university told me that they didn't want to give us advice because they were sued in the past." Many universities fall somewhere in between, offering some advice and funds (such as a portion of the "start-up" funds some faculty receive when they are first hired).

This haphazard approach is particularly disadvantageous for early-career faculty. It places a considerable burden on their time during a period when they are supposed to be getting a good start in research and teaching. As one interviewee said, "It's such a challenge, you have to do everything yourself and to read all those documents when you're supposed to be starting a new job." Furthermore, international faculty cannot apply for some types of research funds until they are permanent residents or citizens and, for early-career faculty who need to travel internationally for conferences and field research, there can be restrictions on travel during the waiting periods when paperwork is being processed for visas and change of citizenship status. As one interviewee engaged in considerable international research noted:

> If I go for a conference in Europe I have to apply for a new visa. Normally the visa application process itself is a week, so this means that after this conference I have to stay in this location for another week to get an interview at the embassy where they would decide whether to give me the visa or not. I'm going to go to Ghana in about two weeks and I told my head of department that I can't guarantee that if I go to the embassy in Ghana I'll get the visa I need to return next semester.

Other participants were critical of the USCIS itself. As one participant noted, "It's the worst, the most incompetent bureaucracy in this country, it's absolutely amazing the process that I went through and then how they bungled everything just about every week."

Making funds available in start-up packages to help new hires move through the immigration process is useful but it can still disadvantage international faculty. Sometimes departments try to be scrupulously fair in allocating available funds among all faculty, irrespective of domestic or international status. But if international faculty need to use funds for visas and domestic faculty can use theirs for advancing their research and teaching, inequities can result.

I raise these issues because it is important for department leaders and US colleagues to understand how the visa and immigration process can affect international faculty. This does not mean that department chairs need to keep up with immigration law and ever-changing US policy, but it does mean knowing enough to be able to: (1) point international faculty to knowledgeable staff, advisors, or lawyers who can help; and (2) understand how visa and citizenship issues can potentially affect the work of international faculty, particularly during the early-career period.

It is also important to note that dealing with the USCIS, as well as other agencies within the Department of Homeland Security, does not necessarily end for international faculty when they have a visa, permanent residency, or citizenship. Two factors are significant. First, visa restrictions and limitations can create barriers to sustaining personal, family, and professional relationships abroad since any visitor must negotiate US border security—a sometimes frustrating and uncertain process. In some cases, it can even affect immediate family when spouses, partners, parents, or children have different visa and citizenship status. One geographer interviewed during a GFDA workshop focused on these problems:

> I am here on an H1-B visa, which means that my spouse, no matter how qualified, is a dependent and cannot work and that's all. So basically she can sit at home and watch TV. So my spouse decided to stay in Canada because it didn't make sense for her to come and watch TV in a small town where there's not much to do anyway. But that's not the end of the story. My daughter is Canadian so she gets medical services for free, whereas here even with insurance you have to pay...It just does not make financial sense.

Second, travel across borders, even for short visits such as for professional meetings, can still be slow and unpredictable, even when international faculty have residency, citizenship, or necessary visas (Jacobson 2003; Castles and Davidson 2000).

In the Classroom and Working with Students

Visa and immigration issues are at the top of the list of concerns for international faculty, but many other issues revolve around teaching and working with students. Recent public attention has focused on language issues and the perception that some non-US faculty and graduate students are difficult to understand in the classroom because of their poor command of or accented English (Gravois 2005; see also chapter 11 of this book). However, there are many other issues that receive far less attention but are of perhaps equal importance in helping international faculty succeed in American higher education. These include, among others, how courses and degree plans are organized, the types and levels of interaction encouraged in the classroom, expectations regarding workload and grading, and assumptions regarding advising and interaction outside the classroom (Alberts 2008). These issues are not always well addressed for faculty moving into a new job, whether domestic or international, but for non-US faculty these issues can lead to miscommunication and misunderstandings. As one GFDA participant reflected, "I still probably came in with some of the assumption that undergraduate teaching should be done the way I experienced it, even though I probably knew that this was not quite right."

Explicit discussion of these issues can help all faculty, but particularly international faculty. This is especially true because assumptions made about experience, background, and ability can work differently for scholars from different parts of the world. For example, faculty arriving from Europe and the British Commonwealth are sometimes perceived (or rather stereotyped) as better educated than geographers coming from other regions, perhaps because US academics tend to know less about the educational systems and universities in Africa, Asia, and South America and rate their quality less highly.

Stereotypes and preconceptions can cut both ways in the classroom. On the negative side, students may make assumptions about the training, competency, and experience of a faculty member based upon nation of origin. One of the most difficult issues is that foreign-born faculty, women, and faculty of color tend to experience far more classroom incivilities than do their domestic counterparts. That is, their authority is challenged or questioned more often than that of professors fitting the White, male, middle-class stereotypes of a university professor (Alberts, Hazen, and Theobald 2010; Chesler and Young 2007; Mahtani 2004; Vargas 2002; Boice 2000, 1996). Sometimes these incivilities have racist or sexist dimensions, but often the biases are more subtle. In the world of today's higher education, overtly racist views that would meet immediate censure are now instead expressed in neo-racist terms—attributing the qualities to a person's nation of origin rather than "race," or objecting to a person's accent rather than their skin color (Lee and Rice 2007). These assumptions may be expressed in other ways as well; for instance, students expecting international faculty to portray life and opinions in their home country in ways that are prejudiced or biased. Sometimes, other issues arise, for example, students reacting negatively to internationals voicing positions perceived to be even slightly critical of the United States. As one GFDA participant—originally from Malaysia—noted:

> You know I haven't found a comfortable way of speaking about American-type things yet, so yeah, I haven't figured it out yet. So I'm always skirting around the Vietnam War and Japan and Hiroshima and all that kind of stuff, even though I'm not Japanese or Chinese.

Another GFDA participant, from Africa and a Muslim, made the point that:

> In my world regional class I don't teach the Middle East...I have an American colleague who teaches the Middle East and...says "I hate what America is doing." The students are OK with his opinion because he's an American. If I did that in my class I don't think they would take it lightly. Because of that I think there is that difference. If you are an American then you can actually voice your opinion and people will be more willing and accepting. But, as a foreigner, if you voice those same concerns I don't think everybody will really accept that and accept it lightly.

But, as this participant notes, "Aside from addressing certain controversial or political issues, I think everything is fine."

This point suggests that only particular issues are sources of friction or even, on the positive side, that international faculty can offer different viewpoints to students. As Alberts (2008) points out, foreignness can be viewed as a teaching resource and as a means of offering contrasting perspectives and information. This is of particular value to geography, a discipline where expanding student awareness and comprehension of national, international, and global issues is often of paramount concern. As one interviewee stated: "I think it is generally true that they value the different cultural perspective as illuminating."

Working with Colleagues Inside and Outside the Department

Issues outside the classroom can also lead to misunderstandings. These include how budgets and schedules are set; how decisions are made, by whom, and by which committees; performance expectations regarding research and service; and general assumptions about how a particular department, college, or university operates. These procedures and expectations vary greatly by institution type, both nationally and internationally. My point is that, because of this great variability, there is perhaps a need to be more explicit in addressing these issues. The assumption that new faculty, whether domestic or international, will become familiar with these procedures and expectations on their own may be too optimistic. I am not suggesting packing all of these topics into some sort of orientation course for international faculty because I think such an approach would be counterproductive. These topics cannot be addressed all at once when a faculty member first arrives on campus, nor can they be addressed through a one-size-fits-all program. I would argue instead for a more nuanced approach, one that considers (without making assumptions) the background of international faculty and addresses relevant issues in dialog with chairs, colleagues, mentors, and administrators.

The attitudes of colleagues toward international faculty are also important to consider. These attitudes can be influenced by the same preconceptions and misperceptions as are held by students. In some cases, these attitudes may be expressed in assumptions that internationals will be most interested in particular fields of research, instruction, or service. For instance, one GFDA participant from Asia, but with research interests far removed from regional geography, recounted that:

> My first teaching assignment was teaching the geography of Asia. I think I have a department chair who just assumed, "Well you are from Asia so you can teach geography of Asia." There was a guy in my department who was from Zimbabwe, well, actually he was British but he had lived in Zimbabwe and had a passport from Zimbabwe, so he was assigned to teach the geography of Africa.

In addition to expecting international faculty to teach about their home nations or regions, there can also be an assumption that they should serve on committees where international perspectives are valued, even if these extra service requests are unwanted or become a burden.

In other cases, constant but subtle reminders of a faculty member's difference can undermine a sense of community. I am reminded of one friend—now a longtime US citizen—telling me how almost every time she made a comment in a faculty meeting, someone would almost immediately chime in, "So I guess that's the British perspective," even though the joke had long-since worn thin. Other friends have mentioned how frustrating it is for them that their colleagues will not make the effort to learn how to pronounce their names correctly, or even joke about how they cannot or will not use the correct pronunciation. These may be small slights but, taken together, they are serious, persistent problems that can undercut bonds of collegiality. But disparaging attitudes toward colleagues and their accomplishments can also affect pay, merit, promotion, and tenure if, for example, international faculty do not get credit for books and articles that are not published in English.

Professional Practice and Disciplinary Contexts

There is a range of topics related to professional practice that go beyond the context of particular departments and universities. One of the most important is differential access to funding and research opportunities. As already noted, international faculty may be ineligible for some funding opportunities reserved for US citizens and permanent residents. Also, travel for research and meetings may be impossible or complicated during some stages of the immigration process due to paperwork and travel restrictions. But disciplinary practice also involves being aware of relatively small, though important, factors such as which meetings to attend, how to get involved in a new professional association, and how to engage in effective networking in a new setting.

Relatively small issues for domestic academics can loom large for their international counterparts. Among these is the job search. In the first place, it can be difficult for international faculty to understand differences among institutions of higher education within the United States in terms of their mission and quality. Second, it can be equally difficult to judge desirability of local and regional living environments. Finally, interviews—though stressful for all candidates—pose additional challenges for international faculty. The unstructured and somewhat unpredictable way interviews are arranged in US universities means that language problems, problems understanding context, and even understanding when someone is joking can present significant barriers. Furthermore, international faculty may encounter prejudices and stereotypes during interview, lack strategies for "selling" themselves in the United States, not know what information should and should not be listed in their CVs, and not realize that in the United States certain questions and topics cannot be raised during interviews.

Making the Implicit Explicit: Exposing the Hidden Curriculum of Higher Education

Many if not most of the issues outlined in this section revolve around *implicit* knowledge and skills needed to succeed in an academic career. These topics are not always covered explicitly in graduate curricula or professional life. The assumption seems to be that if graduate students and faculty cannot figure out these issues on their own, then they are probably not well suited for a career in higher education. As Lovitts (2007, 2001) and Margolis (2001) have argued, the implicit knowledge needed for advancement might be seen as a hidden curriculum comprising the unwritten norms, lore, and values essential to surviving and thriving in academia. There is nothing necessarily wrong with expecting people to master a hidden curriculum, but inequities arise if access to this knowledge is privileged by reason of international or domestic status, just as it often is by gender, sexuality, age, family status, race, ethnicity, and other factors.

I would argue that making explicit the implicit norms of academic life is one of the key ways of supporting international faculty. Exposing this hidden curriculum underlies many, if not all, of the topics discussed above in this section. But I would also argue that exposing this hidden curriculum to greater openness is good for all academics, international or domestic. It levels the academic playing field so that qualified, talented individuals can contribute to higher education without being excluded by arbitrary characteristics such as nationality.

Beyond Work and into the Community

A host of challenges face international faculty beyond their work and professional lives. Living in the United States also involves sharing that life with spouses, partners, children, and extended families, as well as often maintaining connections to friends, family, and colleagues in the home country. International faculty I have worked with as colleagues and as participants in workshops I have led often reported a sense of culture shock when getting started in the United States. One GFDA participant related that:

> My first semester was kind of a culture shock. In Asia students are quiet, we don't eat, drink or read newspapers in class; we are all quiet and sit up straight and take notes and we're all good and respectful and everything. So it's really different seeing American students eating

and drinking in class with legs on the table. To me, this is disorder, chaos and all that, so a little bit of a culture shock.

Others report a tremendous sense of loneliness and isolation as they get started on their careers (Collins 2008), particularly before they have time to build professional and personal support networks. Beyond this it is nearly impossible to list the possible effects of professional decisions on spouses, partners, and families. There are the issues of searching and finding work for a partner or spouse, finding suitable schools for children, and dealing with all the place-making issues that allow people to establish lives in a new setting—all of which vary considerably depending on a person's experiences and background.

Another issue is the sometimes greater efforts needed to maintain contacts and connections with distant family and friends outside of the United States. The more subtle point is that many international faculty develop transnational and hybridized identities that involve cultivating and sustaining multiple professional and personal identities. How much do they want to become "American" and how much do they wish to sustain a different identity? For example, many migrants from China as well as other parts of Asia are encouraged to pick and use an English nickname because Americans are so little concerned with pronouncing their real names correctly. So in this situation international faculty are immediately faced with choosing the degree to which they wish to assimilate into the dominant culture and the degree to which they wish to sustain their previous identity.

Given the complexity of these issues and the diversity of international faculty I do not think it is possible to offer clear guidelines for mentoring and supporting international faculty. Instead, the key points are to be aware of the issues, to offer support as necessary, and to help find solutions as challenges and opportunities arise.

Conclusion

The issues I have listed cannot be addressed all at once, but they do provide some guidance and direction for improving support for international faculty. Perhaps the biggest struggle is convincing colleagues and administrators that these are serious issues that both impede the careers of international faculty and work to the detriment of their own colleges and universities. Too often, when I raise these issues, I hear the refrain, "But I treat all the faculty equally, they all have access to exactly the same resources, support and funds"; "I don't want to seem like I'm playing favorites"; or "If these faculty can't succeed on their own in academia, then they should probably look elsewhere." My point is that treating all faculty "equally" in terms of access to basic resources and professional support may not be fair in the sense of giving each faculty member the same opportunities for promotion and advancement. As I mentioned earlier, some universities offer financial and legal help in applying for visa and citizenship, and some expect faculty to use their "start-up" funds. Sometimes the choice is between using the moneys for visas and citizenship or for research; sometimes there is no support at all. This is "equal" in a very strict sense, but it is not fair to international faculty, who end up having to make hard choices.

In this chapter I have only scratched the surface of these issues. More research is needed to study these topics in greater detail. We need a clearer idea of exactly how the experiences of international faculty compare and contrast with domestic faculty, how the experiences of international faculty in the United States differ from international faculty living in other countries, and how the experiences of international faculty differ from those of other highly skilled immigrants. Other issues highlighted for further investigation by Foote et al. (2008, 174–5) include:

1. What are the full range of professional opportunities and difficulties international faculty face in their academic work—especially in teaching and service—due to differences of language, cultural values, political beliefs, educational expectations, and other factors?
2. What social, disciplinary, departmental, and institutional policies, programs, and support systems do foreign-born academics find most useful?
3. To what extent and in what ways do foreign-born faculty members develop hybridized identities? In developing hybridized identities, how do they maintain professional contact with their home country and with family and friends overseas, and what challenges do they face in adjusting to living in American communities?
4. What role do place and context (e.g., type of institution, departmental culture, community in which institution is situated) play in the experience of foreign-born faculty?
5. How do foreign-born faculty view their role in the American higher-education system in general, on their campuses, and in their communities? Are they expected to promote international and diversity perspectives or play a part in community outreach?

This is an auspicious moment to focus on these topics. Considerable attention is now focusing on the causes and consequences of globalization, particularly globalization's effect on intellectual migration within the context of expanding "knowledge economies." Focusing on these issues within higher education would be an important contribution to research into the effects of globalization, as well as a step forward in terms of supporting international faculty. And while I focused here on the situation in the United States, the issues I raise are relevant to foreign-born academics in other nations experiencing similar growth in intellectual immigration. Supporting international faculty as they transition into new academics settings is a global issue that needs to be addressed more systematically worldwide, not just in the United States.

References

Abel, C. 2002. "Family Adjustment to American Culture." *New Directions for Higher Education* 117: 71–7.

Alberts, H. 2008. "The Challenges and Opportunities of Foreign-Born Instructors in the Classroom." *Journal of Geography in Higher Education* 32(2): 189–203.

Alberts, H., H. Hazen, and R. Theobald. 2010. "Classroom Incivilities: The Challenge of Interactions between College Students and Instructors in the U.S." *Journal of Geography in Higher Education* 34(3): 439–62.

Association of American Geographers. 2006. *Guide to Geography Programs in North America*. Washington, DC: Association of American Geographers.

Boice, R. 2000. *Advice for New Faculty Members*. Needham Heights, MA: Allyn and Bacon.

———. 1996. "Classroom Incivilities." *Research in Higher Education* 37(4): 453–86.

———. 1992. *The New Faculty Member: Supporting and Fostering Professional Development*. San Francisco, CA: Jossey-Bass.

Bystydzienski, J., and E. Resnik, eds. 1994. *Women in Cross-Cultural Transitions*. Bloomington, IN: Phi Delta Kappa Educational Foundation.

Castles, S., and A. Davidson. 2000. "Immigration, Minority Formation and Racialization." In *Citizenship and Migration: Globalization and the Politics of Belonging*, edited by S. Castles and A. Davidson, 54–83. New York: Routledge.

Chapman, A. and D. Pyvis. 2006. "Dilemmas in the Formation of Student Identity in Offshore Higher Education: A Case Study in Hong Kong." *Educational Review* 58(3): 291–302.

Chesler, M. and A. Young, Jr. 2007. "Faculty Members' Social Identities and Classroom Authority." *New Directions for Teaching and Learning* 111: 11–19.

Collins, F. 2006. "Making Asian Students, Making Students Asian: The Racialisation of Export Education in Auckland, New Zealand." *Asia Pacific Viewpoint* 47(2): 217–34.

Collins, J. 2008. "Coming to America: Challenges for Faculty Coming to United States' Universities." *Journal of Geography in Higher Education* 32(2): 179–88.

Cooper, J. and D. Stevens. 2002. *Tenure in the Sacred Grove: Issues and Strategies for Women and Minority Faculty.* Albany, NY: State University of New York.

Dillon, S. 2004. "U.S. Slips in Attracting the World's Best Students." *New York Times.* Available at: http://www.nytimes.com/2004/12/21/national/21global.html. Accessed: May 2012.

EDGE [Enhancing Departments and Graduate Education in Geography Project]. 2012. Association of American Geographers. Available at: http://www.aag.org/edge. Accessed: May 2012.

Fink, L. 1984. *The First Year of College Teaching.* San Francisco, CA: Jossey-Bass.

Fleming, D., and B. Bailyn, eds. 1969. *The Intellectual Migration: Europe and America, 1930–1960.* Cambridge, MA: Harvard University Press.

Foote, K. 2010. "Creating a Community of Support for Early Career Academics." *Journal of Geography in Higher Education* 34(1): 7–19.

Foote, K., and M. Solem. 2009. "Toward Better Mentoring for Early Career Faculty: Results of a Study of U.S. Geographers." *International Journal for Academic Development* 14(1): 47–58.

Foote, K., W. Li, J. Monk, and R. Theobald. 2008. "Foreign-Born Scholars in U.S. Universities: Issues, Concerns, and Strategies." *Journal of Geography in Higher Education* 32(2): 167–78.

Garcia, M., ed. 2000. *Succeeding in an Academic Career: A Guide for Faculty of Color.* Westport, CT: Greenwood Press.

GeographyFaculty Development Alliance (GFDA). 2012. Available at: http://www.colorado.edu/geography/gfda/gfda.html. Accessed: April 2012.

Germain-Rutherford, A., and B. Kerr. 2009. "Faculty Development E-Module for Professional Acculturation in Canadian Higher Education." *FormaMente: International Research Journal on Digital Future* 4(3–4): 181–215.

Gravois, J. 2005. "Teach Impediment." *The Chronicle of Higher Education*, 8(April). Available at: http://chronicle.com/article/Teach-Impediment/33613/. Accessed: May 2012.

Iredale, R. 2001. "The Migration of Professionals: Theories and Typologies." *International Migration* 39(5): 7–26.

Jacobson, J. 2003. "In Visa Limbo." *Chronicle of Higher Education*, 19(September): A37–A8.

Lee, J., and C. Rice. 2007. "Welcome to America? International Student Perceptions of Discrimination." *Higher Education* 53: 381–409.

Lim, S., and M. Herrera-Sobek, eds. 2000. *Power, Race, and Gender in Academe: Strangers in the Tower.* New York: Modern Language Association of America.

Lovitts, B. 2007. *Making the Implicit Explicit: Creating Performance Expectations for the Dissertation.* Sterling, VA: Stylus.

———. 2001. *Leaving the Ivory Tower: The Causes and Consequences of Departure from Doctoral Study.* Lanham, MD: Rowman & Littlefield.

Mahtani, M. 2004. "Mapping Race and Gender in the Academy: The Experience of Women of Colour Faculty and Graduate Students in Britain, the U.S. and Canada." *Journal of Geography in Higher Education* 28: 91–9.

Manrique, C., and G. Manrique. 1999. *The Multicultural or Immigrant Faculty in American Society.* Lewiston, NY: Edwin Mellen Press.

Margolis, E., ed. 2001. *The Hidden Curriculum in Higher Education.* New York: Routledge.

Menges, R., and Associates. 1999. *Faculty in New Jobs: A Guide to Settling in, Becoming Established, and Building Institutional Support.* San Francisco, CA: Jossey-Bass.

Meyer, J.-B. 2001. "Network Approach versus Brain Drain: Lessons from the Diaspora." *International Migration* 39(5): 91–110.

Mills, N. 1994. "Introduction: The Era of the Golden Venture." In *Arguing Immigration: The Debate over the Changing Face of America,* edited by N. Mills, 11–28. New York: Touchstone Books.

Moody, J. 2004. *Faculty Diversity: Problems and Solutions.* New York: Routledge.

National Association of State Universities and Land Grant Colleges. 2000. "H1B Letter to Congress." Available at: http://www.aila.org/content/default.aspx?docid=22304. Accessed: May 2012.

National Science Foundation. 2000. *Science and Engineering Indicators—2000.* Arlington, VA: National Science Board.

Pulido, L. 2002. Reflections on a White Discipline. *Professional Geographer* 54(1): 42–9.

Richardson, J., K. McBey, and S. McKenna. 2006. "International Faculty in Canada: An Exploratory Study." Ottawa: Industry Canada, HRSDC-IC-SSHRC Skills Research Initiative. Available at: http://www.ic.gc.ca/eic/site/eas-aes.nsf/eng/h_ra01877.html. Accessed: April 2012.

Robison, M. 2003. *Changing Intellectual Paradigms.* Los Angeles, CA: University of Southern California.

Scheyvens, R., K. Wild, and J. Overton. 2003. "International Students Pursing Postgraduate Study in Geography: Impediments to their Learning Experiences." *Journal of Geography in Higher Education* 27(3): 309–23.

Solem, M., and K. Foote. 2009. "Enhancing Departments and Graduate Education in Geography: A Disciplinary Project in Professional Development." *International Journal of Researcher Development* 1(1): 11–28.

———. 2004. "Concerns, Attitudes and Abilities of Early Career Geography Faculty." *Annals of the Association of American Geographers* 94(4): 889–912.

Solem, M., K. Foote, and J. Monk. 2009. *Aspiring Academics: A Resource Book for Graduate Students and Early Career Faculty.* Upper Saddle River, NJ: Pearson Prentice-Hall.

Solomon, B. 1985. *In the Company of Educated Women: A History of Women and Higher Education in America.* New Haven, CT: Yale University Press.
Subedi, B. 2006. "Theorizing a 'Halfie' Researcher's Identity in Transnational Fieldwork." *International Journal of Qualitative Studies in Education* 19(5): 573–93.
Theobald, R. 2009. "New Faces in Academic Places: Gender and the Experiences of Early-career Foreign-born and Native-born Geographers in the United States." *Journal of Geographical Science* 57: 7–32.
———. 2007. "Foreign-Born Early-Career Faculty in American Higher Education: The Case of the Discipline of Geography." PhD dissertation, University of Colorado at Boulder.
Tichenor, D. 1994. "Immigration and Political Community in the United States." *The Responsive Community: Rights and Responsibilities* 4(3): 16–28.
U.S. Citizenship and Immigration Service (USCIS). 2012. "Employment-Based Immigration: First Preference EB-1." Available at: http://www.uscis.gov/portal/site/uscis/menuitem.eb1d4c2a3e5b9ac89243c6a7543f6d1a/?vgnextoid=17b983453d4a3210VgnVCM100000b92ca60aRCRD&vgnextchannel=17b983453d4a3210VgnVCM100000b92ca60aRCRD. Accessed: April 2012.
Vargas, L., ed. 2002. *Women Faculty of Color in the White Classroom: Narratives on the Pedagogical Implications of Teacher Diversity.* New York: P. Lang.

11

TEACHING AND LEARNING WITH ACCENTED ENGLISH

Heike Alberts, Helen Hazen, and Rebecca Theobald

The accent of international university instructors has been an issue of public debate in the United States for several decades, with concerns raised over the teaching effectiveness of nonnative English-speaking instructors (NNIs). Although little evidence supports the idea that NNIs are inferior educators, teaching with an accent clearly presents distinct challenges for both instructors and students, making it a topic worthy of exploration. Recognizing that both NNIs and students are integral to communication in the classroom (Kavas and Kavas 2008; Rao 1995), we report the findings of two surveys: the first assessed undergraduates' attitudes to and experiences with NNIs in geography classes at six Midwestern universities, the second asked nonnative English-speaking geography instructors to discuss their accent and the strategies they use to address communication problems. We chose geography as a useful case study for analyzing the challenges faced by NNIs owing to its large proportion of international faculty from a wide range of countries.

BACKGROUND

Since the 1980s, the impact that foreign-born teaching assistants and professors have on American students has become a topic of public debate because of the assumption that it is more difficult to learn when the instructor has a foreign accent (e.g., Gravois 2005; Clayton 2000; Rubin 1998; Neves and Sanyal 1991; Rubin and Smith 1990; Jacobs and Friedman 1988). Certain cases of students who could not understand their NNIs because of strong accents have been widely publicized (Neves and Sanyal 1991), but other evidence suggests that accent may be less significant than students' attitudes toward those from other cultures. As such, it is not only communication but also cultural difference that is significant in considering the challenges facing NNIs (Kavas and Kavas 2008; Jacobs and Friedman 1988). Regardless of cause, concerns with foreign instructors among students are well documented. In 1995, Rao coined the term "the oh-no! syndrome" to reflect the response of some students to finding that their class will be taught by a nonnative instructor.

Researchers have begun to systematically assess the potential impacts of foreign-born instructors on US students (e.g., Grossman 2011; Alberts 2008; Fleisher, Masanori, and Weinberg 2002; Borjas 2000; Gill 1994; Jacobs and Friedman 1988). Some studies, mostly undertaken in communication or related disciplines, conclude that being taught by an instructor with an unfamiliar accent may indeed have some negative effects. For example, Gill (1994) found that recall rates were lower when students listened to accented English. However, the results of many studies are inconclusive (Munro and Derwing 1995), and acknowledge that factors other than accent may play a role. For example, Grossman (2011) found that students considered lectures delivered in accented English more difficult to comprehend, but the results differed according to the content of the lecture. Similarly, Rao (1995) found that students minded accented speech less in classes in their major than in general education classes as they were more familiar with the content.

The findings of studies that look more broadly at the impact of international instructors on American students are also mixed, although most researchers conclude that nonnative instructors pose few disadvantages for student learning, or affect learning only in very specific ways or contexts. For instance, Jacobs and Friedman (1988) found little evidence that foreign teaching assistants are less effective than their domestic counterparts, nor did they uncover significant student dissatisfaction with nonnative teaching assistants. Borjas (2000), whose conclusions about international instructors are among the most negative, concluded from his study of student perceptions of NNIs that student learning may suffer when students are taught by NNIs, but even he reported that grades of nonnative English-speaking students and students with higher grade point averages (GPA) were not affected by having an NNI, suggesting that this effect may be limited to specific student populations.

Even where concerns with NNIs have been noted, problems may be more imagined than real. For example, Munro and Derwing (1995) found in their study of accented English that strength of accent was correlated with students' *perception* of the comprehensibility of nonnative speakers, but did not alter how much students were actually able to understand in an objective test. However, they acknowledge that the amount of effort the student has to put in may vary with the strength of the accent. Other studies (reported in Cargile 1997) found that people evaluate accents according to factors other than objective strength—for example, some accents are associated with a high status (e.g. a British accent) while others are seen more negatively.

Whether problems are real or imagined, they can nonetheless be influential on student decisions. For example, Jacobs and Friedman (1988) report students staying away from courses taught by people with foreign-sounding names. In another study, about 40 percent of the undergraduates stated that they had dropped a class when they found it was taught by a nonnative speaker, although students who had actually taken a nonnative speaker's class often did not hold such negative views toward NNIs (Rubin and Smith 1990), again suggesting that perceptions of NNIs may differ from actual experiences. Rao (1995) suggests that high rates of dropping NNIs' classes may reflect group dynamics rather than widespread concerns: as some students complain about foreign-born instructors and drop their classes, others are likely to follow. Bresnahan and Kim (1993) suggest that lack of experience with foreign accents may also partially explain undergraduates' concerns with foreign-born instructors.

Ethnic or racial bias may provide another explanation. Rubin (1992) and Rubin and Smith (1990) showed that students perceive accents to be stronger when they are shown the face of a non-White instructor with a particular recording of spoken English, even when the recording is of standard English. Studies have not developed a consistent picture of the role of ethnic bias, however, with some researchers reporting clear same-ethnicity preference among students and others failing to identify a significant association (see Labouvie-Vief 2006; Anderson and Smith 2005; Galguera 1998). Nonetheless, why some students should hold negative views toward NNIs remains a critical question, leading de Oliveira et al. (2009) to argue that investigating ethnocentric bias toward college instructors is a critical area for further research.

Other biases may also influence students' attitudes toward NNIs. McCalman (2007) found that some American students have difficulty accepting NNIs because they believe that international instructors come from inferior education systems and are in the United States to learn. Similarly, de Oliveira et al. (2009) suggest that foreign-born instructors have to work harder than their domestic counterparts to convince students of their competence. Alberts (2008) reports how some students express dislike of non-Americans making critical comments about the United States and consider them biased. Overall, evidence such as this indicates that student assumptions about international instructors may be as influential for student learning as the objective strength of instructors' accents.

Some scholars have proposed ways to try to tackle problems associated with student stereotypes about international instructors or foreigners in general. Recommendations include greater exposure to foreign-born instructors (de Oliveira et al. 2009) and participation in study-abroad programs (de Oliveira et al. 2009; Chieffo and Griffiths 2003). However, we should not overestimate the impact of study abroad on students since students participating in study abroad are likely to be those with low levels of prejudice and ethnocentrism even before they participate in the experience abroad (Goldstein and Kim 2006). To realize their full potential, such opportunities must be carefully designed and integrated with broader curricular goals (Pandit 2009; Veeck and Biles 2009).

How instructors deal with the topic of their language proficiency and accent may also be significant. In Alberts' (2008) study, students resented NNIs assuming that students would understand them, but took a positive outlook when professors admitted that they had a different accent and took measures to help them understand. NNIs therefore have significant agency in influencing the classroom dynamics that develop around their accent. Examining which strategies NNIs can most effectively employ to enhance communication with their students is therefore critical. A few publications have offered guidance for international teaching assistants and professors (e.g., Alberts 2008; Collins 2008; Kavas and Kavas 2008; Wu 2003; Sarkisian 2000), with some attention paid to linguistic issues, but overall this topic remains under-researched.

As this brief literature review indicates, there remains considerable controversy, and indeed confusion, over the influence of NNIs on student learning, although many studies point to a mismatch between US students' perceptions of NNIs and the objective influence of NNIs on students' education. In this chapter, we systematically investigate how US students' preconceptions of NNIs differ from their actual experiences with them, considering a variety of factors that could influence student attitudes, including students' age, GPA, and previous exposure to NNIs. We then consider measures that could be taken to improve communication between NNIs and their students. These measures include specific pedagogical techniques the

NNI could employ in the classroom but also approaches that increase students' exposure to people different from themselves.

Methods

Inspired by Rao's (1995) and Kavas and Kavas' (2008) assertions that both instructors and students have to contribute to successful learning, our study uses a two-pronged approach to explore the impact of NNIs and to make recommendations for how to improve communication between NNIs and their students. In order to investigate student attitudes toward and experiences with NNIs, we conducted a survey at six universities in the Midwestern United States (two each in Minnesota, Illinois, and Wisconsin). We selected two large research universities, two midsized state universities, and two selective private institutions for the study in order to investigate the degree to which characteristics of different institutions play a role. All surveys were administered by native English-speaking instructors in undergraduate human geography classes. In order to increase the likelihood of students answering candidly, the surveys were completed anonymously. In total, we received 285 completed questionnaires from the six universities.

The survey consisted of three parts. The first part elicited background information about the student respondent such as age, class standing, and current GPA, as well as the student's exposure to foreign languages, cultures, and instructors. The second part gauged the student's *attitudes* toward NNIs. We gave respondents a number of statements (derived from student opinions expressed in other studies) and asked them to mark whether they agreed with the statement, were neutral, or disagreed. Some statements were framed negatively, such as "I try to avoid classes taught by NNIs"; others listed potential benefits of being taught by foreign-born instructors, such as "I believe that it is important to learn to understand foreign accents." A final set of statements elicited information about whether students see differences between American-born and foreign-born instructors in terms of teaching effectiveness, friendliness, knowledge, competence, standards, and expectations of students. In using these comparative statements we are aware that we were encouraging students to generalize from their personal experiences with individual instructors to all American and all foreign-born instructors. Nonetheless, we felt that it was important to see whether students *perceived* systematic differences between NNIs and native English-speaking instructors (NEIs)—again working on the assumption that student perceptions may be more critical than actual differences in classroom behavior or pedagogic approaches. The second part of the survey concluded with a list of strategies NNIs might use to put their students at ease and help them understand accented English. Students were asked whether or not they would recommend that NNIs use these strategies.

The last part of the survey asked students about their actual *experiences* with NNIs. In order to avoid students reporting their most extreme experience, we asked respondents to fill out these questions in reference to the NNI by whom they had most recently been taught. Students evaluated their instructor's English proficiency and strength of accent and were then asked whether they had experienced specific comprehension problems with this particular instructor. Finally, student respondents marked the strategies their professor had used to help students understand them in class.

To look at the issue from the perspective of instructors, we surveyed early-career geography NNIs to find out the techniques they employ to improve communication with their students and how effective they consider these strategies to be. The anonymous web-based survey included a number of closed questions to collect background information about the respondents and their institutions, as well as their self-reported English proficiency and strength of accent. We then asked respondents to identify the strategies they use to enhance classroom communication, and to use rating scales to assess the effectiveness of these strategies.

Characteristics of Survey Respondents

Student Respondents

Our 285 student respondents were fairly representative of the overall population of US undergraduates in terms of age and sex, with a slight bias toward more advanced undergraduates and males (50.5% male; versus 44.0% in the US university population, as reported by Davis and Bauman 2008). The vast majority of our respondents were American-born (93.0%) and native speakers of English (94.7%), a higher percentage than would be expected of the overall US undergraduate population. Most respondents reported some foreign language skills (91%); almost half claimed to be proficient in one or more foreign language. About two-thirds of our respondents had traveled to a country where English was not the dominant language, and a similar percentage had friends whose native language was not

English. Most respondents had taken a class with an NNI at the university level (90%).

Faculty Respondents

As part of a larger survey investigating strategies employed by early-career geography instructors to address academic and behavioral problems arising in the classroom (Alberts, Hazen, and Theobald 2010), we identified 195 early-career foreign-born geography faculty through membership lists of the Association of American Geographers as well as web searches of individual geography departments in the United States. A total of 78 respondents completed the survey (a response rate of 40% for the foreign-born population). Only 44 of these respondents were nonnative speakers of English, so we acknowledge that our findings in this section are based on a relatively small number of responses. More than three-quarters (77.3%) of our nonnative speaker faculty respondents were male. Almost half (47.7%) were originally from Asia, 34.1 percent from Europe, 11.4 percent from the Middle East and Africa, and 6.8 percent from Latin America. Almost 60 percent of our respondents identified themselves as non-White. It is impossible to tell how representative this sample is of the broader population of NNIs working in the United States owing to lack of data on the population from which the sample was drawn.

Student Attitudes to and Experiences with NNIs

Student Attitudes toward NNIs

While many students in our sample (59.3%) rejected the idea that there is a systematic disadvantage to being taught by an NNI, an even larger proportion (63.5%) nevertheless reported some concerns about being taught by a nonnative speaker. For some students these concerns translated into avoidance strategies, with 15.8 percent stating that they actively avoided classes taught by NNIs; a further 8.1 percent stated that they would consider dropping a class if the instructor was an NNI.

Students' concerns with NNIs included a range of issues such as clarity of assignments, fear of bias, and differing expectations, with most concerns centered on being taught by a person who speaks accented English. Roughly a third of student respondents felt that

NNIs were generally hard to understand because of their accents (31.9%), about one-third were neutral on the topic (33.0%), and the remaining third believed that NNIs were generally not difficult to understand (35.1%). Whether these differences in opinion are due to students being exposed to different strengths of accents or largely the result of students' ability (or willingness) to understand their NNIs is open to question.

In contrast to the fairly large proportion of students reporting some comprehension problems, 88.7 percent of our NNI respondents considered their accent to be barely noticeable or noticeable but presenting no problems with comprehension; only 11.4 percent of NNI respondents felt that students struggled with understanding their accents. Furthermore, NNI respondents were generally confident of their spoken and written English, with 40.9 percent stating that they speak and write English almost as well as a native speaker, and another 56.8 percent reporting that they are very comfortable speaking and writing English or struggle only occasionally. Whether students are overestimating the challenge of coping with NNIs' foreign accents and style of English or whether faculty are overconfident in self-assessing their accents and language ability is hard to ascertain, but there is clearly a disjunction in perceptions.

Students did not always see foreign accents as a barrier, however. Almost half (48.8%) of all student respondents said that they enjoyed listening to a foreign accent. Furthermore, three-quarters (73.3%) agreed that it is important to learn to understand foreign accents. Most student respondents (91.3%) also agreed that it is advantageous to learn from people who might bring different perspectives to the classroom, although almost a quarter of respondents (23.2%) stated that they are bothered by international professors criticizing the United States, suggesting that this acceptance of alternative perspectives does not hold true in all situations.

As noted in the literature (e.g., de Oliveira et al. 2009; McCroskey 2002), some American students question the teaching effectiveness of NNIs. We therefore asked student respondents to compare their perceptions of NNIs to those of NEIs by agreeing or disagreeing with statements such as "Generally, NNIs are as effective as teachers as NEIs." The majority of student respondents reported that they do not perceive systematic differences between NEIs and NNIs in most regards. Over 70 percent indicated that NEIs and NNIs are, in their view, comparable in terms of competence, academic standards, and academic and behavioral expectations, with only very small minorities actively disagreeing with these statements.

Students were slightly more critical of NNIs' effectiveness as teachers, however, with 60 percent agreeing that they are comparable to NEIs in this regard and about 10 percent actively disagreeing. Another area in which some respondents perceived differences between NNIs and NEIs was in the appropriateness of NNIs' expectations of students' background knowledge, with 10 percent of student respondents stating that NNIs and NEIs differ in their expectations. Research with international instructors has shown that the instructors, too, often believe that they have different expectations of their students compared with many American instructors, precisely because they come from different educational systems, which some international instructors perceive as more demanding than the US education system (see Alberts 2008). Preconceived ideas about the effectiveness of different education systems can be found among instructors as well as students.

In summary, while most students express some level of concern about being taught by an NNI, mostly in relation to language, for the majority of students these concerns are not serious enough to try to avoid NNIs as teachers. Most students also believe that there are some benefits to having NNIs as instructors, for example in helping students to learn to understand foreign accents and exposing them to different perspectives. Notably, however, students' perceptions of their interactions with NNIs frequently differ from NNIs' assessment of their own interactions with students.

Student Experiences with NNIs

Having investigated student *attitudes* toward NNIs, we asked the 90 percent of our respondents who had been taught by an NNI at the university level about their actual *experiences*. More than a third of these student respondents reported that they perceived that their most recent NNI had a very strong or quite strong accent (7.4% and 36.1%, respectively), 36.5 percent described their instructor's accent as perceptible but not difficult to understand, and 12.3 percent considered the accent mild. (For comparison, nearly 90 percent of our NNI respondents rated their accents as insignificant.) Students were generally quite positive in evaluating their instructor's English proficiency: 8.8 percent judged their NNI's English as native-like, 25.3 percent as excellent, and a further 35.1 percent as good. Only 5.6 percent complained that the English proficiency of their most recent NNI was poor, suggesting that press reports of widespread problems with NNIs' English skills may be exaggerated.

Having said this, almost a fifth (17.2%) of student respondents claimed that they struggled with understanding their NNIs' English for the entire semester. A further 10.5 percent of respondents stated that they struggled with the clarity of NNIs' assignments and 7.0 percent with their phrasing of questions on exams. Admittedly, ambiguous or unclear instructions and questions can be a problem with NEIs too, but clearly some students found that being taught by an NNI brought significant challenges in this regard.

Factors Influencing Student Interactions with NNIs

In order to suggest measures to improve communication, an understanding of which factors influence students' attitudes toward NNIs is necessary. Some of the existing literature suggests that characteristics such as age (as a proxy for maturity level), gender, GPA, and previous experience with foreign cultures and foreign-born instructors may influence student attitudes toward foreign-born instructors. In order to investigate this, we cross-tabulated student respondents' demographic and educational characteristics with their attitude statements. We accepted relationships where the chi-square value was significant at the 95 percent level, and discuss these below. We also briefly report some of the relationships tested that did not reveal significant results.

Most cross-tabulations suggested that personal and educational characteristics (such as age or GPA) are not significantly correlated with student attitudes toward NNIs. However, class standing, international background, native language, and gender did show a significant relationship with *some* student attitudes. More advanced undergraduates were more likely to judge NNIs' competence as similar to NEIs' than were less advanced students, with 90.4 percent of seniors agreeing that the two groups were comparable, compared to just 67.7 percent of freshmen. Whether this difference is attributable to greater maturity or more experience with NNIs is hard to tell, as more advanced students were significantly more likely to have had NNIs than were freshmen and sophomores. Unsurprisingly, American-born students were more likely to be concerned about being taught by NNIs than were foreign-born students (64.9% versus 45.0%), and native English-speakers more likely to be concerned than nonnative English-speakers (64.8% versus 40.0%). Female students were more likely to report that they enjoyed listening to foreign accents than were male students (61.0% versus 36.8%), and were more likely to consider it beneficial to learn to understand foreign accents (80.9% versus 66.0).

While demographic indicators were generally not strongly correlated with attitude statements, students' experiences with foreign languages and exposure to foreign-born instructors did significantly influence their attitudes toward NNIs (table 11.1), as evidenced by the large number of cross-tabulations that resulted in statistically significant chi-square values. For example, while 53.5 percent of those who spoke a foreign language expressed concerns about NNIs, the respective figure was 68.0 percent for those without foreign language skills. Similarly, 68.5 percent of students with foreign language skills would not consider dropping a class taught by a NNI, versus 52.0 percent of those who do not speak a foreign language. Students proficient in foreign languages were also more likely than their monolingual counterparts to see NNIs as equally friendly and approachable as their American-born professors (79.5% versus 68.0%). Having traveled to a country where English is not the dominant language made students less likely to be concerned about being taught by a NNI and less likely to report problems with understanding foreign accents. It also gave students a more positive attitude toward NNIs, and made it more likely that they would evaluate the teaching effectiveness and friendliness of NNIs as similar to those of NEIs. Similarly, those students with nonnative English-speaking friends reported fewer concerns with NNIs, were less likely to avoid classes taught by NNIs, and held more positive attitudes toward foreign accents.

The factor that mattered most in explaining student attitudes toward NNIs was whether the student had actually been taught by an NNI at the university level (table 11.1). Students who had been taught by NNIs had fewer concerns about NNIs and were less likely to avoid them or consider dropping their classes. They reported fewer problems with understanding foreign accents, and were more likely to report enjoying listening to them. They were also considerably more likely to report NNIs as equivalent to NEIs in teaching ability. These differences in attitudes were also influenced by the *number* of NNIs a respondent had had at university, with those students with greater exposure to NNIs expressing more positive experiences and attitudes overall. For instance, while only 26.7 percent of those who had never been taught by an NNI thought that they were generally as effective as NEIs, 74.0 percent of those who had been taught by three or more NNIs judged them as equally effective. Similarly, 46.7 percent of those without exposure to NNIs considered them equally as competent as NEIs, compared to 88.6 percent of those who had three or more NNIs.

Table 11.1 Correlation between student attitudes and exposure to foreign languages and NNIs (significance of χ^2)

Attitudes of student respondents	Speaks language other than English	Has traveled to country where English is not dominant	Has friends whose native language is not English	Has been taught by an NNI at the university level
Concerned that it may be difficult to understand an NNI	0.004	0.046	0.000	0.024
Has avoided classes taught by an NNI	0.021	~	0.002	0.004
Would consider dropping a class taught by an NNI	~	~	~	0.002
Feels disadvantaged when taught by an NNI	~	~	~	~
Finds it hard to understand foreign accents	~	0.010	0.009	0.005
Enjoys listening to a foreign accent	~	0.026	~	0.044
Believes it is important to learn to understand foreign accents	~	0.044	0.050	~
Believes it is beneficial to learn from people with a different perspective	~	0.040	~	~
Believes NNIs to be as effective as teachers as NEIs	~	0.034	~	0.000
Believes NNIs to be as friendly and approachable as NEIs	0.031	0.034	~	0.002
Believes NNIs to be as knowledgeable and competent as NEIs	~	~	~	0.000
Believes NNIs to have same academic standards as NEIs	~	~	~	0.000
Believes NNIs to have same expectations of student behavior as NEIs	~	~	0.037	0.000
Believes NNIs to have same expectations of student knowledge and skills as NEIs	~	~	0.014	0.002

Note: Only results significant at the 95% significance level are reported in the table.

Within the group of students with no experience of NNIs, it is probable that there were some who have actively avoided classes with NNIs precisely because of their negative preconceptions of what their classes would be like. It is hard to assess whether or not these students' fears would be allayed if they actually took a class with an NNI. Similarly, it is impossible to say to what extent the positive attitude among those taking multiple classes with NNIs developed during the classes and how much was a result of these students having preexisting international outlooks. However, it does appear that perceptions of problems associated with being taught by an NNI may be far stronger than the reality of problems when taking a class with an NNI. Furthermore, greater exposure to NNIs, on balance, appears to allay fears rather than reinforce poor expectations.

The importance of exposure to NNIs and international matters more generally in shaping positive attitudes toward NNIs is also supported by differences among institutions. We found no systematic differences in student attitudes toward NNIs according to type of institution (e.g. research-oriented, teaching-oriented), size of institution, or size of the metropolitan area where the institution is located. However, there were highly significant differences among universities, with students at two of the six institutions reporting much more positive attitudes toward NNIs. One of these two institutions defines itself as being strongly international in outlook, has a high percentage of students participating in study-abroad programs, and a high percentage of international students. The other institution has an unusually high proportion of international faculty in the department where the surveys were carried out, so that respondents had, in total, been exposed to a larger number of NNIs than at the other universities surveyed.

In summary, exposure to foreign languages and cultures appears to be significant in developing positive student attitudes toward NNIs. Personal decisions concerning travel destinations and friends are obviously beyond the control of educational institutions. However, institutions can encourage study abroad and create opportunities for American students to meet and interact with foreign-born students. Our results also suggest that requiring students to take foreign language classes may have positive effects beyond the intrinsic benefit of speaking a foreign language, through encouraging students to be more open-minded toward other peoples and languages. Being taught by NNIs similarly seems to help students become less ethnocentric and help them build skills (such as understanding a foreign accent) that may be valuable in an increasingly diverse world and workplace.

While being taught by an NNI may initially be difficult for a student, in the long run many students appear to benefit from the experience and to appreciate their interaction with NNIs.

Strategies to Enhance Communication between Students and NNIs

Hoping that students will benefit in the long run from being taught by NNIs is no excuse for ignoring problems that may occur in the classroom in the short term. Instead, we argue that it is critical to address students' immediate concerns with NNIs to ensure that long-term benefits are realized. We consider here suggestions made by students regarding what they believe would help their comprehension of NNIs, as well as assessments made by NNIs of their success with various strategies to enhance communication.

We gave NNI respondents a list of potential strategies for facilitating student understanding and asked them to mark the strategies they used. Almost all NNIs in our survey reported using strategies to assist their students in understanding them. The majority (86.4%) reported asking students to raise their hands if they did not understand something. A similar proportion of student respondents agreed that this is a helpful strategy (87.4%). Roughly two-thirds of our NNIs reported making an effort to speak more slowly to enhance student understanding, with a similar proportion of student respondents (63.9%) advocating this strategy. Two-thirds of NNI respondents reported writing out notes for their students to assist with comprehension; 79.6 percent of students valued this strategy. Professors who reported seeing their accents as a potential problem for students more commonly employed strategies to help their students understand them in the classroom.

Despite the large proportion of our NNI respondents who reported using strategies to enhance student comprehension, a far smaller proportion of our student respondents claimed that their most recent NNI had actually used them—further evidence of disjunction in perceptions between faculty and students. Just 56.5 percent of students claimed that they had been encouraged to raise their hands when they had difficulty understanding their NNI, only 40.4 percent reported that their most recent NNI had made an effort to speak more slowly, and 51.6 percent had had notes written out for them to help them understand.

Most strategies were rated positively by NNIs. Writing brief notes received the highest ratings, with 77.8 percent of respondents judging this strategy to be very effective, the remainder believing that it was somewhat effective. Evaluations of writing extensive notes were somewhat more mixed, perhaps because of concerns of overwhelming students with too much text or of spoon-feeding them with information. Most instructors saw some value in asking students to raise their hands if they had problems understanding, as well as making an effort to speak more slowly.

Strategies that more explicitly acknowledge that an instructor's English is not perfect were less popular among NNIs and received lower effectiveness ratings, perhaps reflecting the belief that they undermine an instructor's authority in the classroom or could embarrass the NNI. Nonetheless, slightly more than one-third of NNI respondents (37.2%) reported that they asked their students to correct their mistakes, and 11.4 percent had nominated a specific student to take on the task of stopping the professor when they heard words that they thought others in the class may not have understood. Students were similarly divided in their opinion of whether instructors should ask students to correct mistakes, with just 42.8 percent of students recommending the strategy, and over 20 percent arguing that this is not a good idea.

Conclusion

Debates over whether American students are disadvantaged by being taught by NNIs resurface periodically, with press reports typically focusing on sensational cases where students cannot understand instructors with particularly strong accents. As a result, the public often perceives the problem to be serious and widespread. However, most research, including ours, suggests that these extreme cases are the exception rather than the rule. Nonetheless, those speaking with a strong accent face challenges in the classroom, both because of genuine communication problems and student prejudices that accented English is associated with poorer teaching skills or a weaker academic background. Addressing the challenge of communication between students and instructors who come from different backgrounds is a two-way process, requiring the effort of students and instructors (Rao 1995).

While most of our student respondents had some concerns about NNIs and their accents, the vast majority did not believe that they were at a systematic disadvantage because their instructor was a non-native speaker of English, nor did they avoid being taught by NNIs. While students perceived many of their NNIs' accents to be quite strong, relatively few claimed to have struggled with understanding an accent over the long term. Students who had been taught by NNIs had far more positive attitudes toward them than those who had no experience of NNIs, suggesting that preconceptions of NNIs may be more problematic than the reality. Overall, few respondents suggested that the experience of being taught by an NNI had an overall negative impact on their learning.

Still, student and NNI perceptions of the problems associated with classroom communication were often mismatched. In particular, while NNIs tended to underplay the importance of their accent in the classroom, many students perceived NNIs' accents to be strong. In addition, while instructors claimed to be using techniques to address potential communication problems at high rates, students reported their NNIs to be using these techniques less frequently. This mismatch in expectations and experiences likely exacerbates tensions between NNIs and their American students. While it is hard to realign expectations, the simple effort of an instructor acknowledging that his or her accent may be a problem for students may go a long way toward generating a positive classroom atmosphere around the issue. A variety of practical techniques can also be employed to lessen the impact of an accent, such as asking students to raise their hands when they do not understand, writing out brief notes, and making an effort to speak more slowly (see also Kavas and Kavas 2008). Such techniques provide instructors with some agency to initiate change and signal the instructor's willingness to address the issue, which in turn might have positive effects on student attitudes (see also Alberts 2008).

A further key question emerging from current literature is whether demographic and educational characteristics of students influence their attitudes toward NNIs. Our results suggest that these factors matter less than expected. Instead, our findings indicate that the most critical factors in shaping student attitudes are exposure to foreign languages (through foreign language classes or travel abroad) and exposure to nonnative speakers of English, both within the classroom and outside. Fostering such experiences could be an important step toward encouraging more fruitful interactions between students and NNIs. Increasing diversity at the institutional level is clearly beneficial in this respect (Cargile 1997), as well as encouraging study abroad and maintaining foreign language requirements.

International instructors provide insights into different cultures and alternative perspectives on life in their students' home country—valuable contributions to any student's education. Ensuring that accents do not pose a barrier to effective cross-cultural communication is critical (Gill 1994). The experiences of NNIs might be significantly improved if they received mentoring to familiarize them with strategies to address communication problems from the start. While advice on improving communication skills is useful for all new faculty, assigning experienced and successful nonnative English-speaking faculty to mentor new NNIs could be especially helpful considering the unique challenges this group faces. In turn, employing strategies to improve classroom communication signals to students that their concerns are taken seriously by faculty, which could help open up channels of communication and enable more students to see foreign instructors as an asset rather than an obstacle to learning.

Works Cited

Alberts, H. 2008. "The Challenges and Opportunities of Foreign-Born Instructors in the Classroom." *Journal of Geography in Higher Education* 32(2): 189–203.

Alberts, H., H. Hazen, and R. Theobald. 2010. "Classroom Incivilities: The Challenge of Interactions between College Students and Instructors in the US." *Journal of Geography in Higher Education* 34(3): 439–62.

Anderson, K., and G. Smith. 2005. "Student Preconceptions of Professors: Benefits and Barriers According to Ethnicity and Gender." *Hispanic Journal of Behavioral Sciences* 27(2): 184–201.

Borjas, G. 2000. "Foreign-Born Teaching Assistants and the Academic Performance of Undergraduates." NBER Working Paper No. W7635, Harvard University. Available at: http://ksghome.harvard.edu/~GBorjas/Papers/Foreign-Born_Teaching_Assistants.pdf. Accessed July 6, 2008.

Bresnahan, M., and M. Kim. 1993. "Predictors of Receptivity and Resistance toward International Teaching Assistants." *Journal of Asian Pacific Communication* 4(1): 3–14.

Cargile, A. 1997. "Attitudes toward Chinese-Accented Speech. An Investigation in Two Contexts." *Journal of Language and Social Psychology* 16(4): 434–43.

Chieffo, L., and L. Griffiths. 2003. "What's a Month Worth?" *International Educator*. Fall: 26–31.

Clayton, M. 2000. "Foreign Teaching Assistants' First Test: The Accent." *Christian Science Monitor* 92 (June 5): 14. Available at: http://www.csmonitor.com/2000/0905/p14s1.html. Accessed: July 8, 2008.

Collins, J. 2008. "Coming to America: Challenges for Faculty Coming to United States' Universities." *Journal of Geography in Higher Education* 32(2): 179–88.

Davis, J., and K. Bauman. 2008. "Current Population Reports: School Enrollment in the United States." United States Bureau of the Census,

Washington, DC. Available at: http://www.census.gov/prod/2008pubs/p20-559.pdf. Accessed: August 12, 2009.

De Oliveira, E., J. Braun, T. Carlson, and S. de Oliveira. 2009. "Students' Attitudes toward Foreign-Born and Domestic Instructors." *Journal of Diversity in Higher Education* 2(2): 113–25.

Fleisher, B., H. Masanori, and B. Weinberg. 2002. "Foreign GTAs Can Be Effective Teachers of Economics." *Journal of Economic Education* 33(4): 299–325.

Galguera, T. 1998. "Students' Attitudes toward Teachers' Ethnicity, Biliinguality, and Gender. *Hispanic Journal of Behavioral Sciences* 20: 411–28.

Gill, M. 1994. "Accent and Stereotypes: Their Effect on Perceptions of Teachers and Lecture Comprehension." *Journal of Applied Communication Research* 22: 348–61.

Goldstein, S., and R. Kim. 2006. "Predictors of U.S. College Students' Participation in Study Abroad Programs: A Longitudinal Study." *International Journal of Intercultural Relations* 30: 507–21.

Gravois, J. 2005. "Teach Impediment. When the Student Can't Understand the Instructor, Who Is to Blame?" *Chronicle of Higher Education* 51(31): A1, A10–12.

Grossman, L. 2011. "The Effects of Mere Exposure on Response to Foreign-Accented Speech." Masters' Thesis. Paper 4051. Available at: http://scholarworks.sjsu.edu/etd_theses/4051. Accessed: July 6, 2008.

Jacobs, L., and C. Friedman. 1988. "Student Achievement under Foreign Teaching Associates Compared with Native Teaching Associates." *The Journal of Higher Education* 59: 551–63.

Kavas, A., and A. Kavas. 2008. "An Exploratory Study of Undergraduate College Students' Perceptions and Attitudes toward Foreign Accented Faculty." *College Student Journal* 42: 879–90.

Labouvie-Vief, G. 2006. "Emerging Structures of Adult Thought." In *Emerging Adults in America: Coming of Age in the 21st Century*, edited by J. Arnett, and J. Tanner, 59–84. Washington, DC: American Psychological Association.

McCalman, C. 2007. "Being an Interculturally Competent Instructor in the United States: Issues of Classroom Dynamics and Appropriateness, and Recommendations for International Instructors." *New Directions for Teaching and Learning* 110: 65–74.

McCroskey, L. 2002. "Domestic and International College Instructors: An Examination of Perceived Differences and their Correlates." *Journal of Intercultural Communication Research* 31(2): 63–83.

Munro, M., and T. Derwing. 1995. "Foreign Accent, Comprehensibility, and the Intelligibility in the Speech of Second Language Learners." *Language Learning* 45(1): 73–97.

Neves, J., and R. Sanyal. 1991. "Classroom Communication and Teaching Effectiveness: The Foreign-Born Instructor." *Journal of Education for Business* 66(5): 304–8.

Pandit, K. 2009. "Geographers and the Work of Internationalization." *Journal of Geography* 108(3): 91.

Rao, N. 1995. "The 'Oh No!' Syndrome: A Language Expectation Model of Undergraduate Negative Reactions toward Foreign Teaching Assistants." Paper presented at the 79th Annual Meeting of the International Communication Association, Albuquerque, NM, May.

Rubin, D. 1998. "Help! My Professor (or Doctor, or Boss) Doesn't Talk English!" In *Readings in Cultural Contexts*, edited by J. Martin, T. Nakayama, and L. Flores. Mountainview, CA: Mayfield Publishing.

———. 1992. "Nonlanguage Factors Affecting Undergraduates' Judgments of Non-Native English Speaking Teaching Assistants." *Research in Higher Education* 33: 511–31.

Rubin, D., and K. Smith. 1990. "Effects of Accent, Ethnicity, and Lecture Topic on Undergraduates' Perceptions of Nonnative English-Speaking Teaching Assistant." *International Journal of Intercultural Relations* 14: 337–53.

Sarkisian, E. 2000. *Teaching American Students: A Guide for International Faculty and Teaching Assistants in Colleges and Universities.* Cambridge: Derek Bok Center for Teaching and Learning, Harvard University.

Veeck, G., and J. Biles. 2009. "Geography, Geographers, and Study Abroad." *Journal of Geography* 108(3): 92–93.

Wu, X. 2003. "Challenges of Accommodating Non-Native English Speaking Instructors' Teaching and Native English Speaking Students' Learning in College, and the Exploration of Potential Solutions." Master's Thesis. Available at: http://www.uwstout.edu/lib/thesis/2003/2003wux.pdf. Accessed: July 12, 2008.

12

CONCLUSION

Heike Alberts and Helen Hazen

The international migration of students and other academics is common in today's globalized world. While this process provides an important mechanism for sharing skills and knowledge, as well as deepening cross-cultural understanding, it also has significant social, economic, and cultural impacts. Better understanding the process of academic migration and its outcomes, at both individual and societal levels, is therefore an important task.

With over 700,000 international students studying in the United States in the 2010/11 academic year—a large share of the entire international student market—the United States is currently the prime destination for international students in the world. The United States also attracts a large share of globally mobile faculty. There is widespread agreement that these two groups are pivotal in maintaining the United States' global competitiveness. To maximize their contributions to the US higher-education system and economy it is important to gain a thorough understanding of the issues they face and develop effective strategies to overcome any difficulties.

In this volume, we have brought together recent academic scholarship on international students and scholars in the United States, focusing on migration trends, the particularity of experience of different migrant groups, the contributions they make to internationalization efforts, the challenges faced by those migrating, and strategies to maximize the benefits of these migrations. Here, we draw out crosscutting themes from the book.

CHANGING TRENDS IN MIGRATION PATTERNS

International students and faculty have long played an important role in the US higher-education system. Over the last several decades, the number of international students and faculty in the United States has increased steadily with few exceptions. The terrorist attacks of 9/11 led to a brief decline in international student and faculty flows owing to tightened regulations, but numbers soon rebounded. Recently, however, some commentators have expressed concern that numbers may again be declining as economic difficulties in the United States, coupled with global competition for talented individuals, reduce the United States' attractiveness.

Beyond these trends in overall numbers of international students and faculty, other trends can be observed at finer scales of analysis. For example, as Wan Yu described in her chapter, Chinese students are now not only the largest group of international students in the United States, but the characteristics of this group have also changed over time. In particular, while international student flows from many countries were strongly dominated by graduate students in the past, undergraduate students are now playing an increasingly important role. Significant shifts in migration patterns can also be observed among faculty members. As Rebecca Theobald and Ken Foote pointed out in their respective chapters, international faculty were once predominantly White males from European countries. Today, however, international faculty are increasingly female, non-White, and from low-income countries. Indeed, the US faculty as a whole has become much more diverse in terms of race, national origin, gender, sexual orientation, and other characteristics. The greater diversity of international students and faculty offers great opportunities but also presents new challenges.

Under-Researched Groups

In recent years, international students, and to a lesser degree international faculty, have attracted a lot of research attention. Much of this research has concentrated on broad trends or on case studies of particular subgroups. Most research focuses on the groups that are most numerically important in the United States, such as Chinese and Korean students. Other groups, such as students from Africa, have received less attention. As Jane Irungu made clear in her chapter, this gap has to be addressed as different subgroups of international students face different issues.

Another gap in the literature is research on international students and faculty from countries with a similar level of development to the United States. Russell King, Allan Findlay, Alistair Geddes, and Jill

Ahrens discussed the motivations of British students to study in the United States. They argued that, while the United Kingdom has world-class universities and is itself a major recipient of international students, the excellent reputation of the US university system as well as the wish to gain international experience have resulted in a flow of British students to the United States. Among faculty and other scholars, there is an even stronger circulation of talent among high-income countries, as Heike Alberts explored in her examination of German faculty in the United States. She argued that, even though Germany has a strong academic tradition and is a major producer of knowledge, many German faculty with US experience prefer the United States' greater degree of job security in entry-level academic jobs as well as the high degree of independence in research. The fact that even students and faculty from other prestigious education systems feel drawn to the United States suggests a new strain of "brain circulation."

Return Migration and Brain Circulation

Even though international students are assumed to be temporary migrants, in reality a large proportion of international students in the United States adjust their status to become permanent residents and even citizens after completing their degrees. Because of this, international student migrations have long been framed in the "brain drain" discourse, which interprets these migrations as a permanent loss to the home countries and a "brain gain" for the United States. Increasingly, researchers are revealing this assumption to be overly simplistic. While there is great variation among nationality groups and different academic fields, overall, return flows are increasing and academic migrants often maintain complex transnational networks during and after their migration. For example, Wan Yu described how improving opportunities in China are drawing increasing numbers of Chinese students back to their home country, resulting in brain circulation. Helen Hazen and Heike Alberts argued that many international students see themselves as transnational, and specifically seek out careers that allow them to spend time in different countries. Heike Alberts, in her research on German academics, showed that the creation of knowledge networks represents another form of brain circulation, which does not necessarily require the migrant's return home.

In considering the circulation of global talent, return migration decisions take on great significance and yet remain understudied.

As Helen Hazen and Heike Alberts argued, the decision-making process for return migration may be even more complex than the decision to make the initial migration. In deciding whether or not to return to their home country, students have firsthand experience of both their home and host country. In addition, their personal circumstances may have changed over time, for example through marriage to a partner of another nationality or changing attitudes, resulting in strong ties to both societies. Evaluating a return migration thus involves considering a complex set of personal and professional factors that are embedded in the broader cultural and economic settings of both countries under consideration. International faculty consider similar factors to students, as Heike Alberts showed in her chapter on the return migration intentions of German faculty, but typically put greater emphasis on professional factors, particularly job security, working conditions, and research opportunities.

Internationalization and Diversity

Recruiting international talent clearly has potentially significant economic benefits, but can also be part of a broader cultural agenda. As Kavita Pandit and Rebecca Theobald described in their respective chapters, international students and faculty are often seen as critical components of the internationalization strategies now common at US institutions of higher education. Unfortunately, simply recruiting international students does not by itself achieve internationalization and diversity goals. As Kavita Pandit pointed out, a comprehensive internationalization strategy must go beyond simply recruiting a diverse group of people to also creating opportunities for meaningful interaction among different groups. Furthermore, internationalization goals need to permeate all aspects of university life rather than be restricted to bringing people to campus from overseas.

It is also important to appreciate the tensions that exist between internationalization and diversity agendas. Clearly the two are interlinked, but they are not synonymous. As Rebecca Theobald discussed in her chapter, different institutions have very different interpretations of what constitutes diversity. In some cases, international faculty and students are seen as the core of diversification strategies, while in others international faculty are not even counted when reporting diversity figures. Kavita Pandit argued that assuming that recruiting international students can achieve diversity goals via a "check-the-box" approach to race can actually end up alienating and marginalizing underrepresented domestic subpopulations. Moreover, she suggested that increasing numbers of international students on American campuses do not necessarily contribute to greater understanding among different groups of people as there is often little meaningful interaction between international students and domestic students. Indeed, domestic minority students and international students may actually hold strong prejudices against one another that can worsen rather than improve intercultural communication if stereotypes remain unquestioned and unaddressed. Universities need to create programs that help both sides to maximize the benefits of intercultural interactions.

Adjustment as a Two-Way Street

Any migrant must make significant adjustments to settle in a new society. It is increasingly clear, however, that meeting internationalization goals requires adjustments on the part of both international migrants and the host population. As noted above, Kavita Pandit argued that successful intercultural communication can only take place when both sides critically examine their previously held beliefs about one another and adjust accordingly. This is also true for interactions in the classroom specifically.

As Alisa Eland and Kay Thomas explained in their chapter, many international students come from countries with fundamentally different classroom cultures. As a result, they have very different understandings of the role of the instructor, what is expected of them as students, and what they have to do to succeed academically. It is important for international students to understand these differences so that they can adapt to them, but it is also crucial for faculty to understand migrants' backgrounds so that they can identify and respond to their specific problems and acknowledge different, but equally valid, approaches to learning.

Similarly, international instructors must work in concert with their students to tackle adjustment issues. For instance, as Heike Alberts, Helen Hazen, and Rebecca Theobald described, it is important for international instructors to be aware that their accented English may pose problems for their students and to take measures to help their students understand them. However, students must also play their part in making sure that communication is successful through maintaining an open outlook toward international instructors and providing constructive feedback to them.

Supporting International Students and Faculty

While all parties involved have to make an effort to ensure the successful integration of international students and faculty on US campuses, much of the burden undoubtedly lies on the shoulders of international migrants themselves. For this reason, there is widespread recognition that international students and faculty greatly benefit from targeted support on campus. As Alisa Eland and Kay Thomas discussed, international students experience a wide range of difficulties associated with living abroad, ranging from legal restrictions to homesickness, as well as academic problems such as comprehension problems and difficulties in dealing with US classroom culture. In order to address this wide range of issues, it is critical that different offices on campus collaborate in offering support.

It is also crucial that such support is targeted toward specific subgroups of international students and students' individual circumstances. For instance, as Jane Irungu showed, African students often experience problems in adapting to the United States related to their race and cultural backgrounds. It is therefore important to have support staff available who have some understanding of the different cultural backgrounds that international students come from in order to properly target support and make others across campus aware of the issues international students may be facing.

International faculty struggle with many of the same issues as international students, including immigration-related problems, culture shock, and prejudice, as Ken Foote showed in his chapter. As such, they benefit from similar programs geared toward easing their transition to the US academic setting as well as mentoring, which can target the specific needs of individual faculty members.

Future Research

While international academics face many of the same challenges as other highly skilled migrants in adjusting to a new setting, they also experience unique challenges and bring specific opportunities. This volume has demonstrated the importance of combining theoretical and practical approaches to help understand the issues that international academics face and to provide the expertise needed to tackle these issues effectively.

Significant gaps remain, however. Considerably less has been written on international faculty than students, despite their important role in US higher education and the US economy more broadly. Many commentators expect the proportion of international faculty to increase further in the future, underscoring the need for more research on this group. In particular, it is important to examine more carefully how various aspects of their identities shape their experiences in the United States. More in-depth research is needed not only about international faculty's challenges and opportunities in the classroom, but also about particular issues that might present themselves in service and research. In regards to research, in particular, a much more careful analysis of international collaborations and other aspects of brain circulation is warranted if the potential of international academics is to be maximized. Finally, we know very little about how international faculty evaluate the support that is available to them and how they see their own contributions to US higher education and the global production of knowledge.

In regards to international students, more research about specific subgroups is still needed, particularly under-researched groups such as students from Latin America and Africa. To date, most research has focused on graduate students, but recent trends indicate that undergraduate students are increasing significantly in number, and not much is known about how their experiences differ from those of graduate students. We also still know relatively little about international students from industrialized nations with good educational opportunities in their home countries.

Most research about international students has been carried out at institutions that attract large numbers of international students, typically large research universities. However, international student numbers are also increasing at smaller state institutions and community colleges. Exploring the experiences of international students in less diverse settings, where they do not have a peer group from their home country for support, would provide another valuable contribution to the field.

More broadly, to date, most studies on international students and faculty have been carried out in the main recipient countries, particularly English-speaking countries (especially the United States, United Kingdom, Canada, and Australia). Little is known about international students' experiences in non-English-speaking countries such as the Netherlands, Germany, and France; even less is known about those studying in low-income countries, many of which attract only small numbers of international students and faculty. Comparative studies of international students in different host countries are also largely absent from the literature. These gaps are even more significant for international faculty.

Addressing these gaps in the literature will require a concerted effort from both academics and those working with international students and faculty on a day-to-day basis. As academic settings, and indeed society more broadly, become increasingly diverse, meeting this challenge becomes more and more important. There exists huge potential within the population of international academics in terms of the diverse perspectives and approaches toward creating knowledge that they bring. Unlocking this potential requires attention to the particular challenges faced by international academics, but also offers the opportunity to enrich the teaching and research agendas of US higher education.

Contributors

Jill Ahrens is a doctoral student in migration studies and an associate tutor in the School of Global Studies, University of Sussex, United Kingdom. She has worked as a research assistant on two projects related to student mobility. For her PhD she is researching Nigerian migration to and within Europe.

Heike Alberts is an associate professor of geography at the University of Wisconsin Oshkosh. She received her MA from the Free University of Berlin in Germany and her PhD from the University of Minnesota. Her research interests focus on international migration and education as well as urban issues.

Alisa Eland is associate director of International Student and Scholar Services at the University of Minnesota. As head of counseling and advising, she supervises staff, oversees student programs, and provides training and consultation for university faculty and staff on cross-cultural and mental health issues. Her research focuses on international students' academic and cross-cultural experiences.

Allan Findlay is a professor of geography at the University of St. Andrews, United Kingdom. He is founder and coeditor of the international journal *Population, Space and Place* and chair of the International Geographical Union Commission on Population Geography. He has carried out several research projects focusing on international student mobility.

Ken Foote is a professor of geography and former department chair at the University of Colorado at Boulder. He has served as president of both the Association of American Geographers (2010–2011) and National Council for Geographic Education (2006). Much of his work focuses on improving geography in higher education. Among his current projects is the Geography Faculty Development Alliance (GFDA), begun in 2002 with the sponsorship of the National Science Foundation to provide support for early-career faculty in higher education. It is through this project that he became aware of the issues facing international faculty in US higher education.

Alistair Geddes is a lecturer in human geography at the University of Dundee, United Kingdom. His research focuses on human mobility, including recently completed work on UK students abroad for the UK government, and current projects on the scope and experience of forced labor among migrant workers in the UK funded by the Joseph Rowntree Foundation. He holds a PhD in geography from the Pennsylvania State University.

Helen Hazen is a research scholar at Macalester College, Minnesota. Following undergraduate training in geography at Oxford University, United Kingdom, she received her MA and PhD at the University of Minnesota. She has participated in research projects on international students and international faculty; other research interests include issues of health and environment.

Jane Irungu is the director of the Division of Graduation and Post-graduation Success in the Center for Multicultural Academic Excellence at the University of Oregon, and a native of Kenya. She is also a linguist and instructor of Swahili and Kikuyu. Her research focuses on students' experiences in higher education with a focus on historically underrepresented populations and international students.

Russell King is a professor of geography at the University of Sussex, United Kingdom. He is editor of the *Journal of Ethnic and Migration Studies*. He was lecturer and professor at the University of Leicester and Trinity College, Dublin, before moving to the University of Sussex, where he was the founding director of the Sussex Centre for Migration Research.

Kavita Pandit is Associate Provost for International Education at the University of Georgia and a native of India. She is a geographer and has served as president of the Association of American Geographers. Her research interests are in the areas of internationalization, higher education, population, and migration.

Rebecca Theobald is an assistant professor adjoint in the Department of Geography and Environmental Studies at the University of Colorado, Colorado Springs, as well as the coordinator of the Colorado Geographic Alliance. Her research interests center on global systems of education, public services and public policy, as well as political geography.

Kay Thomas recently retired as director of International Student and Scholar Services at the University of Minnesota. She was affiliate faculty in the Counseling and Student Personnel program in the Department of Educational Psychology, where she taught cross-cultural counseling for over 30 years. Her research interests are in the areas of cross-cultural counseling and the adjustment needs of international students. She served as national president of NAFSA: Association of International Educators and has had Fulbright scholarships to Japan and Korea.

Wan Yu is a PhD candidate in the School of Geographical Sciences and Urban Planning of Arizona State University. She received her MA from Miami University of Ohio and her BS from Peking University, Beijing, China. Her research interests are Chinese Americans, highly skilled international migrants, and return migration.

Index

Note: references in bold text refer to figures or tables.

academic
  atmosphere, 70, 77, 80, 96, 104, 214
  challenges, 12, 133, 146–7, 155, 166, 224
  dishonesty, 147, 152–3, 172
accent, foreign, 13, 171–2, 188, 199–215
acculturation, 118, 170, 174
adjustment, 12, 36, 115, 118–19, 123, 133, 149, 151, 160, 166, 171–2, 176, 223
admission standards, 41, 99, 146
advising, academic, 133, 136, 146, 149, 173, 181, 188
Africa, 13, 71, **72**, 74, **75**, **76**, 77, 80, 123, 163–6, 220, 224, 225
Asia, 7, 9, 11, 12, 13, 38, 54, 57, 70, 71, **72**, 74, **75**, **76**, 77, 78, 82, 117, 122, 137, 153, 155, 167, 188, 192, 193
Australia, 13, 30, **34**, 35, 38, 41, 51, 52, 133, 225

bias, 137, 139, 188, 201–2, 205
  see also prejudice
brain circulation, 3, 15, 47, 48–9, 50–1, 60–1, 66, 89–90, 92–3, 100–3, 105, 221, 225
brain drain, 3, 14, 26, 27, 41, 42, 47, 48–50, 51, 66, 89, 92, 93, 100–3, 104, 105, 221
  see also optimal brain drain
brain exchange, 3, 92

brain gain, 47, 49, 50, 221
brain overflow, 49, 93
Britain, *see* United Kingdom
bureaucracy, 94, 98, 186

Canada, 7, **8**, **9**, 13, 30, 38, 41, 51, 52, 117, 167, 187, 225
capital, 36, 101
  cultural, 31
  economic, 31, 50
  human, 31, 43, 47, 48, 49, 51, 53, 165
  intellectual, 13, 14, 67, 133
  mobility, 31, 39, 101
  social, 31, 36, 59
career
  aspirations, 38
  prospects, **34**, 35, 38, 73, 77, 104
China, 2, 7, 8, **8**, 9, **9**, 12, 47–61, **53**, 68, 69, 71, 73, 74, 77, 78, 79, 82, 83, 84, 91, 137, 193, 220, 221
citizenship, 43, 52, 90, 113, 115, 117, 182, 185–7, 194
civil rights, 133, 138
class discussion, **152**, 155, 156, 158, 171, 172
classroom
  culture, 149–54, 171–2, 182, 194, 223, 224
  dynamics, 147, 149, 153–4, 202
  incivilities, 188, 205
collectivism, 150–4, 158
collegiality, 96, 104, 191

communication, 66, 105, 149, 199
  challenges, 132, 155–6, 160, 171, 181, 213–15, 223
  strategies to improve, 156, 202, 204, 208, 212–13, 215
  see also cross-cultural communication; low-context versus high-context communication
competition for academic talent, 2–3, 42, 112, 131, 133, 183, 220
counseling, 146, 149, 156–7, 159, 173, 175
credit mobility, 26, 43
critical thinking, 150–2, 172
cross-cultural
  communication, 132, 133, 135, 200, 215, 223
  issues, 132, 184, 219
  teams, 156
cultural alienation/dislocation, 2, 75, 79, 80, 160, 166
culture shock, 79, 172, 192–3, 224

degree mobility, 26–7, 31, 41, 42
demographic change in higher education, 11–12, 52–5, **53**, 114
destination country, 5, 26, 28, 41–2, 59, 93, 133, 163, 176, 219
diaspora networks, 67, 105
  see also knowledge networks
discrimination, 13, 14, 80, 83, 115, 133, 138, 139, 166, 168–70, 171, 172, 175, 176, 184
discussion, *see* class discussion
diversity, 11, 15, 111–24, 131–40
  measuring of, 16, 120–3, 132

English as a second language, 13, 78, 79, 82, 135, 147, 155, 156, 160, 171–2, 175, 187, 191, 199–215, 223
English-speaking countries, 5, 42, 225
ethnocentrism, 136, 201–2, 211

exchange, educational, 1, 4, 13, 14, 53, 54, 55, 71, 132–3, 138, 139, 145, 157, 184

F-1 visa, 54
financial issues, 7, 10–11, 13, 33–4, 37, 41, 52, 55, 98, 148, 165, 167, 169, 173–4, 175–6, 194
  see also funding issues
foreign-born faculty, 9, 90, 111–12, 114–5, 116–24, 181, 183, 188, 194–5, 199–215
  see also international faculty
friendship, understandings of, **75**, 79, 80, 135
Fulbright Program, 118, 132
funding issues, 2, 5, 7, 10–11, 31, 33–4, **33**, 41, 57, 70, 71, 72, 91, 93, 97, 98–9, 104, 115, 169, 174–6, 186, 191, 193–4
  see also financial issues

gender issues, 12, 80–1, 83, 99–100, 111, 114, 115, 116, 117, 120, 122, 135, 138, 139, 184, 188, 208, 220
Germany, **9**, 43, 89–105, 221, 225
globalization, 10, 15, 42, 47, 67, 78, 111, 124, 183, 195
grants, **33**, 99
  see also funding issues
"green cards," 6, 57, 58, 114, 121

H1-B visa, 7, 54–5, 57, 121, 187
health issues, 148, 157, 173
  see also mental health
hierarchies in academia, 77, 94, 96–7, 104
high-income countries, 47, 61, 71, 89, 92, 101, 221
highly skilled migrants, 1, 3, 7, 14, 47–51, 57, 60–1, 65–6, 91–3, 104–5, 112, 194, 224
hiring practices, 95–6, 97, 100, 103, 104, 113, 116, 122–3, 124, 185
  see also spousal hiring

Index

identity, 28, 39–40, 82, 117–18, 148, 150, 159–60, 169, 170, 193
immigration
  policy, 2, 5, 11, 13, 49, 52, 54, 55, 56–8, 59, 65, 78, 115, 118, 183, 185–7
  restrictions, 2, 5, 11, 52, 55, 59, 115, 158, 174, 183, 185–7, 191
  status, 6, 54, 56, 90, 93, 114, 115, 121, 148, 182, 186, 187, 221
India, 2, 7, 8, **8**, 9, **9**, 13, 54, 69, 70, 71, 79, 80, 81, 82, 83, 91
individualism, 79, 150, 153–4
informal atmosphere in the classroom, 35, 154
Institute of International Education (IIE), 4
interactions
  between American and international students, 132, 134–9, 172, 175, 223
  between students and international faculty, 207, 208–15, 223
Intercultural Sensitivity Model, 136
international
  career, 1, 4, 10, 11, 12–13, 16, 26, 28, **29**, 30, **34**, 35, 38, 39, 77–8, 182, 221
  faculty, 2, 3, 4, 5, 8–9, 10, 11, 14, 16, 89–105, 111–24, 181–95, 199–215, 219–26
  scholars, 2, 4, 8–10, **9**, 89, 90, 91, **91**, 92, 93, 113–15, **113**, 184, 221
  student services, 132, 136, 138–9, 157–60, 164, 174, 224
internationalization, 4, 15, 16, 89, 116, 119, 131–40, 219, 222–3
isolation, 13, 82, 147, 175, 182, 193

job security, 97, 103, 104, 221, 222

knowledge-based economy, *see* knowledge economy
knowledge diasporas, 15, 67

knowledge economy, 7, 50, 66, 85, 195
knowledge networks, 89, 92, 103, 105, 221
  see also diaspora networks

language
  issues, 2, 11, 12, 56, 78, 79, 81, 100, 147, 156, 171, 175, 185, 187, 191, 202, 203, 206–12, **210**, 214
  partners, 135
Latin America, 13, 71, **72**, 75, 76, 78, 137, 225
learner-centered pedagogical approaches, 151, **152**
low-context versus high-context communication, 155–6
low-income countries, 3, 8, 14, 61, 66, 71, 72, 74, 76, 92, 104, 113, 164, 220, 225

mental health, 157, 173
mentoring, 111, 115, 118, 124, 181–95, 215, 224
Middle East, 13, 167, 189, 205
migration
  barriers, 1, 2, 5, 10–11, 83–4, 115, 183, 185–6
  challenges of, 10, 12–13
  impact of, 10, 13–14, 48, 50–1, 67, 92
  motivations, 10–11, 29–34, **29**, 42–3, 49, 70–2, **72**, 74–83
  trends, 1, 2, 3, 4–5, 9, 11–12, 52–4, 90–1, 183–4, 219–20
  see also return migration
minority populations, 100, 111–24, **114**, 131–40, 159, 184, 223
mobility, 1, 3, 14, 26–8, 39, 42, 47, 50, 93, 164, 165
  see also credit mobility; degree mobility
multiculturalism, 13, 119, 184

neo-racism, 169
nonresident alien, 114–5

optimal brain drain, 50
optional practical training (OPT), 54–6, 65
orientation programs, 124, 135, 148, 157, 159, 164, 174, 176, 190

Patriot Act, 5
pedagogical approaches, 149, 151, **152**, 172, 202, 204
people of color, 14, 111, 114, 115, 116, 120–4, 168–70, 188
   see also minority populations
permanent residency, 6, 65, 90, 93, 114, 185–7, 191, 221
plagiarism, 152–3, 172
positional advantage, 8, 38
postdoctoral work, 2, 65, 90, 93, 95, 103
postgraduate work, 30, 32, 33, 39, 53, 57
power-distance, 150–1, 153, 154
prejudice, 115, 132, 138, 139, 166, 167, 168, 171, 172, 176, 188, 191, 202, 213, 223, 224
promotion, 103, 112, 191, 194
psychological issues and migration, 12, 73, 82, 166, 171, 172–3, 175

quality of life, 11, **75**, 76, 79, 80

racism, 13, **75**, 80, 169
   see also discrimination; prejudice
recruitment, 6, 54, 57, 112–3, 118, 131–3, 134, 139, 163
remittances, 50, 173, 176
reputation
   of individual institutions, 11, 30, 91
   of US education, 4, 52, 94, 221
research funding, access to, 2, 5, 10, 11, 33–4, 57, 70, 71, **72**, 91, 93, 97, 98–9, 104, 115, 191
   see also funding issues
research networks, 89, 105
retention
   of faculty, 113, 116, 118, 119
   of students, 41, 164

return intentions, 12, 68, 72–83
return migration, 26, 55–60, 65, 67, 68, 72–3, 83–4, 89–105, 221–2
   incentives for, 57–8, 78
return rate, 56, 68

scholarships, 4, 33, 37, 54, 164, 175, 176
screening of immigrants, 5, 52
sending countries, 9, 14, 47–8
senior faculty, 11, 96–9
September 11th 2001 terrorist attacks, 5, 52, 55, 68, 78, 80, 113, 183, 220
sexual harassment, 12
sexual identity, 120, 138, 148, 159, 185, 192, 220
South Korea, 7, 8, **8**, 9, **9**, 91, 220
spousal hiring, 94, 100, 103
staff who work with international faculty and students, 16, 133, 135, 136, 145, 146, 149–50, 154, 155, 156, 157, 174, 175, 185, 187, 224
   see also international student services
standard of living, 74, 75, **75**, 76, **76**, 79, 92, 104, 176
stay rates, 11, 68, 91
STEM disciplines, 55, 115
stereotypes, 170
study abroad, 26–9, 34, 42, 131, 135, 138, 176, 184, 202, 211, 214
   see also exchange, educational

teacher-centered learning, 151, **152**
teaching effectiveness, 199, 203, 206, 209
temporary migrant, 65, 68, 69, 72, 73, 93, 97, 221
tenure system, 94, 96–7, 102, 103, 104, **114**, 115, 118, 191
terrorism, *see* September 11th 2001 terrorist attacks

transmigration, 66, 73
transnationalism, 3, 66–7, 73, 77, 82, 84–5, 105, 193, 221
travel restrictions, 115, 148, 185, 186, 187, 191
tuition revenue, 7, 48, 52, 53, 54, 60, 133, 145, 163

undergraduates, 2, 7, 11, 16, 32, 33, **33**, 36, 38, 47, 52–3, **53**, 54, 60, 118, 134, 137, 147, 158, 199, 201, 204, 208, 220, 225
United Kingdom (UK), 5, **9**, 25–43, 184, 221, 225

United States Citizenship and Immigration Service (USCIS), 185, 186, 187

visas, 4, 5–6, 7, 12, 52, 54–5, 56, 57, 65, 68, 93, 115, 121, 136, 148, 185–7, 194
temporary, 12, 65, 68, 93
see also H1-B visa; F-1 visa

world-class
education, 3, 14, 16
university, 29–31, **29**, 42, 43, 113, 221

GPSR Compliance

The European Union's (EU) General Product Safety Regulation (GPSR) is a set of rules that requires consumer products to be safe and our obligations to ensure this.

If you have any concerns about our products, you can contact us on

ProductSafety@springernature.com

In case Publisher is established outside the EU, the EU authorized representative is:

Springer Nature Customer Service Center GmbH
Europaplatz 3
69115 Heidelberg, Germany

www.ingramcontent.com/pod-product-compliance
Lightning Source LLC
LaVergne TN
LVHW012059070526
838200LV00074BA/3765